Religion as Art Form

Reclaiming Spirituality without Supernatural Beliefs

Carl L. Jech

RESOURCE *Publications* · Eugene, Oregon

RELIGION AS ART FORM
Reclaiming Spirituality without Supernatural Beliefs

Resource Publications
An Imprint of Wipf and Stock Publishers
199 W. 8th Ave., Suite 3
Eugene, OR 97401
www.wipfandstock.com

ISBN 13: 978-1-62032-910-8

Manufactured in the U.S.A.

To Eric Markham Simpson
And my grandchildren, Talisynn, Ayanna, Mahkayla, and Scotty

Modern man suffers from a kind of poverty of the spirit, which stands in glaring contrast with a scientific and technical abundance.

MARTIN LUTHER KING JR.

CONTENTS

Preface

THIS IS A THOROUGHLY revised version of my 2011 book *Spiritual Non-believer,* a title based on Albert Einstein's description of himself as "a deeply religious nonbeliever." Einstein's references to "God" are often misunderstood or misused by those who want to make it appear that this most eminent of scientists believed in a traditional personified deity, in spite of his clear statements to the contrary. The current title and subtitle, *Religion as Art Form*: *Reclaiming Spirituality without Supernatural Beliefs,* provide a more clear and explicit description of this book's main thesis. Another appropriate title could have been "Spiritual Naturalism," reflecting the views of Jerome A. Stone in his book *Religious Naturalism Today.* A basic premise underlying such titles is that in our postmodern age, belief in supernatural worlds, entities, or ideas is rapidly fading. In spite of the popularity of supernatural themes in the realm of entertainment, actual belief in anything that smacks of superstitious nonsense is on the wane. The amazing results produced by scientific methods have called into question any non-empirical means of ascertaining real truth. When religions claim to provide supernatural or revealed truth they are encountering increasing skepticism, in particular because the scientific study of sacred texts themselves has seriously called into question their supposed supernatural origin or unique inspiration. All indications are that a growing number of people now identify as agnostics, atheists, secular humanists, free-thinkers, or as "spiritual but not religious."

Ironically (and disingenuously.) some religious people claim that there is nothing supernatural about their religion, because their beliefs are about things that are in fact aspects of the natural world rather than of some super-natural "dimension" or "other world." Heaven or Paradise is on another planet, in another galaxy, or will be established on a renewed earth. God and Jesus are actual persons also somewhere "out there" (sitting on a throne?) in the physical/material world (on a star or planet named Kolob according to Mormonism). Many scholars studying Christianity have observed that precisely in response to the scientific revolution, some fundamentalist believers have developed the very unscientific notion that scriptural material can be "scientific" evidence. They have read the Bible more literally as fact than it typically was before the age of enlightenment and reason (the age of science). In other words, this kind of biblical literalism is more modern than traditional. Much of the earlier history of Christianity displayed a great deal of appreciation for metaphor, symbolism, and analogy—for a poetic understanding of religious language. Early Christianity was also a far more diverse, imaginative, and creative phenomenon than has been generally understood.

To deny that any of one's religious beliefs are supernatural by claiming that religious language and scriptural texts are empirical, natural, scientific, and factual, is simply dishonest. It totally muddies the waters and turns language upside down. This approach ignores the clearly supernatural element in the thinking of those ancients who wrote and edited the now-sacred texts, not to mention their scientifically incorrect notions about things such as firmaments, a flat earth, and the sun standing still. It obscures the distinction between facts and interpretations, science and poetry—between natural and supernatural. Taken at face value, many religious claims and beliefs can only be properly understood as supernatural. To the degree that they *may* be based on facts (such as the crucifixion of Jesus) they are *interpretations* of those facts. Supernatural claims are about believing things for which there is no real evidence and, more often than not, these claims fly in the face of whatever real evidence does exist. Assertions put forward about supernatural truth do not pass the test that says extraordinary claims require extraordinary proof!

I have written here for those who can relate to a description such as "spiritual nonbeliever." I am addressing those who are strongly inclined to affirm both spirituality and science. I am also writing for those who may not have the time or inclination to keep up with all the recent well-publicized books that deal with the relationship between religion, atheism, and science—and also for those who may be overwhelmed by the scholarly depth of Richard Rorty (Stanford University) and Gianni Vattimos' daunting 2005 book *The Future of Religion*. This book can serve as an accessible state-of-the-art guide for those struggling with the current theism-versus-atheism and religious-versus-spiritual debates. Instead of using footnotes, I have simply mentioned books and their authors in the text itself, offering summaries of salient points along with some criticism and commentary. To be frank, this book is also a promotion of sorts for the scintillating and timely writings of folks such as Richard Dawkins, Daniel C. Dennett, Sam Harris, Christopher Hitchens, Karen Armstrong, Elaine Pagels, Harvey

Cox, Gordon D. Kaufman, Bart Ehrman, John Shelby Spong, Marcus Borg, and John Dominic Crossan. I have drawn upon other media sources of information as well, and my special fondness for contemporary movies will be evident.

What I hope makes this more than just another book for the pile is my emphasis on understanding religion as primarily a creative art form. As uniquely self-conscious human beings, we create religions and ideas of God to meet some of our most basic needs—especially our need to feel secure or at home in the universe and to be meaningfully engaged with the Ultimate Mystery of life and death.

Religion is more about interpretations, values, and meaning than about facts. Science and religion both deal with a combination of speculation and data, imagination and knowledge, interpretations and facts. There is much truth in Einstein's famous observation that "Imagination is more important than knowledge," but this does not mean that we don't need both. The intelligent collection of mere facts and data (information) may give us only trivia. On the other hand, pure imaginative speculation seldom if ever produces any real or tangible results. It is when imagination and facts come together in imaginative interpretation of data that we achieve amazing results such as medical marvels, going to the moon—and the creation of a spirituality that can thrive without supernatural beliefs.

Sudhir Kakar makes this point about the relationship between imagination and critical reasoning, with particular attention to the poets John Keats and Samuel Coleridge, in an article "The Resurgence of Imagination" published in the Harvard Divinity Bulletin, 2009 Winter edition. What Coleridge called "primary imagination" and Keats called "unitive imagination," Kakar calls "connective imagination," which connects spirituality, art, science, empathy, and compassion, reflecting the attitude encouraged by the Upanishads that speak about seeing all beings in our own self and our own self in all beings. Instead of viewing the religious and spiritual imagination of others as a threat, understanding religion as primarily a creative and imaginative art form allows us to walk in each other's shoes, and to appreciate the combination of unique and universal themes, images, and metaphors in our various religious cultures. I think it would be fair to say that each religion can be attractive in somewhat the same way as Garrison Keillor says that in Lake Wobegon "all the women are strong, all the men are good-looking, and all the children are above average." H. L. Mencken similarly observed that we can respect and appreciate the other guy's religion "in the sense and to the extent that we respect his theory that his wife is beautiful and his children smart." The beauty and truth of a religion is in the eye and the imagination of the beholder.

While not all aspects of religion are purely speculative and imaginative, the *focus* of religion is on the imaginative, creative interpretation of our situation in the universe, our relationship to Reality and to Eternity. Without artistic imagination and speculative creativity there would be no religion. On the other hand, the *focus* of science is on facts, and the speculative, deductive imagination only comes into play *after* inductive research has provided solid data. (Einstein's $E=mc^2$ is an imaginative interpretation of data.) Without hard evidence there would be no real science. Science and religion each involve both facts and interpretations, but without creative interpretation there is no religion, and without data there is no science! The relationship of science and religion needs to be understood in this context.

In various other places throughout this book I have explicitly described groups of people for whom I am writing. It makes sense to mention some of them right here at the outset.

I am writing for those who only occasionally attend religious services, perhaps just at Christmas and Easter or on other special holy days (holidays) such as *Yom Kippur*. I am writing for those who, like American founding father Thomas Jefferson, are troubled by the supernatural aspects in many religious stories. I write for those who may attend church regularly, but who squirm in their pew because they feel they are being asked to accept a scientific worldview that is at least two thousand years out of date. I am writing for the rapidly growing number of people, especially younger ones, who consistently describe themselves as "spiritual but not religious." Those who want to continue enjoying many aspects of their traditional religion but feel uneasy and somewhat hypocritical—perhaps because more often than not it seems they are merely pretending to believe major features of their tradition—should find this book to be just what they have been looking for. Folks who fill churches and other religious venues for concerts and other artistic events but who otherwise seldom if ever find themselves in such surroundings will also appreciate reading these pages. Many churches, mosques, synagogues and other religious communities and their leaders offer various support services and opportunities for involvement in the wider world. This book calls attention to the importance of supporting and participating in these kinds of spiritual communities. I am also writing for religious leaders, teachers, and preachers who need support, insight, and encouragement in finding ways to serve and speak more effectively to the kinds of folks I have just described.

I also wish to address the traditional believers who may be troubled or upset by the notion of religion as an imaginative and creative art form. If you prefer to affirm the traditional supernatural aspects of your faith, I encourage you to recognize that it is, in fact, simply what you prefer. None of us understands the world perfectly. All I would ask is that you don't take your marbles and go home, or insensitively intimidate those in your family or community who are uncomfortable with your traditional beliefs. There is no need to split faith communities apart when confronted with those in our own community, or with other thinkers, who question the supernatural assumptions that have seemed to be at the heart of true faith. If religious people can't be sensitive to others and remain in community in spite of differences in the way they interpret or practice religion, how can we expect society and cultures at large to preserve the absolutely essential celebration of our common humanity! "People of faith" do not need to have an identical degree of appreciation for metaphor and symbolism in order to share a passion for their spiritual tradition.

The themes of religion do indeed deal with many great truths. But they tend to be subjective, "existential" truths, often expressed in artistic, mythological and supernatural storytelling. An important part of seeing religion as a creative art form is understanding that divinely revealed authorities (prophets, holy books, etc.) are not a reliable alternative to empiricism (scientific methods of testing) as a means by which we might be able to ascertain *objective* truth. The concept of "special revelation" as a source of solid knowledge has been rendered untenable by the tested and proven ability of scientific methods to reliably distinguish between fact and fiction. "Supernatural truths"—by definition beyond the scope of the natural sciences—cannot be proven to be objectively factual. Such truths clearly belong in the realm of art and of subjective/emotional ex-perience—the realm of spirituality. A personal vision or "revelation" may include the kind of imaginative insight that Einstein says is more impor-tant than intelligence, but it would have to be connected with proven facts, reliable data, and real-world results if it is going to have anything more than subjective meaning for some individuals or groups of believers. It might well be argued that the chaotic plethora of competing and often contradictory supernatural religious beliefs, all claiming to be divinely re-vealed, proves that *not even one* of these beliefs or claims is *objectively true*.

We can no longer think of ourselves as living in two separate worlds, the natural and the supernatural world, this world and a next world. We live in one world, one global village, one universe, one home—*now*! Supernatural language is best seen as artistic, subjective, symbolic, and metaphorical language. When it comes to the relationship between fact, myth, and metaphor, Marcus Borg likes to quote the aphorism, "The Bible is true, and some of it happened." The Native American version is, "I'm going to tell you a story. This never happened, but it is still true." Some stories are historical facts—although we must understand that history is "layers of complexity," as film-maker Oliver Stone says. Other stories, such as the boy who cried wolf, could have actually happened, but typically are not based on actual or specific events. Then there are stories that almost certainly never did happen or never could have happened literally (myths, etc.), stories that can only be properly understood as supernatural, but stories that can be reinterpreted in a way that makes them meaningful in a scientific age. It is these supernatural stories that often become a major problem in religion because the relationship between facts, interpretations, and truth can be tricky. Theologians, such as Karl Barth, who have insisted upon the objective, factual existence of God—even if God is objectified or personified only as, say, "the Mind of the Universe"—are losing the evidence argument to those like Tillich and Armstrong (and philosophers like Heidegger or Feuerbach) who understand specific Gods and religions as basically the products of humankind's artful and creative imagination. Intending to convey great truths, we make up stories—oftentimes containing supernatural elements—stories that are not and could not be factual. My point in this book is that the use of our imagination in this way is all well and good, as long as we remember what we are doing.

Religion—which ties, binds and links us to traditions, communities, and to all of reality—involves a never-ending process of appreciating and *interpreting* life. Jerome Stone writes: "Our religious traditions are neither to be accepted nor rejected, but to be reconstructed." Religions can no longer be about special pleading for the unique objective validity of supernatural truth claims. Such claims do not mark the way to world peace. The reinterpretation of supernatural themes and stories, together with the use of those themes wherever possible to help solve pressing problems, can mark *the Way* to making this a better world. Much will be said in these pages about distributive justice, compassion, love, peace—and about freedom from oppression and domination. It is my hope that this book will help readers affirm the kind of spirituality that fosters both real-world solutions to one-world problems and an appreciation for the amazing potential of science to enhance human life as we move into the twenty-first century and beyond. Religion is a *practical* art form.

It will become obvious to the reader that I have great admiration and affection for folks such as John Shelby (Jack) Spong, John Dominic Crossan, Elaine Pagels, and Bart Ehrman. But while they have more or less limited themselves to Christian and biblical perspectives, I have been teaching world religions for many years. Two of my college courses are "Global Religious Perspectives" and "Introduction to World Religions." I have found some of the books by Karen Armstrong to be particularly valuable resources for these courses. While I too may give more attention in this book to biblical perspectives than to other sacred texts and religious traditions, my more global perspective should be evident. The understanding of religion as a creative art form liberates every religion to celebrate its unique perspectives without the kind of dangerous arrogance that does more harm than good.

For a kinder, gentler, or perhaps I should say more "diplomatic" version of what I am doing here I refer the reader to the books of Marcus Borg. His focus is more narrowly on the Bible and Christianity, but transforming how folks understand the biblical tradition is so vitally necessary in today's world that he is to be applauded for his important contributions to this process of transformation. Borg has stated quite bluntly, by the way, that the main reason people nowadays leave the church, or never get involved to begin with, is because biblical literalism no longer makes sense to them! Yet most church publications that I see never seem to tackle this issue when they discuss dwindling church membership and participation (preferring instead the churchly equivalent of rearranging deck chairs on the Titanic). Borg is a strong advocate for and practitioner of adult Christian *re-education*.

Other very helpful books along these lines are Jim Burklo's *Open Christianity* (2000) and *Everything Must Change* (2007) by Brian D. McLaren. For a more scholastic and historical approach to the issue of spirituality without supernatural beliefs see Jerome A. Stone's *Religious Naturalism Today*.

ACKNOWLEDGMENTS

PAUL TILLICH AND RUDOLF Bultmann were two of the most controversial and transformative biblical theologians of the twentieth century. Prolific critic and champion of Christianity, Episcopal Bishop Emeritus John Shelby Spong, started writing his books in part to popularize the contributions of scholars such as Tillich and Bultmann, much as his friend and mentor Bishop John A. T. Robinson had done with his mid-twentieth century book *Honest to God*. Bishop Spong also has many concerns in common with his British friend Don Cupitt whose 1997 book *After God* explains why we must move beyond the supernatural beliefs that have shaped our values and our vision of the world. Richard Dawkins, outspoken atheist author of *The God Delusion*, is also a popularizer whose academic position at the time of that book's publication was Professor of the Public Understanding of Science at Oxford University in England. My goal here is to provide a synthesis of the work of these and many other scholars and authors who have "wrestled with God." I have tried my best to contribute to the public understanding of religion by writing in a way that I hope will connect with any and all thoughtful readers. In the interest of full disclosure, I want to point out that it took me quite a long time to understand the kind of Buddhist enlightenment and consciousness that I present in chapter 5. Some may want to reread this chapter and a few other sections of the book that, I admit, may be somewhat challenging. As I think is typical with Buddhism, it can take a while to overcome resistance to a new way of seeing Reality. It certainly took me some time and struggle to do so, but I hope readers will agree that it is more than worth the effort.

William Weiblen, one of my professors of systematic theology at Wartburg Theological Seminary in Dubuque, Iowa, had been a student of Tillich's at Harvard Divinity School and he encouraged me to go on for further graduate work at Harvard myself. Weiblen had an aura of being shy or reserved, but he was also congenial, caring—and deep. My buddy Mike Sherer and I still laugh about the time during a lecture when Doc Weiblen attempted to explain a major theological concept by saying, "Let us call it simply the hermeneutical prolegomena to existentialistic realized eschatology." Mike and I rolled our eyes at his prefacing of this collocation of verbiage with the word "simply."

"Realized eschatology" is a major theme in this book, and it actually can be described rather simply. Eschatology, based on the Greek word *eschaton*, refers to "end time" or "last things" and is about coping with our human mortality, with death, and with thoughts about endings, including "the end of the world." In slightly more than one hundred years from any given time, every person who had been alive at that time will have died. This reality is not much different from a scenario in which the entire planet would be destroyed all at once. The fact that seven billion people who are alive at any given moment will all be dead in just over a hundred years can make end-of-the-world scenarios seem both less far-fetched and less frightening in a way. But it also can increase our apprehension about how fragile and vulnerable life is. Given ecological, nuclear, technological, and other threats, it is not surprising that at this beginning of a new century we are seeing a large number of movies hitting the theaters that focus on apocalyptic disasters—films such as "Wall-e" and "Melancholia," with special effects featuring the destruction of world famous landmarks or even of the entire planet earth. Famed anthropologist Margaret Mead (who I was privileged to meet a number of times) always insisted that the "generation gap" of the 1960s was not about parents and children but rather about whether you were born "before or after the bomb." The specter of nuclear annihilation has haunted us ever since the Manhattan Project. Of course, a lot of people throughout history have mistakenly and embarrassingly, with self-aggrandizing presumption, thought that the end of the world was near. Another reality, however, is that human and other forms of life have proven to be highly resilient! The human race has managed to muddle through somehow and we may well be around for many long ages to come, perhaps even until our sun burns out—which it eventually will.

Realized (also called participatory) eschatology means "simply" that we are to participate fully in the present time, that all life is an ongoing process (interaction) of beginnings and endings. It is about realizing that basic reality is always *now* and that although we remember the past and anticipate an unknown future, life is always happening in the present moments of *this* world. In Weiblen's verbose phrase, "existentialistic" refers to the personal experience of being fully alive in what Tillich called the "eternal now;" "hermeneutics" refers to principles of interpretation; and "prolegomena" is a fancy term meaning critical introduction. So Professor

Weiblen was "simply" talking about an introduction to the process of interpreting realized eschatology.

This realized "already present eternal now" is associated especially with the John Gospel's Jesus who says that a person of faith already "has" (present tense!) eternal life—now! What is translated in the John Gospel as "eternal or everlasting life" would often be more accurately translated as "the life of the age to come," the future transformation of this world—not "another" world. The John Gospel is the fourth and latest of the New Testament gospels, and as we will note again later, by the time it was written and reedited, the notion of a soon to occur and literal "second coming" of Jesus was beginning to be replaced by the idea of a "second presence" *(parousia)* of Jesus in the form of his "Holy Spirit of truth" (see John 15—some Muslims imagine this as a reference to Mohammed). When the Mark Gospel (which was used as a source by both the Matthew and Luke Gospels) describes the "*kairos* moment," the time being fulfilled, the Kingdom of God as being "at hand," "in your midst," or "within you," the basic point is "now is the time that matters!" Now is the time for changing our way of thinking and acting in this world (*metanoia*/repentance). The Mark Gospel uses the word "immediately" (now!) many times. I suggest that realized eschatology is the most viable approach left to us in Christian theology for understanding and participating in the real world as our science has shown it to be. Realized, participatory eschatology sees the word "end" as being about a *process* of moving toward a *goal—a goal that includes peace, justice/fairness, love, compassion, and ecological sustainability.*

Bill Weiblen was a serious guy, yes. But he also did not take himself too seriously. Following a seminar-type course he taught on the theology of Paul Tillich, instead of a final exam we had barbeque and beer with Bill and his wife Ilah at their home. He may at times have been "inebriated with the exuberance of his own verbosity," but we quickly learned to take that in stride. I have heard it said that Tillich was more respected at Harvard for his deeply spiritual nature than for his intellectual achievements, although his intellect was remarkable. I think one might say something similar about Bill Weiblen who never missed daily chapel services, even though I now wonder how he put up with the many naïve and amateurish things that were said and done there by students (myself included) who were still very wet behind the ears. My subsequent encounters with him reinforced my appreciation of his scholarly depth, open-mindedness and willingness to change in response to new situations and new insights. I also have reason to suspect that he was significantly more "progressive" in his theology than many of his students and colleagues may have recognized—although this is not to suggest that he necessarily would have agreed with everything I have written here.

Another major theme of this book is that we need to lighten up when it comes to religion. I have taught numerous courses on the subject of humor and I think humor is one of the main fruits of a theology of grace. We have to learn the paradoxical art of combining a sense of moral urgency with a sense of humor. Weiblen was teaching at a time when the insights of theologians such as Tillich were just beginning to challenge many traditional religious notions and, therefore, he tread somewhat lightly when introducing them to us (with only occasional and perhaps deliberately whimsical lapses into linguistic exuberance). Our young Wartburg professor of New Testament theology, Duane Priebe, would also on occasion take a whimsical tone when challenging us with the existential and "demythologizing" biblical scholarship of Rudolf Bultmann. It was Priebe who first impressed upon me the importance of realizing that a diversity of theologies is developed in the New Testament—a development better understood when we pay attention to the order in which its twenty-seven books were written and chosen (canonized).

It is high time that we develop a sense of urgency about treading lightly when it comes to religion. Our scientific and pluralistic age requires ever evolving perspectives on religion and spirituality. This book is about taking religion both seriously and not so seriously. We need to have a sense of urgency about confronting no longer viable religious ideas and world views. There is too much at stake when it comes to issues of human spirituality not to say things plainly. (I realize that some things I will be saying may at times upset the reader.) It is my contention that understanding religion as a creative art form is the best way to "tread lightly"—the main way to avoid taking religion so seriously, so literally as supernaturally derived truth, that it becomes a destructive force in the world. We need to remind ourselves regularly that we can take religion *seriously* without taking everything about it *literally*!

No doubt some Wartburg Seminary folks will think that I have gone too far in these pages, but I think it is a tribute to this seminary with an odd-sounding German name that its spirit of openness and honest inquiry has "brought me safe thus far." Wartburg is the name of a castle in Eisenach, Germany, Bach's birthplace. The castle is associated with Elizabeth, a thirteenth century patron Saint of the poor, and with Martin Luther. The name has been said to come from "warten" (to wait) because the builder of the castle had to wait a long time for permission to build it. I like to relate this image of waiting to the fact that it has taken me a long time as a third generation Lutheran pastor, preacher, and college chaplain to move from my earlier certainties to the Mystery that I now embrace.

Another major acknowledgment must be made at the outset. Now that psychology is so widely understood and appreciated, religion cannot be properly understood without bringing psychology into the equation. (I see limited value in the dredging-up-memories form of psychology—especially as scientology uses it.) My good friend and advisor in psychology has been Dr. Dennis Hinkle. He has been particularly helpful to me in broadening my appreciation of the basic Buddhist approach to understanding reality that will be described in chapter 5. But most significant has been his guidance on the subject of what motivates people to change and grow. In these pages I am going to present a point of view that is intended to help as it also challenges many religious people to change the way they view and practice their religion. The many advantages that come with adopting the approach to religion that I am recommending will be described early in chapter 1. Dr. Hinkle's skill in helping people envision and construct different and better options for their lives ("personal construct psychology") is a skill that I hope to emulate in this book. Religion itself can be the cause of deep personal and social problems. We all need to work and play at constructing better ways of practicing our religious spirituality as we move into the twenty-first century.

I want to acknowledge the important role played in the development of my thinking by my college philosophy teacher, Clifford T. Hansen. In addition to his patient mentoring of the rather narrow-minded theological person I was at that time, I am particularly grateful to him for introducing me to H. Richard Niebuhr's classic book *Christ and Culture*.

While a graduate student at Harvard Divinity School I spent a larger portion of my time with Gordon D. Kaufman than with any of my other professors. Ironically, I did not always understand or appreciate his approach to theology at the time, but it is now apparent to me that as we both developed our understandings over the years we turned out to be increasingly on the same wavelength. I have made an effort in this book not to quote Kaufman too frequently in order that I might chart my own course, but I do want to acknowledge and applaud him for his theological insights which I now appreciate and share to an almost startling degree.

I also want to express my profound gratitude to all the other creative thinkers and artists whose works I have referenced or quoted in these pages. In his 1983 book *A Sociable God*, Ken Wilber develops an elaborate and complicated scheme for evaluating religious worldviews. At its apex is his discussion of *legitimate* and *authentic* religion, with guidelines for determining relative degrees of legitimacy and authenticity. Wilber's system, which in his later writings leads to the concept of "Integral Spirituality," provides complex criteria for making value judgments about what constitutes "higher" forms of spirituality. He is careful not to demand that everyone agree with his conclusions about what constitutes higher or highest religion, but he does his best to validate and defend his personal judgments. I greatly appreciate Ken Wilber's masterful and challenging analysis of spirituality and will be referring to his insights often.

To keep this book as readable as possible I have chosen not to use footnotes. Instead I have referred to books, articles, movies and other sources in the text itself and have provided a thorough index. In this computer age we have virtually instant access to any subject imaginable. I encourage the reader to use the Internet for following up on anything I have written here. Surf away!

Many professional and personal friends and family members too numerous to mention have encouraged and helped me in my life, some in particular by reading and sharing extensive comments on various drafts of this book. They know who they are, and they know how grateful I am for their support and assistance. In particular I must thank my sister Mary Jech for her computer savvy and for her heroic (if not always successful) efforts to reign in my longwinded tendencies, my cousin Laurence Angell for his helpful comments about the first version of the book, my "informal" research assistant Marjorie Cagan, my expert advisor in philology (languages) Edward Jajko, and my many students with whom I have shared the learning process. Without the constant presence and technical expertise of Eric Simpson I can't imagine how this book could have ever made its way into print. I am also especially indebted to my great friend and expert editorial consultant, Michael Sherer, who has been critiquing and encouraging my writing since we were college and seminary classmates—and who gave me my first opportunities to be a published author.

Although I have referred to the creative work of many others, as noted throughout these pages, the ideas expressed here are my own, and I take sole responsibility if there are any errors or misrepresentations. I hope my firmly stated thoughts and opinions never come across as harsh, upsetting, or insensitive.

I also express my deep gratitude to Christian Amondson at Wipf and Stock publishers for seeing merit in what I have written and offering to publish this book. I thank Kristen Brack for her marvelous cover design with the star trails time-lapse photography. Thanks also go to Tina Campbell Owens, Raydeen Cuffe, and those in other departments at Wipf and Stock who have been very patient with me during the process of typesetting, marketing, and those aspects of publishing about which I have little knowledge.

Some of the pre-publication editorial feedback I've received has been critical of the way I weave together personal (folksy) and serious academic elements. I hope it is clear, however, that I have done this deliberately. This book is intended to be in part a personal memoir of my own spiritual journey. (I think there is bound to be an element of autobiography in even the most academic or fictionalized writing.) I have attempted to summarize the insights gained during a lifetime in which religion and music together have been an abiding presence.

Religion—A Creative Art Form

IN 2008 I VISITED Rome for the first time together with my artist friend Sidney. I was not surprised but very much impressed by the degree to which many churches there as elsewhere in Europe are not so much vibrant houses of worship as they are architectural art museums reflecting past glories. I have long noticed signs that much of North America shares a similar tendency toward secularism, especially in the ever-expanding urban areas. This lively appreciation of art, together with the movement toward secularism, is actually a fortunate trend in my opinion. I think that religion at its best approaches (spiritual) truth in an essentially artistic way and is focused on dealing with reality in the (secular) here and now.

While I am adamant about the principle of the separation of church and state, I think that the typical distinction between sacred and secular, between spiritual and material, has been too rigid. Martin Luther wisely said, "God is interested in a lot of things besides religion." One of my professors in Graduate School, Harvey Cox, had just written a popular book in 1965 titled *The Secular City* which helped to clarify that sacred and secular are not mutually exclusive (and that loving your neighbor does not mean that you have to hug everyone you meet). The secular religion or "spiritual non-theism" that I will be outlining here is an approach to spirituality that does not involve a supernatural world distinct from the empirical, physical, natural world. Artistic Spiritual Non-theism works from the premise that spirituality and science do not have to be at odds with each other. Embracing the *spiritual dimension* of life is *not* about conjuring up a *supernatural world* of magic, ethereal entities and agents, paranormal experiences, heaven, hell, purgatory, and so forth. Spirituality embraces *Transcendent Mystery*, not supernatural superstitions. At best, we can perhaps say that some supernatural images and stories might serve as meaningful metaphors (symbols)—as more or less ham-fisted ways of expressing this Mystery.

For many years I have been teaching college humanities courses, mainly in world religions, in the Silicon Valley and larger Bay Area of northern California. A majority of college humanities courses tend to be about art. It has come to me as something of an epiphany that religion itself is best understood as an art form! For a number of years I have been using Karen Armstrong's classic *A History of God* as a textbook in one of my courses. Here are some of her observations that helped spark my epiphany:

> "... human beings are spiritual animals ... they created religions at the same time as they created works of art." (page xix)

> "... in an important sense God was a product of the creative imagination, like the poetry and music that I found so inspiring." (page xx)

> "... it should be obvious that the imagination is the chief religious faculty ... the cause of our major achievements in science and technology as well as in art and religion." (page 233)

> "Greek Christians ... found that God was better expressed in a work of art than in rationalistic discourse." (page 223)

> "... God is to be approached through the imagination and can be seen as a kind of art form, akin to the other great artistic symbols that have expressed the ineffable mystery, beauty and value of life." (page 396)

Armstrong's 2009 book *The Case for GOD* restates the point when she writes: "Like art, religion is an attempt to construct meaning in the face of the relentless pain and injustice of life." I quibble only with the notion that religion is merely "like" art or a "kind of" art form. My thesis here will be that religion *is* an art form because it is ultimately a product of creative human imagination.

A principal way in which religion differs from other art forms is in the degree to which it is practical and intends to affect our morality, our ethical behavior. In defense of artistic freedom it is said that art should be independent of moral concerns (that art *per se* is neither moral nor immoral but "amoral"). Since art is often deliberately provocative, we are indeed wise to look for its possible meaning and insight without rushing to judgment. This does not mean, however, that the creators of art can be indifferent to the possible uses or effects of their work. This book is partly about how religion can be misused or misunderstood—as can any art form.

In *The Case for GOD* Armstrong significantly updates some of her earlier views, but she is also responding to the contemporary atheist writers with whose irritation she sympathizes. She makes the point I will echo in these pages that "religion is not going to disappear," but she also warns against religion's "violent and intolerant strain." Although Islamic extremism has been the most immediate and widespread concern at the beginning of the twenty-first century, Christian hate groups picket funerals, pastors are forced by their doctrine-obsessed denominational leaders to apologize for participating in ecumenical responses to tragedies, and bigoted politics masquerade as a defense of scriptural tradition and principle.

Armstrong has come to describe herself as a "freelance monotheist." Despite my preference for more paradoxical terms such as "spiritual nonbeliever" or "high church atheist," I highly recommend *The Case for GOD*. It provides many detailed insights into the specific ways that the great monotheistic religious traditions that dominate Western culture have essayed the depths of religious experience and have created their notions of One God in a well-intentioned if sometimes deeply flawed effort to bring peace and harmony to the world. I say "deeply flawed" because the idea that all the people in the world would ever recognize the same specific "One God" is at best naïve. Even efforts such as the Sikh attempt to replace specific names for the One God with a neutral phrase such as "the True Name" have not succeeded in preventing religious wars and other serious conflicts. Furthermore, we shall see that when we expand our view and include the Asian (Eastern) and other non-monotheistic understandings of the sacred ("God"), there are even more reasons to wonder if religion has lived up to its intention of being a force for peace and unity in the world.

In both her history of God and case for God, Armstrong does a wonderful job of validating much of the imagery found in monotheistic traditions—often including helpful comparisons to other types of theology. She illustrates what I will be saying here about reclaiming our particular religions when we don't believe in them quite the same way we once did. In spite of identifying herself specifically as a monotheist, her overarching point is that God-language is always metaphorical and mythic. (I frequently find it helpful to put the word "God" in quotes—and perhaps we should always imagine the word as being in quotes.) Armstrong writes: "It may not be empirically true, it may defy the laws of logic, but a good myth will tell us something valuable about the human predicament. Like any work of art, a myth will make no sense unless we open ourselves to it wholeheartedly and allow it to change us. . . . The desire to cultivate a sense of the transcendent may be *the* defining human characteristic." "Like art," she continues, "the truths of religion require the disciplined cultivation of a different mode of consciousness." She uses the Greek word *ekstasis* (ecstatic) to describe "stepping out" beyond normal experience, and I would add how this is similar to the Greek word *ekklesia* (English—church; Spanish—iglesia) where Christians are "called out" to move beyond the norm in more ways than one.

In his book *After God*, Don Cupitt writes about the need to redefine religion in terms of artistic practice and symbolic expression. He suggests that we see religion less as ideology and more as a "tool kit" of techniques (such as imagining a "God's-eye-view") that can enhance our lives. John Herman Randall similarly views religion as "an art, a technique" that teaches us how to see "a unified vision of the Divine" and "to discern better the qualities and possibilities of the world"—to celebrate, consecrate, and clarify the splendor we experience in this world. Cupitt resurrects Augustine's phrase "poetical theology." His discussion of art and aesthetic philosophy shows how religion is indeed an art form closely bound up especially with literature, poetry, and music. He observes that "the magical supernatural world of religion was...a mythical representation of the world of language." In other words, it was precisely the appearance in our species of words and language that made both possible and inevitable the creation of an imaginary, supernatural world which we now must demythologize by emphasizing the metaphorical nature of religious language. Cupitt's "linguistic analysis" suggests that *the creation of religion was identical with the creation of metaphor and symbolism.* We imagine "God creating with a Word" because we create our world with words.

To put it another way, *Mystery forces us to make do with metaphor, symbolism, and personification.* My graduate theological colloquium at Harvard Divinity School was led by Professor Gordon D. Kaufman. Kaufman spent his career developing an understanding of "God" not as a supernatural entity but as an "ultimate point of reference for understanding everything" and as "serendipitous creativity"—a metaphor that includes reverence for imagination as well as an understanding of "big bang" theories and quantum science. Artist Don Bachardy stated in a 2011 "Gay and Lesbian Review" article that his life companion, writer Christopher Isherwood, "always felt that the religious life and the artist's life were parallel, that you could build one or the other on more or less the same principles."

In 2009 at age 90, Huston Smith, who has been described as the dean or even rock star of religion scholars, published an autobiography titled *Tales of Wonder: Adventures Chasing the Divine*. The San Francisco Chronicle review characterized the book as written in a spirit of "intellectual playfulness" and noted also that when Smith touches on the great issues "his wonderings are better than his answers." My focus in this book will not be on "religious art" but on religion itself as innately playful, imaginative and artistic. (Sadly, much religious art can be quite banal and tedious.) In these pages I will be reinforcing and drawing out the proposal by Armstrong, Cupitt, and others that religion itself is best understood as an art form. The issue becomes not whether God exists, but how any notion of God plays out—what it means and how it functions.

The most basic meaning of "art" is human work or effort, whether in the form of craft or "fine" art. Great Books educator Thomas Simpson defines a work of art as a high quality conception or product of our creative imagination, as opposed to a purely given fact of nature. Art is about interpretation and imagination. In their textbook introduction to the philosophical theories of art and aesthetics, editors D. Bronstein, Y. Krikorian, and P. Wiener write that "before the products of art we stand in rapture; the word that expresses our feelings is *ineffable,* and the ineffable is not prone to analysis." Just like religion, which is the next and final topic of their book, aesthetics is said to include the full range of that which inspires awe. Art is not only about "beauty" as this word is typically understood. That which may be neutral or even ugly may nevertheless express a sense of awe or of the sublime. Hebrew poets spoke of "the beauty of holiness," but this is the kind of sublime beauty that goes far beyond "pretty." Aesthetics includes everything that inspires awe and wonder. Specific religious traditions have their own special take on holy awe, such as the Buddhist contemplation of "the Seamless Whole" which we will encounter later.

Religion and Art together are perhaps the most comprehensive expressions of our love of wisdom because they typically pay attention to all the forms of intelligence—intellectual, emotional, and social. Aesthetics is arguably the most holistic and multi-dimensional branch of philosophy, partly because it affirms and celebrates ineffable mystery. As a creative and imaginative art form, religion has great practical effect on our personal, social, and political behavior in the here and now. As an art form—with its vision of reality, its themes of compassion, serenity, and wholeness, its stories and myths—religion touches every aspect of what it means to be human. The phrase "arts and sciences" includes the humanities, philosophy, psychology, sociology, literature, physics—everything! God and religion represent our audacious yet self-critical attempt to have Kaufman's "ultimate frame of reference for understanding everything." By understanding religion as an art form we are not reducing it to a narrow, one-dimensional version of aesthetics. We are, however, seeking to keep religion from taking itself too seriously as it struggles to comprehend the largest possible vision (with a nod to the Superman myth) of truth, justice, and the human way.

Armstrong's *A History of God* is more fully and accurately described as a history of how we humans have worked and played around with great ideas or fine conceptions about God and religion. The major religious traditions of the world are historical not in the sense that all their stories—such as those where angels speak to humans—are historical facts, but in the sense that they are incredibly influential and long-lived art forms. There may be certain core facts behind some of the stories, but religion presents us mainly with artistic, playful, and imaginative interpretations related to those core facts. The element of playfulness associated with art is in stark contrast to the certainty which is the stock in trade of religion that typically panders to our lesser instincts or to our delusions of grandeur. Among many other things, this understanding of religion as art or play means that a major function of religion is to keep our pride in check as we endeavor to comprehend the mystery of existence. Healthy religion does not promise to give us all the answers to life's persistent questions. It helps us rather to be at peace and comfortable with not having all the answers—with not being, well . . . God!

Music, Theology, and Imagination

I have grown up in the Lutheran tradition of Christianity. I am also a life-long musician—singer, conductor and organist. The fact that we speak of "playing" music reinforces the connection between religion, theology (God-talk), music, art, and playfulness. One of my favorite Schubert art songs is "To music" which in the usual English version begins with "O art divine!" ("The Divine" as Art!) Martin Luther wrote this in the preface to a collection of hymns first published in 1538:

"Experience testifies that after the Word of God music alone
deserves to be celebrated as mistress and queen of the emotions
of the human heart."

For a long time I thought Luther's line was "Next to theology, music
is the greatest." While this pithy phrase does capture the gist of what Luther meant, the quote apparently does not exist in this short form. Luther's
"Discourse in Praise of Music" puts it this way: "I give music the highest
and most honorable place . . . for music is a gift and grace of God, not an
invention of men." I suggest music might also be poetically described as
"divine grace notes." Jesus sings! (See Mark 14:26)

As both theologian and musician, my experience suggests to me that
theology and music are creative art forms which more than any other art
forms can be seen as two sides of the same coin. Furthermore, if there is a
"heads" or "tails" to this coin I am inclined to reverse Luther's observation
and declare music to be "heads" and theology "tails." I am thinking of great
or classic music in whatever genres, allowing, of course, for differences in
artistic taste. Almost any kind of music might have the potential to touch
the spiritual core of our being. Consider the incredible, ecstatic spirit often
found at the typical rock concert. My long experience with both music and
theology has led me toward the conclusion that in many respects music,
and in particular truly great religious music (think Bach, for example),
can be more effective than religious doctrine for putting us in touch with
the Divine Mystery that surrounds us. This Mystery can include even an
ecstatic sexual component. Musician friends and I have joked about how
some conductors seem to become virtually orgasmic when conducting
great music.

In her *History of God* chapter on "The God of the Mystics," Karen
Armstrong says that the visions, symbols, paradoxes, and poetic imagination that we find in the stories of all great religious literature are attempts
to bypass the intellect and to transcend language itself in order to invoke a
mood or experience of wonder, awe, and Ineffable Mystery. She describes
how this happens in Islam, Christianity and Judaism, even though there
has also been a literalizing tendency to think of stories as plain and simple
facts. Nevertheless, many Christians and Jews down through history have
indeed understood that biblical stories are usually much better and more
accurately seen as symbolic—as psychologically, imaginatively, themati-
cally and artistically true rather than as literally factual. Armstrong's book
Islam includes a history showing that many Muslims have allowed for
some highly symbolic, metaphorical, philosophical, or at times dubious

allegorical interpretations of the Qur'an and of Islam. Mutazilites and many other Muslim thinkers have rejected anthropomorphic images of Allah in favor of a more impersonal and transcendent understanding of divinity. As Irshad Manji describes in her 2003 book *The Trouble With Islam*, the "independent reasoning" called *ijtihad* has traditionally been encouraged in Muslim communities. In *The Case for GOD* Armstrong again notes "the long religious tradition that stressed the importance of recognizing the limits of our knowledge, [the importance] of silence, reticence, and awe." She adds: "It is not easy to talk about what we call 'God,' and the religious quest often begins with the deliberate dissolution of ordinary thought patterns."

All sacred scriptures are first and foremost works of literature, and literature is a highly metaphorical and symbolic art form! Metaphors and symbols are imaginative comparisons using images that do not include the qualifiers "like," "as," or "represents." For example, in explaining one of his parables Jesus is pictured as saying "The seed is the Word of God." We look pretty silly if we vehemently insist that "is means is" when, as in this case, it so obviously means "represents." An opera metaphor for the literature of sacred scriptures would be to describe holy books as *libretti* which when combined with *music* produce in us an awareness of Transcendent Mystery. Opera, whether grand or soapy, is storytelling. When I was a child, I listened faithfully to a Sunday afternoon radio program called "The Greatest Story Ever Told" in which the voice of Jesus always sounded as if it were coming from an echo chamber. I venture to say that the greatest and most popular form of literature is the art of storytelling—with or without music. Great preachers and speakers of any kind always tell stories. I love movies because they tell stories (and often so expensively that it seems a form of poor stewardship not to see and appreciate them). Stories do not always have to be factual in order to be great. Even movies with stories based on fact frequently use disclaimers such as "based on true events," and they inform the audience that some scenes and characters are "composites" created either for dramatic effect or to condense timelines. When the movie version of her novel *The Joy Luck Club* came out, Amy Tan told a radio interviewer that it is an occupational hazard of novelists to become confused over what in a story is fact and what is imagined. She implied that the truth lies not merely in the facts, but in the larger picture created by artistic imagination.

We will see that the great stories told in sacred scriptures are created by writers and editors who exercised a lot of artistic freedom as they developed their theological worldviews. One of my consistent objectives in this book will be to help the reader see that any stories where God is treated as an active agent or character need to be understood as symbolic. The themes of the story are the point, and to insist on the literal existence of the "God character" in the story is to risk missing the point. Recognizing themes is a primary key to understanding any form of literature.

The "music of the spheres" image which played a central role in Steven Spielberg's movie "Close Encounters of the Third Kind" clearly suggests that awe, wonder and transcendent imagination are perhaps best expressed in music. In the 2007 edition of his book *A Brief History of Everything*, Ken Wilber describes the universe as "one song" (page 34). But while I do feel that music trumps theology in some ways, I don't think that it is necessary for music and theology to play a bruising game of one-ups-man-ship with each other. Both endeavor to transcend the limitations of language. It will remain, however, an overall objective in this book to underscore the essentially artistic nature of religion and to highlight music as the singular art form most compatible, and virtually even synonymous, with religion.

When we see religion and theology as art, we are better able to appreciate the unique contributions of the various world religions. Religion understood as art is much less likely to "poison everything," as Christopher Hitchens said it does. Of course, religion can also become a benign and more positive force in the world if we concentrate on the striking similarities among religious traditions, as Joseph Campbell does in his 1948 classic *The Hero With A Thousand Faces*. But it is the differences between religions that cause the major problems and, sadly, the disagreements sometimes become even more intense when spiritual traditions actually have a great deal in common. Krister Stendahl, who was the dean of Harvard Divinity School when I was there, liked to speak of "holy envy." He meant that beyond mere toleration we should actually celebrate—yes, even envy—the wonderful things in religious traditions other than our own. (Our church history professor at Wartburg Seminary, Bernard Holm, sometimes expressed envy of Roman Catholicism, wishing, for example, that we Lutherans had more statues in our churches—Holm also loved to improvise on the piano and whimsically hoped that his first experience in heaven would be to meet Mozart.)

Great art is often simultaneously both particular and universal. *Understood as art forms, distinct religions can celebrate their unique stories, symbols, rituals, holidays and the like—their "local color"—as absolutely meaningful and beautiful while also allowing others to do the same!* An artistic mindset makes it possible for followers of a religion to embrace their worldview without engaging in hard-sell missionary activity and special pleading about how their particular religion, with its sometimes embarrassingly violent or all too parochial back-story, is uniquely superior. Now that we live in a global village, the various faith traditions must learn to share their stories and symbols in a spirit of dialogue without arrogance or condescension. When this happens people inevitably find that many of the particulars which they don't share in common are just different aspects of, or approaches to, the same universal issues and concerns. The theme of divine grace is found in virtually all religions, even though it is expressed in different ways. Muslim scholar Fethullah Gulen pictures inter-religious dialogue as a "symphony" of divine mercy. In *The Future of Faith* Harvey Cox says that religious myths are "a symphony of symbols."

Understood as uniquely congruent art forms, theology and music together produce charms to sooth the savage religions. John Lennon's song "Imagine" struck a chord that continues to resonate. He imagines a world of peace without war, of people living fully in the moment—a world with no religion and no heaven! Lennon's controversial remark about the Beatles being more popular than Jesus may have been a greater clue about the future of religion than even he imagined. When he back peddled somewhat on his remarks he was probably conceding that religion does not necessarily have to be a destructive force in the world. Imagination is about vision, and we surely would be bereft without our artistic, spiritual, and political visionaries who imagine "God's dream" for a world of justice and peace.

Mystery, Metaphor, and Music

When Karen Armstrong says that the imagination is the chief religious faculty, she challenges us to be both quite modest and very adventurous when we talk about God and religion. She is not dismissing God or religion as mere figments of our imagination. The word "figment" comes from the Latin meaning "to form, mold or fashion." But rather than being the "fine or high quality conception" I mentioned previously, "figment" has the connotation of being a fabrication or arbitrary notion that is simply made up with no solid evidence or rationale behind it, that is, an idea with no *Referent*. But God and religion *are not just mere figments* in this sense. Armstrong echoes Paul Tillich's point that religious symbols or imaginative metaphors must not be denigrated with modifiers such as just, merely, or only. *There is a basic Referent, a basic Reality behind God and religion, and that Referent is the Quality of Sacred, Ineffable Mystery—which Joseph Campbell describes as "beyond all categories of thought."* This Referent is no "thing" or any specific version of God. It is not the "Unknown God" of the Athenians who erected a statue to represent any deity they might have missed when they compiled their list of gods (Acts 17:23).

When Gordon Kaufman says that the word "God" represents our human attempt to create a symbol that serves as "the ultimate point of reference for understanding everything," he is being "holistic"—the root meaning of "catholic" (cat, in Greek *kata*–like, as, or according to; *holos*– whole or universal). He is talking about coming to terms with Reality as a whole. We can imagine such an ultimate point of reference, but we almost certainly will never achieve, possess, or fully comprehend "everything!" It was in this sense that Kaufman also called God the "relativizer" because our understanding of "everything" will almost certainly never be absolute. It is also in this sense that the opening lines of the *Daodejing* (Tao Te Ching) insist that "The Tao that can be spoken of is not the eternal Tao. The name that can be named is not the eternal name." In Taoism, all names and concepts are flexible. Tao is typically said to mean "the way things are," but there is no one, absolute, comprehensive way to understand or express this "Reality." Reality is mysteriously flexible. Even the terms good and evil are relative to situations, perceptions, and our comparative value judgments.

There is a big difference between a metaphor and a lie, between creative, supple imagination and deceptive balderdash. Creative and imaginative religious metaphors and symbols such as "God" are focused on the most challenging aspects of Reality—on the mysterious flexibility or fluidity of Reality, and on the haunting questions that even science likely will never answer! The Ultimate Mystery in which these symbols "participate" (as Tillich would say) is best viewed as a positive, uplifting, creative Reality. We may not fully comprehend why there is something rather than nothing, but we do know that there *is* something and that this Reality is to a significant degree naturally supportive, flexible, hopeful, and energetic.

Harvey Cox writes that both fundamentalists and atheists are often "deficient in their capacity for metaphor, analogy, and the place of symbol and myth in human life." He describes religious stories as "artifacts human beings have crafted to try to wring some meaning from the mystery." But even our imagination cannot fully capture Reality. Somewhat as Reality TV is not total reality, artistic theological symbols and metaphors also are never identical with Ultimate Reality. Ultimate Reality is an Ultimate Mystery, and not mystery in the sense of a riddle or detective yarn that can be solved if we are especially clever, or if we merely gather more information. The *Quality* of Ultimate Mystery is about questions such as why there is something rather than nothing, questions that almost certainly have no totally satisfying answers. This Great Mystery challenges us with the realization that neither our wildest imaginings nor our mind-boggling forays into theoretical physics (sub-atomic "God-particles," big bangs, string theory, "eloquent equations," dark matter/energy and black holes) are likely ever to fully comprehend Ultimate Reality.

In his 2012 book *A Universe from Nothing: Why There Is Something Rather Than Nothing*, Lawrence M. Krauss displays his knowledge of math and physics in an attempt to answer this question, but he basically ends up playing with the meaning of words such as "nothing," "infinity," or "empty space." Like masterful theologians and philosophers, physicists and mathematicians typically run up against the limits of language. They end up struggling with paradoxes (apparent contradictions). They use metaphors such as "big bang," "black hole" and "dark matter." They try to explain how "empty doesn't necessarily mean empty" or "nothing doesn't mean nothing" (which does make sense up to a point), often failing to recognize, however, that ultimately they are up against Mystery. Krauss admits the need for appropriate humility on the part of scientists, but I think his idea that we can or should turn all "why" questions into "how" questions betrays a refusal to face the reality of Ultimate Mystery (see *The Tao of Physics*, 35th anniversary edition, pages 287 and 334). To deny that there can ever be "why" questions without answers amounts to a categorical denial that there can be any such thing as Ultimate Mystery. Rather than simply recognizing that science will continue to make astounding discoveries, the attempt to reduce everything to "how" questions seems to make the arrogant claim that the scientific method can and will eventually provide adequate answers to absolutely every question we human beings are capable of asking, no matter how "ultimate" those questions might be and despite the fact that every discovery often raises a host of new questions. "Why" questions are more existential than practical—they require not so much answers as ongoing discussion.

If you need help coming to terms with the notion of Ultimate Mystery, consider whether outer space never ends or does end at some point. If it does end and there is nothing beyond, is that nothing something? When astronomers talk about galaxies numbered in the billions, aren't they really moving beyond the very category of "number"? Or does the universe curve back upon itself—and what does that mean? What does it mean to talk about moving beyond the categories of time and space—beyond all categories of thought (Campbell)? Do contemporary physics and astronomy force us to use the term multiverse rather than universe? (See "Scientific American," January, 2010.) If there is other intelligent life in the universe (with its Billions and Billions of galaxies), as astronomer Carl Sagan fondly hoped (see his 1995 *The Demon-Haunted World: Science as a Candle in the Dark*), what are we to make of his admitting that there is absolutely no evidence for it so far, in spite of all our sophisticated explorations? How can it seem impossible to believe that we are the only intelligent life in the universe and at the same time, so far, seem necessary to believe it? Perhaps the simple fact is that we are the only beings in the universe capable of asking this question about other intelligent life in the universe.

If you want an example of Mystery that is similar to the big bang but closer to our immediate experience, consider a microscopic sperm and egg turning into the incredibly complex body and brain (!) of a human being in just nine months or less. We may understand more than we once did about cellular biology and genetics, but many who help deliver babies still experience a profound sense of awe each time. (I find it amazing in a rather opposite way that Francis Collins, who directed the successful mapping of the human genome, defends a supernatural notion of God, and of Christianity in particular as a literal and factually true revelation of this supernatural God. Collins and others like him are frequently criticized in this regard for illegitimately compartmentalizing their ideas into separate categories with differing rules of logic.)

Religious imagination creates many comforting poetic fantasies. In answer to those who would tell me that they could exercise their spirituality by enjoying a beautiful sunset rather than by going to church, I used to point out that the same sun that creates warmth and beauty can also fry you to death—nature is neutral, whereas "God's Word" can tell you in clear terms that you are loved. Religion has typically provided this type of counterpoint to the neutrality and randomness of nature. But the comforting poetic fantasy that imagines God telling you how much "He" loves you is more about the power of positive thinking than it is about the existence or reality of any particular notion of God. It is about creating an image in our minds that provides strong encouragement and support. The image may be fantasy as opposed to fact, but it can have real power.

(The placebo effect will be mentioned more than once in this book.) To those who would denigrate this power by saying that it is all in one's head, I would point out that our heads contain our brains, which are as mysteriously amazing as anything in the universe!

British science writer Philip Ball says in *The Music Instinct* that music is a mystery unique to humans. Scans show that our entire brain is activated by music. Barbara Hagerty has a lot to say about our brains in her 2009 book *Fingerprints of God: The Search for the Science of Spirituality*. The book is not so much about whether God exists as it is an update on the science of religious experience. She concludes that the human brain is hardwired to produce transcendent experiences but that many things, including psychedelic drugs, can produce such experiences. She cannot resist the urge to personify a source of our religious experiences as "One who longs to be known," but this is predictable since we seem hardwired to personify everything from ducks (Donald) to Ultimate Mystery (God).

To praise imagination is to recognize the power of images that we hold in our minds. Relaxation therapy, for example, may suggest that I imagine a calm and peaceful scene until my imagined calm becomes real calm. Some psychologists who survived Hitler's death camps observed that those who survived were the ones who imagined surviving, while the "realists" who did not expect to survive generally did not. Honest hope is not the same as mere wishful thinking. Ironically, the imaginers sometimes turn out to be the realists. This is one of the many paradoxes we will be considering in these pages. Hagerty, perhaps because she comes out of a "mind-over-matter" Christian Science background, documents that religious beliefs and practices can have significant positive effects on our well-being even if they are products of creative, artistic imagination. On the other hand, while positive thinking and imaging may have beneficial effects, careful studies have shown that positive attitudes in and of themselves can let us down. If you are told that positive thinking will cure a disease but despite all your positive thinking or believing you are still sick, you may have done nothing but add guilt to your suffering, berating yourself for not having enough faith. This can be another form of taking religion too literally. Religious metaphors and images can be very meaningful and helpful, but they can let us down if we over-indulge in what Joan Didion described as "magical thinking" when she wrote about her efforts to cope with her husband's death.

When B. F. Skinner wrote that there is no such "thing" as freedom and dignity he meant that these words describe ways of behaving rather than things, that they are more verbs than nouns (and that these ways of behaving are limited by the primitive part of our brains and by our environmental and genetic conditioning). When Freud said that there is no such thing as an Oedipus Complex he meant that this mythic *allusion* was shorthand for describing a form of behavior. Freud sometimes said that many of his concepts were, like religious ideas such as God, *illusions*, but that his were better, more pragmatic and functional illusions. He could have called them "allusions," "constructs," or "metaphors" because all these terms involve a kind of indirect meaning. When Richard Dawkins talks about the "God *Delusion*" he is saying that there is no such "thing" as God. But the God *Allusion* suggests that we see "God" as a playful, creative, metaphor with unique potential for putting us in touch with Ultimate Mystery. While it may not be a "thing," Ultimate Mystery is absolutely Real! This is why music celebrating The Power and The Glory is so inspiring. This is why religion is not going to go away!

But while neither religion nor concepts of God will go away, we must not engage in battles about which particular image of God or religious belief system is "The Truth." The Zoroastrian wise-men story in the Matthew Gospel needs to be seen as about welcoming all rather than as demanding the conversion of all. I appreciate the attempt of Bahai to highlight what is great in all the major religions, but it seems to me that Bahai unfortunately has come up with its own Truth that superimposes itself above all others as the last word. This tendency of religion to want to convert everyone is a constant temptation that can be avoided by understanding religion as a creative art form. Religions must be criticized whenever they threaten to become absolutist and authoritarian power trips. An awareness of Absolute Divine Mystery should serve precisely to keep anyone from claiming to have a lock on Absolute Truths—or "Final Solutions." Ironically, when Bahai developed out of Shi'ite Islam in Iran the movement was condemned and persecuted precisely because Bahai claimed to have its own later day prophet, which was seen as a denial of the Islamic claim that Mohammed was the last and final prophet! (Shouldn't the theme that Mohammed is just a messenger and not a divine being prevent fanatical hyper-sensitivity regarding his name or image?) Consider how unfair and arrogant it is to ask people to choose between final prophets or true religions when you basically have no solid evidence but only claims based on assumed authority. A person's eternal destiny depends on a guess as to which competing claim is right?

Garrison Keillor tells a joke about castaway Ole showing his rescuers around the deserted island where he has built some buildings. He shows them his house, a church, and then is asked about another large building. "Oh, that's the church I used to go to," he replies. The joke spoofs those who are always in quest of the perfect church or religion, but it also illustrates how all thinkers, philosophers, theologians, and scientists try to make improvements on what has gone before, to get a better handle on truth. Freud and Einstein will always be revered, but not everything they said is considered the last word. Likewise, theology must not claim to have the last word. All wise thinkers who struggle to come up with a history or theory of everything should understand that at best they are charting only one way of moving "Toward The Mystery" (the title of a book by William Edelen). Harvey Cox wisely describes the various religions as "responding to the same mystery…in quite disparate ways."

For truly spiritual people—and I would certainly include John Lennon among them—imagination does not have a negative connotation. The Bible frequently pictures God as being way beyond anything that we can even begin to visualize or imagine! When the original Greek of First Corinthians 2:9 describes God as a Reality that "eye has not seen, nor ear heard, nor has it entered into the heart of man," it reflects the Hebrew notion of "heart" as the basic location of intelligence, understanding or mind. (Nowadays we tend to locate emotion in the heart, but Hebrew writers located emotion in the bowels, in the gut.) So the apostle Paul is clearly saying (as in some translations of this text) that it has not "entered into the mind of man"—that we have not even begun to imagine!—what Divine Mystery is all about. In this same letter St. Paul also writes: "If any one imagines (thinks) that he knows something, he does not yet know as he ought to know." (I Cor. 8:2) To say that God is beyond our imagination is not to denigrate either imagination or God. God is not imaginary in the sense of having nothing to do with Reality. God-talk requires that we engage our imagination to the hilt while at the same time recognizing that the Ultimate Mystery of Life ("God") is beyond our comprehension. Those, such as the comedian and social critic Bill Maher, who find the word "God" too loaded with negative baggage, are not necessarily anti-spiritual just because they ridicule what they consider to be superstitious, naïve or small-minded uses of God-talk. Religious imagination is about stretching our minds. It is about allowing our minds to be boggled. It is not about literal belief in an imaginary friend (or friends) who reside somewhere above the sky.

Alcoholics Anonymous groups typically emphasize the necessity of calling upon a Higher Power of some kind as an aid in resisting temptation. AA folks are encouraged to visualize this Higher Power in whatever way they see fit. It can be anything—a symbolic or actual mountain, a famous landmark, or some kind of God. It is often joked (seriously!) by AA members that because of their terrible behavior while under the influence, any God they might look to would have to be compassionate and forgiving. The power of such imaging or visualization is undeniable. It is the intimation of a Reality that cannot be adequately named. We are forced into paradoxical language of saying that such higher power is both imaginary and incredibly real. Of course, higher power imaging in self-help groups is augmented by the support of individual sponsors and group dynamics, but few in AA would question the reality of this sense of higher power. The kind of radical transformation sought by alcoholics seems inevitably akin to a religious experience.

In his Ingersoll lecture on immortality in 1959 Henry Cadbury stressed that we must not underestimate myths or fairy tales. Walt Disney may have eviscerated many fairy tales, but the deeper levels of meaning in these tales is always there to be rediscovered. Myths are about what William James calls *The More.* Cadbury says:

> "That the dead become angels and exist in heaven would be the kind of mythical views that would be the first to disappear at the hands of modern demythologizing. Probably we are quite prepared to surrender heaven as a place literally in the sky, and the angels as corporeal beings with or without wings. . . .Are not myth and symbol almost universal in religion? . . . imagination naturally plays a part in thinking of life after death. But we must recognize precisely that it is imagination. . . .The purpose of demythologizing is to remove the shell of such notions in order that the spiritual values can be preserved . . ."

If we dismiss myths with a sneer as mere fairy tales we underestimate both myths and fairy tales. We fail to see *the more than* surface meaning and in so doing fail to maintain proper humility in our contemplation of Ultimate Divine Mystery. The tale in Exodus 33 where Moses is placed in a split rock and allowed to see only God's "backside" inspired the hymn "Rock of Ages Cleft for Me." This story where God says that no human can fully see God and survive—along with the Hebrew tradition of not pronouncing the name of the Lord (Yahweh or YHWH)—shows us that even long-ago people were capable of expressing awe when confronted with Ultimate Mystery. Such stories, it seems to me, make it abundantly evident that many if not all of the people who created and told these stories realized that they were basically artful stories intended to interpret the meaning of human life and experience.

Thomas Mann has provided us with one of the best descriptions of myth: "A myth is a story about the way things never were, but always are." Much of the religious writing of India consists of stories and poetry. From earliest times it was a defining characteristic of Hebrew/Jewish culture to prefer storytelling to abstract philosophizing. That tradition is carried on in part today by Jews in the movie industry and in comedy (from Jack Benny and Woody Allen to Jerry Seinfeld, Sarah Silverman, Steven Spielberg, and Mel Brooks). I myself often prefer to have ideas presented in clear prose rather than in symbolic stories. But stories have the advantage of being multi-dimensional. Storytelling involves complex characters and leaves a lot of room for imaginative interpretation. The same is true of music, which is in some ways the most abstract of arts because, except for music combined with a text, the *meaning* of most music is completely open to interpretation. Leonard Bernstein insisted that in spite of its connection with the Lone Ranger, the famous overture to Rossini's William Tell opera doesn't *mean* anything in particular.

It may just be my particular bias that I see creative imagination most often at its zenith in music and theology. Religious stories are indeed among some of the greatest ever told. I also stand in awe of the creative imagination of great composers and I have taught many courses on the lives and music of these artists. In praising music—whether that of Bach, Brahms, Beethoven or the Beatles—I am not claiming that music is absolutely better than all other arts. The ability to appreciate any particular art form can depend on an individual's basic sensory equipment, temperament, education, etc. The architects of great cathedrals, poets, and writers in various genres might well insist that they too are hand in glove with theology. The Paleolithic cave paintings in southern France and northern Spain reflect the amazing antiquity of the connection between art and spirituality. But since, together with its many other attributes, music is perhaps one of humankind's even earlier artistic activities, and since one of the elements of music, namely rhythm, can be experienced by virtually any living being, it might be fair to say that music is the most universally accessible of the arts. I remember visiting a church for the deaf in my home town and there were band instruments set up in the chancel to be played very loudly so that the vibrations and rhythms could be felt.

The physics of string theory and the mathematics of Pythagoras provide us with an image of the whole universe vibrating in rhythmic harmony, and I am aware of a prominent cancer researcher who describes healthy body organs as involving "special primitive 'tunes' played out within the genome." We should also note that music can be combined with all the other forms of art. Grand opera, movies, and dance come particularly to mind. Many artists such as painters, sculptors and architects also frequently listen to music while engaging in their creative processes, and music is often heard in the places where their creations are on display.

Ponder these famous quotations in praise of music that echo those of Luther:

"We have fallen into the place
where everything is music."
Rumi, thirteenth century Islamic Sufi poet

"Music, the greatest good that mortals know,
And all of heaven we have below."
—Joseph Addison: "Songs for St. Cecilia's Day"

"Some to church repair
Not for the doctrine,
but the music there."
—Alexander Pope from his "Essays on Criticism

"Music resembles poetry; in each
Are nameless graces which no methods teach . . ."
—Ibid. Alexander Pope

"Music must take rank as the highest of the fine arts—as the one which, more than any other, ministers to human welfare."
—Herbert Spencer "On the Origen and Function of Music"

"Music is well said to be the speech of angels."
—Thomas Carlyle "Essays. Death of Goethe"

"Music is the universal language of mankind . . ."
—Henry Wadsworth Longfellow "Outre-Mer"

"Music is heaven's best gift to humanity."
—Pyotr Ilyich Tchaikovsky

"Without music life would be a mistake."
—*Friedrich Nietzsche "Maxims and Missiles"*

"If music be the food of love, play on;"
—*Shakespeare "Twelfth Night"*

"Music hath charms to soothe a savage breast/beast"
(the original is uncertain)

—*William Congreve "The Mourning Bride"*

"When music speaks to you, you are at peace with the universe."
—*Nicola Luisotti, Music Director and Conductor of the San Francisco Opera*

"Music is a more sublime divine revelation than all wisdom and philosophy."
—*Ludwig Van Beethoven* (my translation)

And as an organist and choir conductor I must finally add:

"There let the pealing organ blow,
To the full voiced quire below,
In service high, and anthems clear,
As may with sweetness, through mine ear,
Dissolve me into ecstasies,
And bring all Heaven before mine eyes."
—*John Milton "Il Penseroso"*

In a welcoming address given to entering freshmen music students at the Boston Conservatory, Karl Paulnack noted that the Greeks understood how "music has a way of finding the big, invisible moving pieces inside our hearts and souls and helping us figure out the position of things inside us." He added: "Music is a basic need of human survival. Music is one of the ways we make sense of our lives, one of the ways in which we express feelings when we have no words, a way for us to understand things with our hearts when we cannot with our minds." Famed researcher Dr. Oliver Saxe discovered that music engages more of the brain than does language alone. He found that stroke patients who can't speak are able to sing, and that this phenomenon is related to the fact that persons who stutter when they speak often can sing without stuttering. Paulnack concluded his address by saying:

"If there is a future wave of wellness on this planet, of harmony, of peace, of an end to war, of mutual understanding, of equality, of fairness, I don't expect it will come from a government, a military force or a corporation. I no longer even expect it to come from the religions of the world, which together seem to have brought us as much war as they have peace. If there is a future peace for humankind, if there is to be an understanding of how these invisible, internal things should fit together, I expect it will come from the artists…"

The arts also provide us with perhaps the most enduring legacy from our human past. My only quibble with this assessment is that Paulnack seems to separate the role of religion from the role of the arts and sciences. While not all artists or scientists necessarily want or need to be seen as religious, when religiously inclined people see themselves as involved in an art form, their religion can become the kind of spirituality capable of bringing a future wave of wellness, harmony, peace, and justice to this planet. It will take more than choirs singing the many beautiful versions of *dona nobis pacem* (grant us peace) to bring about this reality of peace and justice, but the popularity and persistence of such songs tells me that there is still great hope for humanity.

CHAPTER 1

"High Church Atheism"

THOSE WHO SET THE art, music, ritual, drama, and symbolism of religion above theology have sometimes been dubbed "high church atheists." This description is wonderfully provocative, but also somewhat misleading and unfair. Once upon a time as a budding theologian I occasionally made fun of people who seemed to be worshiping stained glass windows because it seemed to me that their notion of the relationship between religion and art was too shallow. Those in the know when it comes to church-talk recognize the terms high-, middle-, or low-church as referring basically to the amount of ritual and decorative refinement typically found within a particular Christian denomination. "High church" implies a lot of emphasis on ritual, artistic decoration and even theatricality. The Anglican (English) Church in its American incarnation as the Episcopal Church traditionally has appeared most likely to include all three styles among its various congregations. The "high church" tendency reflects the fact that King Henry VIII's break with papal Roman Catholicism was not a break with its rituals. I first encountered the phrase "high church atheist" in the context of performing as a musician in Episcopal churches and Anglican cathedrals. I now understand that there can be a deeper version of high church atheism than what I envisioned when I first encountered the term. Ironically, this deeper version requires first and foremost a more light-hearted and whimsical attitude toward the word atheism.

It is possible to appreciate the concerns of atheists without necessarily being militantly against any version of God or religion as Christopher Hitchens tends to be in his book *God Is NOT Great*. (One wonders if Hitchens noticed the irony that his name Christopher means "Christ-bearer.") Even Richard Dawkins in his best-selling *The God Delusion* will say only that "there almost certainly is no God," and what he specifically objects to is any kind of first-cause, unmoved mover, supernatural father figure/Sky Daddy, *Deus ex machina* (God as intervening agent), or "intelligent designer" concept. Dawkins and others like to point out that virtually all people nowadays are atheists in the sense that they don't believe in many of the famous gods such as Zeus—early Christians were often charged with being atheists because they did not worship the Greek or Roman gods (use of the lower case spelling of "gods" sometimes betrays a clear prejudice). Episcopal Bishop Emeritus Spong is wise to talk about "non-theism" or "moving beyond theism" instead of latching onto the red flag connotations of atheism or atheist. "God" is not going to disappear from our vocabulary any time in the foreseeable future, if ever (although my psychologist friend Dr. Dennis Hinkle would be glad to see the word fade away because he sees supernatural "Sky Daddy" connotations as so inevitable).

My view is that reclaiming spirituality must include an increasingly sophisticated, artistic, and whimsical way of using both God and anti-God language. I suspect that many who consider themselves atheists would nevertheless appreciate Kaufman's observation that the symbol "God" has been specifically created to serve as an "ultimate point of reference for understanding everything"—which, ironically, includes the awareness that we almost certainly will never understand everything, never comprehend the Ultimate Mystery which is "beyond all categories of thought" (Campbell)!

In an insightful article published digitally by The New Yorker magazine titled "God in the Quad" James Woods analyzes the renewed discussion occurring in the wake of the aggressive atheistic books hitting the shelves in the early years of the twenty-first century. He expresses reservations with regard to Richard Dawkin's "intolerant certainty" and "over-weaning rationalistic atheism." "What is needed," he says, "is a theologically engaged atheism that resembles disappointed belief . . . atheism, only a semitone from faith . . ." I, of course, very much appreciate his use of a musical metaphor to describe what I would call a reclaimable rather than a disappointed faith. I think his criticisms of Dawkins are overstated, but he is right on the money when he writes that "abolishing the category of the religious robs nonbelievers of . . . the inexpressible." While he comes close to it with this reference to the inexpressible (enhanced by his description of Mozart as having been sent to earth directly from heaven!), the main criticism I have of Woods' article is that he never explicitly mentions the dimension of Mystery. He deals with the issue of personal versus impersonal concepts of God, but never seems to clarify how the word God can be viewed as the primary metaphor people use to express the dimension or experience of Transcendent Spiritual Mystery.

Living in the moment, in *the eternal now* ("realized/participatory eschatology" as introduced in the Acknowledgments) is about faith as an experience rather than as belief in a set of propositions. Woods refers to the philosopher Wittgenstein as "useful to those who remain attached to the traditions of their upbringing but no longer credit any of the tradition's truth claims." Wittgenstein notes that we do not kiss the photo of a loved one because we think it will affect them but because it expresses a relationship we experience as meaningful and satisfying. Like religion, it is symbolic, metaphorical behavior. Woods uses the term "quasi-believers" instead of "high church atheists," and while it has some value as a description of those who live within the experience and symbolism of Spiritual Mystery, this description too is unfair and misleading. There is nothing "quasi" about Absolute Mystery.

A big part of the problem with the term atheist is that it seems to be mainly about denying and reacting. This is one of the reasons why philosopher Daniel C. Dennett and others are trying to replace it with the term "Bright." Writers such as Dawkins, Dennett, and Sam Harris (*The End of Faith, Letter to a Christian Nation, The Moral Landscape*) and those who appreciate and applaud their wisdom, are not so much against God or gods as they are *for* reason, truth, enlightenment (brightness!), honesty, reality, authenticity and integrity. (Harvard University began as a religious school and its motto is *Veritas*—the Latin word for truth.) We will consider further what is meant by the term "post-modern," but for now we need only note that the modern world is typically defined in terms of the scientific mentality that developed during the so-called age of reason or enlightenment in the eighteenth century, following in the footsteps of the Renaissance. *Post*modernism typically implies a caution against over-emphasizing reason, materialism, or empiricism—caution against a single, purely objective, scientific worldview with no room for a variety of cultural perspectives or non-tangibles such as spirituality. The challenge I am taking up in this book is to show how we can highly value *both* scientific reason (empiricism, materialism, truth-based-on-evidence) *and* spirituality or religion.

Atheism is not itself a religion, as some critics insist. It is not a worship of reason or a "negative faith." Best understood, it simply has to do with replacing supernatural ways of ascertaining truth with more proven and effective ways of gaining knowledge about what is true. Atheism does not have to be about never using the word God! The real issue both for atheists and for those who are religious or spiritual is about being open, cautious, and sometimes even whimsical when using religious or theological language. On the deepest level, God language is about the Great Mystery that is Reality, the Absolute Mystery that surrounds us all—the Mystery that *is* us.

I am concerned about the frequent use of the word "God" in a way that is so far removed from this sense of Absolute Divine/Sacred Mystery. An old Latin phrase is *Magnum Mysterium* (Huge Mystery). We should see the word "God" essentially as shorthand for this Mystery—shorthand to which we should not be too attached. To put it another way, we need to understand God as a personification of this Mystery much akin to "Mother Nature." We should never think of some specific version of "God"—especially God as a mere character in a story, no matter how prominent a character—as fully capturing this Absolute Mystery. This Mystery alone is absolute and, therefore, our particular concepts regarding this Mystery are never absolute. Karen Armstrong writes an entire chapter centered around the theme that the Christian Trinity is not a mathematical riddle but an Ineffable Mystery. The great scholar of world religions, Huston Smith, suggested in an interview with journalist Bill Moyers that Muslims should think of submission to Allah as "submission to Reality with a capital R" rather than as blind obedience to an authoritarian rule maker (as it unfortunately all too often is). This emphasis on Reality with a capital R fits well with the type of Buddhist mindset that we will consider in chapter 5.

Some progressive Roman Catholics such as film director Louis Malle surprised many folks by objecting to the Latin Mass being replaced with vernacular versions that people could supposedly better understand. But the reason Malle and others opposed this change was that they felt the *Magnum Mysterium* better served by a language of great antiquity—a language that has the distinction of both transcending and forming the basis of other languages. Better understanding is a worthy goal, but the most important thing we must understand is that a completely understood God is no God at all! Any true scientist will tell you that the more we learn, the more we discover how much more we don't know. A main purpose of God-talk should be to keep us appropriately humble and open. Unfortunately, too many strongly religious people are anything but humble. Timothy Pantoja rejoiced at receiving his 2009 Master of Divinity degree from Harvard, but his commencement speech emphasized that nobody masters either divinity or humanity.

An article in the April 21, 2000 Wall Street Journal titled "Redefining God" began by citing a market-research study which found rapidly increasing numbers of people, especially younger ones, describing themselves as "spiritual but not religious" and admitting that no standard definition of the deity comes close to their own. ("Deity" comes from the Latin word for God, *deus.* "Theism" and "theology" come from the Greek word for God, *theos.*) A common trend this study found was toward more clearly metaphorical or abstract images such as Radiant Luminosity of the Sacred, Source of All, Ineffable Mystery, Ultimate Sanctuary or Home. The same article also referenced the images of God that Bishop Spong draws from the Hebrew Scriptures—the metaphors of Breath, Wind, and Rock. An important Jewish tradition says that there are 72 or more names for God including abstractions such as "The Divine Presence." Jews, Taoists, and Sikhs are all known for their reticence when it comes to "God talk." Sikhs beat around this burning bush and recognize the limitations of any language about "God" by avoiding specific appellations in favor of the phrase "the True Name." I would add the images of Eternal Spirit or Energy to the list of possibilities for naming the sacred. The New Testament gives us the eloquently simple definition "God is Love." The Power of Divine Love is God—a way of being and acting that expresses compassionate connectedness.

It is important to note that all these images avoid the gender issue. The gender issue regarding "God" has also increasingly been sidestepped by using neutral terms such as Sovereign instead of King or Lord, and Reign instead of Kingdom—although even these gender neutral images are nevertheless somewhat dated and problematic if they are understood in an authoritarian sense rather than as embodying a set of humanistic egalitarian values. Descriptions such as King of kings and Lord of lords supply an appropriate hint of "divine transcendence" but still retain a problematic authoritarian note of gender, domination, and oppression. (Speaking of younger folks, I wonder what it portends that there is a popular brand of jeans labeled True Religion and a music group called Bad Religion.)

God-talk and the God's-eye View

Listening to Invocations and Benedictions during the 2009 inauguration of Barack Obama as President of the United States, it struck me how much of our God-language is about seeing things with the largest possible universal perspective. Religion has as one of its functions to help us stand back and see the big picture, to see humanity and all things as one interconnected whole. Imagine a "God's-eye view" of the gap between the rich countries that consume a hugely disproportionate percentage of the world's resources, and the starving and dying poor on planet earth. Or imagine what God would think of the wealth and income inequality within the United States as compared with the relative equality in Scandinavian countries! It is a viewpoint that can make the problems and complaints of the affluent few seem very small-minded indeed. Cupitt values the "God's-eye view" metaphor as a both tragic and comic vision.

The metaphor of "God's Dream for a better world" imagines an uplifting, positive perspective on life. If we say "*God knows* capitalism has a dark and dangerous side" we mean that by having the broadest possible perspective on things as they truly are we can better understand and more effectively counteract this dark side. (The idea that gung-ho, unregulated capitalism can perfect our world seems incredibly naïve. See Peter Brown's *Through The Eye Of A Needle*, 2012, and Al Gore's *The Future: Six Drivers of Global Change*, 2013.) "God knows" is similar to "Who knows?" or to "Truth is" and none of these idioms necessarily imply that there is some kind of "knower" somewhere. To say "God only knows" or "who knows" is a way of embracing reality, possibilities, and mystery. The God Hitchins rejects, the typical authoritarian or parochial tribal god, may not be great. But the *universal perspective* that accompanies an awareness of *Sublime Sacred Mystery* truly is great. It's "the God's Truth!"

There is a middle ground between strict atheism and doctrinaire theistic belief systems. I don't think agnosticism is the right term for this middle ground. To say one is an agnostic is to say "I *don't know* if God is real." The attitude also tends to be "I don't really care much either since it is so debatable." Agnosticism about God and religion tends to have the connotation of not really wanting to bother with religion at all. High Church Atheism is a striking metaphor which suggests that we can continue to value religion even as we discard its outdated or counter-productive elements! The so-called death of God theologians of the mid-twentieth century were Christian scholars who struggled to come to terms with both the scientific secularism of the modern world and the possible nuances of the New Testament idea that the death of Jesus causes us to think also about the death of God. (The nuance that is not my cup of tea would be the idea that God was literally alive once upon a time, but has now died.)

I think that the terms "bright," "non-theist," or even "anti-theist" are preferable to "atheism." But it would probably be better simply to avoid labels, and instead make use of every opportunity to discuss and promote the notion that *religion is a creative, imaginative art form!* This is the middle ground. If my students ask me whether or not I believe in God, I question labels such as theist, atheist, or agnostic. I suggest that they should focus on what is meant by believing in "God," or what is the purpose of believing in God (a primary purpose, I repeat, is to keep our pride in check, to keep us open-minded and willing to admit how much we don't know—to keep us aware of Absolute Mystery). My goal is that students develop a more nuanced and artistic view regarding the nature of God-talk.

Chris Hedges, author of *American Fascists: The Christian Right and the War on America* and of *I Don't Believe In Atheists*, criticizes New Testament scholar Bart Ehrman for having declared himself an agnostic because of an inability to reconcile the idea of a loving and all-powerful God with the reality of evil and injustice in the world. He accuses Ehrman of being "trapped within the simpleminded belief that religious faith, to have legitimacy, means there has to be something logical and ultimately just about human existence." (What I find incredible is Ehrman's claim that his agnosticism is unrelated to his expanding historical and theological knowledge regarding the complex origins of the Bible.) Hedges' own view is that God is not a Being but an experience, and that it is precisely the loss of this true, experiential spirituality which is often responsible for violent extremism and other evils. Writing in the spring 2008 Harvard Divinity Bulletin, Hedges views God-language as conveying "the hope that permits human beings to cope with inevitable pain, despair and suffering" but also as expressing "the healing solidarity of love and self-sacrifice." The real question for Hedges is not why God allows suffering, but why we are not willing to suffer in order to relieve the suffering of others. The transcendent forces of love, beauty, alienation, loneliness, suffering, good, evil, and the reality of death, says Hedges,

> ". . . are the domain of art and religion. All cultures have struggled to give words, through religion and artistic expression, to these mysteries and moments of transcendence . . . .The best we can do is endure with compassion, wisdom, and humility and accept the mystery and ambiguity of existence . . . . We are not promised a rational world. We are not offered explanations. We are called to act."

Perhaps Hedges is not so much against atheism *per se* as he is against atheism or agnosticism when it becomes a militantly negative, naïve, or overly self-involved form of belief that doesn't participate in the hard work of compassion. My take is that he doesn't "believe in" either theism or atheism, but in *compassionate engagement*. He clearly steers God-talk in the direction of Ultimate Mystery. Hedges would probably appreciate the joke about the inebriated atheist who mentions God during an Irish wake and then defends himself in a thick brogue saying "Sure I'm an atheist, but I don't have much faith in it!" An article in the New York Times of April 27, 2009 titled "More Atheists Are Shouting It From Rooftops" cites polls showing that the ranks of those who call themselves agnostics, atheists and secular humanists are growing, and it highlights the fact that President Obama broke new ground by mentioning and, therefore, validating nonbelievers in his 2009 inaugural address—as he continues to do from time to time. The same article also features a South Carolina card-carrying Secular Humanist church organist who says "I am not one of the humanists who feels that religion is a bad thing."

There may be some atheists or non-theists who make empirical science into a narrow-minded and overly belligerent form of dogmatic faith. But I think it would be more fair and accurate to view most thoughtful atheists primarily as critics of traditional religious people who stubbornly hold onto outdated beliefs, who are too often behind the curve when it comes to science with its notion of truth based on solid empirical evidence. Too frequently it has been religious believers who have stood in the way of civil rights for racial, sexual, and other mistreated minorities—exposing a stunning lack of the empathy and compassion that is (and has to be!) the hallmark of any authentic religion. Karen Armstrong is working to develop a "Charter for Compassion" that she envisions as similar to the Universal Declaration of Human Rights. Such a charter would challenge all religions to produce "the fruits of the spirit," described in the New Testament as love, joy, peace, patience, kindness, goodness, faithfulness, gentleness, self-control—and "God knows" that many religious believers need to control their fearful, repressive, legalistic, self-centered, uncompassionate, and judgmental tendencies!

I am convinced that as we move further into the twenty-first century there will be an increasing number of people who no longer believe in the supernatural but will nevertheless consider themselves to be spiritual— who will identify (whimsically at least) as High Church Atheists, Spiritual Nonbelievers, Non-theists, or Brights. Those who, for whatever reasons, are unable to admit that they merely give lip service to typical notions of God will, sadly, continue just pretending to believe or care about many of the doctrines of their religion. These more or less closeted high church atheists no doubt form a large contingent of the many "C and E" folks who only come to church at Christmas and Easter. I am writing this book for them. I am writing for the folks who don't really believe the supernatural aspect of the stories in their holy books, perhaps because they understand how much of the Bible and other sacred literature is thematic mythical truth rather than mere fact, or because they are more awestruck by the proven miracles of modern science. I am writing for those who squirm in their pew because what they hear from the pulpit seems to presuppose a scientific worldview that is at least two thousand years out of date. I am addressing the spiritual-but-not-religious folks who tend to disparage "organized religion." (I sometimes tease them by asking what is so great about disorganized religion.) I write to lend my support to the many fans of Bishop John Shelby Spong, Marcus Borg, and Thich Nhat Hanh, who understand the need for a new approach to God-talk. My intended audience also includes the folks who fill huge churches for concerts or other artistic events but who otherwise seldom if ever darken the sanctuary door.

By emphasizing the church in High Church Atheist I am challenging folks to come out of the closet as it were and claim the community of church, organized religion, or Scripture, independent of supernatural and other outdated baggage. I am even challenging them to give financial support to progressive communities of organized religion whether or not they themselves attend many gatherings. Churches can be places where all kinds of families and other community institutions receive support in their efforts to build deeper and stronger relationships. Many churches have well-educated leaders and support groups who know how to help people navigate the rough waters of inter-personal dynamics and transform both their personal and communal lives for the better. In his book *Religion for Atheists,* spiritual non-believer Alain de Botton suggests that religion has much to offer in areas such as building community and lasting relationships, finding ways to help people meet their emotional needs, and deepening appreciation of art, music, architecture, and travel. He shows how we can reject the supernatural claims of religion and still look to religions for many valuable insights and ways of enhancing people's lives.

Understanding God-talk (theology) as an art form is key to preserving what is valuable in organized religion—churches, mosques, temples, scriptures—and perhaps even key to saving the world as we move simultaneously into the age of science, culture clashes, and religious pluralism. My goal is to show how followers of all spiritual traditions can reclaim and participate in their own traditional religions when they don't believe in them the same way they did before—or to put it another way, when they don't all want to become Unitarian Universalists (not that there's anything wrong with being a UU). Reformation and reclaiming are both related to the Renaissance. I am being true to my Lutheran roots as I promote this reclaiming and re-imagining of religion. Stephen Greenblatt's Pulitzer Prize winning 2011 book *The Swerve: How the World Became Modern* reveals the history of the anti-supernatural, pro-science, humanistic Renaissance, which "postmodern" religion affirms by placing equal value on both science and spirituality. The highly symbolic and artistic New Testament book of Revelation validates this project by imagining a God who says "Behold, I make all things new!"

The Advantages of Seeing Religion as an Art Form

My friend and colleague, psychologist Dr. Dennis Hinkle, has impressed upon me the necessity of emphasizing early on what a person stands to gain from changing or "converting" to the kind of religion and spirituality that I am outlining here. He has observed over a long career that people are happiest when there is an optimal rate of change in their lives—too little change is intolerable boredom; too much change is chaotic. The famous serenity prayer reminds us that there are two major ways in which change can improve our lives. We can change our situation or we can have the wisdom to see that if we can't change the situation we can change the way we think about our circumstances. Many young GLBTQ (gay, lesbian, bisexual, transgender, queer) people, for example, as they are discovering their sexuality, find it very difficult to face the fact that they are different from most people. However, when they realize they cannot change the reality of their sexuality, but can change the way they think and feel about themselves, they find that the joy of being who they really are outweighs any trepidation they might have felt about making such a big change by "coming out" to themselves and to others.

This book is focused on changing the way people think about their religious beliefs and traditions. Militant atheists who present their case against religion have many valid concerns, but if they want to totally eliminate religion they are probably trying to change a situation that can't be changed. A large percentage of human beings are not going to give up on religion, spirituality, or the word "God." But for some readers the changes I am suggesting here regarding how they view their religion may also seem too militant, too extreme. Does approaching religion as an art form require us to give up the comfort of absolute certainty? Does this understanding of religion risk being accused of promoting immorality or amorality? Are we being asked to give up hope for life after death? On some level the answer to these and similar questions may be "yes." So, what might we gain by changing the way we think about religion that will more than compensate for any apparent losses?

Above all perhaps, by giving up our craving for absolute certainty, we gain the freedom to think and to question. Seeing religion as creative and imaginative art is a way of enjoying the playfulness of multiple perspectives. Creative people look at things from many points of view. Their lives are richer and healthier because they know how to consider constructive alternatives. They don't fall into the trap of seeing themselves merely as helpless victims of forces beyond their control. They understand how kaleidoscopic variety is the spice of life. Dr. Hinkle spent his career using "personal construct psychology" to help his clients increase their ability to think about constructive, creative alternatives in their lives. He likes to describe therapy as "education for one."

Art always involves looking at life and the world from multiple perspectives. Artists and scientists both have this ability, and both make great contributions to humanity by noticing things that others don't, although arts and sciences are not identical to the degree that art (religion) is imagination-based and science is based on hard evidence. Multiple perspective alternatives are the stock in trade of psychologists, but also of comedians. Both are in the business of helping people cope with their problems. In chapter 2 we are going to see how various versions of Christian atonement theology can have relevance for coping with certain aspects of life, whereas reducing the doctrine of atonement to one "truth" is a total dead end. In subsequent chapters we will see how other classic religious traditions (especially Taoism and Buddhism) express multiple perspectives on life and death. One of the important lessons I learned from Dr. Hinkle's expertise as a therapist was that by using provisional phrases such as "it seems to me," "as I see it," "in my opinion," and "it is my impression" we can avoid jumping to false conclusions or assuming that there is only one way of perceiving the motivations or responding to the actions of others. For example, thoughtful reflection (even briefly) on the behavior of others can prevent drivers from getting provoked into road rage.

Mastery is boring. Mystery is exciting. As noted earlier, a completely understood God is no God at all. I've always loved the line from the 1972 movie "Sunday Bloody Sunday" where the mother says to her daughter who has not been able to sustain romantic relationships "You keep throwing your hand in because you haven't got the whole thing. There is no whole thing!" In other words, all-or-nothing attitudes are self-defeating in life where uncertainty, chance, and change are the name of the game. We tend to be like the blind folks feeling different parts of the elephant, mistaking or substituting the part for the whole, and coming to erroneous conclusions. The "whole thing" remains elusive in part because our perception and our imagination are limited. I don't know how frequently curiosity actually kills cats, but those who crave a religion of absolute certainty and security (who demand to have the whole thing) are typically stunted by a lack of curiosity and openness that keeps them from ever being truly alive.

With the freedom to think and to question comes a release from the stultifying effects of blind obedience to authority. We no longer allow ourselves to be manipulated into doing or believing things that are contrary to our own best interests. I grieve for workers who vote for politicians eager to dismantle the social safety net (unemployment insurance, social security, etc), voters who may find themselves unemployed or unable to comfortably retire. I grieve for parents who conform to a culture of hating homosexuality and end up spending their lives tragically alienated from their own gay children. Obedience training, with its attendant guilt and shame, is hard to overcome. If you don't think for yourself you can be a sucker for advertizing. Many folks are psychologically disturbed because they are robot-like slaves to "the rules." They are what I call *pathologically conventional*. I was delighted to see my mother quoted in her 1937 college newspaper saying "a gentleman should not be too conventional." (As a Lutheran Pastor whose nickname in college was Joker, who loved directing plays, and who regularly took his magic act—and me—on the road, my father certainly fit the bill.) By contrast, when Jeanette Winterson told her zealously religious adoptive mother that she was happily in love with a girl, her mother said "Why be happy when you could be normal?" Shakespeare says "to thine own self be true." Socrates would ask those who considered themselves authorities on a subject, "How do you know that?"

In writing about religion as a natural phenomenon (a product of evolution), Daniel Dennett observes that while there is survival value in children learning to believe what they are told, this same conventionality and conformity can become counterproductive, especially in a rapidly changing world. It is possible to be over-socialized. In his one-man show the actor Peter Ustinov obviously relished describing how his entire career was a last laugh on the British schoolmasters who had been determined to destroy his youthful, free-spirited ways. Composer Kirke Mechem took the text of an eighteenth century church rules for "Children's Behavior at the Meeting House" and put them into a whimsical choral setting where leapfrogging repetition of words such as "decently," "listen," and other brief exhortations clearly mock the ridiculously overwrought concern for keeping children under control:

> "Decently walk to thy seat or pew. Run not, nor go wantonly. Shift not seats, but continue in the place where your superiors order you. Fix thine eye on the minister; pray with him when he prayeth . . . and while he preacheth, listen, listen, listen. Walk decently and soberly home without haste or wantonness; thinking on what you have been hearing. Run not!"

Such overwrought concern to teach children the rules of good behavior can sow seeds of fanaticism and perfectionism (a topic that will be considered in the next chapter) or it may lay the groundwork for destructive rebellion later on.

Blind obedience can also create us-versus-them divisions that destroy the awareness of our common humanity. It undermines empathy and among its worst effects often leads to war! Us-versus-them thinking tends to assume that people are either all good or all evil when in general all human beings are a mixture to one degree or another. Even criminals on death row are seldom, if ever, one-dimensional monsters, and while there may be no excuse for their behavior or mitigation of its consequences for them or for their victims, we must recognize that some of these folks suffer from severe mental illness which is something that no one "in their right mind" would choose. If I say "there but for the grace of God go I" it might sound quite humble and yet be an expression of arrogant self-satisfaction. But if I say the same thing as an expression of empathy and compassion, then I am taking it to heart that if I had been born in that time or place, if I had had that chemical imbalance in my brain, if I had been caught in those circumstances, then I too might well have done the things about which I am now tempted to be so harshly judgmental. Thich Nhat Hanh has written some wonderful prose and poetry expressing how true empathy and deep understanding help us avoid us-versus-them, holier-than-thou thinking, and counter-productive anger.

Obedience training also implies that there is only one way of looking at things. Instead of seeing mistakes as part of the process of growth and discernment, we see every mistake as a "sin" and become paralyzed by false guilt. We may also have good reason to feel guilty if we have intentionally or carelessly caused harm, but feeling guilty does not always or necessarily mean that we actually are guilty. Morality should not be mainly about the fear of being punished by authorities. Truly principled ethics are about embracing the values of justice, cooperation, compassion and empathy—positive values that also focus on reducing suffering. These are values that human beings generally prefer over cruelty and cutthroat competition. Evolutionary geneticists believe this preference for justice, cooperation, compassion, and empathy is instinctual because of its high survival value.

Understanding religion as a creative and imaginative art form also frees us to celebrate science and its marvelous accomplishments. We no longer fear the truth as we usually do when we are trying to defend a rigid belief system. We exchange comforting fantasies for truth based on solid evidence, truth that often produces medical miracles which may not give us life after death, but which can give us much more life before death. We find that life becomes more, not less, valuable when we face the reality that our lives do not go on forever—if life went on forever it seems to me that we would be trapped in meaninglessness. Pious life-after-death fantasies blind us to John Keats' insight that "Beauty is truth, truth beauty." In his poem "Sunday Morning" Wallace Stevens tells us that "Death is the mother of beauty"—that the value and beauty of life is heightened by our awareness of its limits. As Dr. Hinkle says, "There is great wisdom in the perspective of a corpse." This perspective makes us grateful for even the smallest moments of life and consciousness here and now, a gratitude enhanced by our awareness of the impermanence of everything and by our wise resistance to imagining a life after death. It makes sense to say "Eat, drink, and be merry, for tomorrow we die." But as I will emphasize again later a better phrase would be: "Eat, drink, and be merry, because today we are alive!" The best funeral or memorial gatherings focus not on pie in the sky, but on the shared joys of life that were particularly valued by the person whose life we celebrate. This remains true even when our grief is intensified because a particular person's life has ended prematurely.

Life as a high church non-theist frees us to find community and a connection with something greater than ourselves in many places besides but also including churches, temples, mosques, shrines. The Internet has amazing potential to build a sense of our common humanity and to help us find communities of mutual interest and understanding. In two films about the gritty San Francisco "tenderloin" area that includes Glide Church, David L. Brown says "we see people finding some form of salvation . . . through community." Understanding salvation in this way through the work of a filmmaker illustrates how the combination of religion and art can open new horizons for our spiritual imagination.

When we think we have nailed down the ultimate answer, the ultimate belief system, we face the frustration of constantly having to defend this system. We let the system get between us and the Supreme Mystery, and this prevents us from having a truly spiritual experience of life. Real peace and serenity come from a mindset that makes us comfortable precisely with not having all the answers. Understanding religion as a creative art is the best way I can imagine to become comfortable with having more questions than answers.

Instead of the bromide of saying that everything happens for a reason or is God's will, Rabbi Harold Kushner in his best selling *When Bad Things Happen to Good People* suggests that we should identify God with the process of moving bravely into the future, regardless of what happens in our lives. He sees God as the source of that amazing ability we discover in ourselves to cope with difficulties and challenges which we originally imagined or encountered as overwhelming and insurmountable. He says those who nervously defend God's almighty power and control would rather have a God who appears to be sadistic, incompetent, or capricious, than to admit that many things happens at random in the universe, things which often can only be given meaning by how we respond with help and support after they happen. Religious God-talk must not be about shallow answers and hollow comfort. It should be about how we can be at home and at peace in the great and mysterious reality that surrounds us. A concept of God that needs our nervous defense is not worthy to be called God. As lecturer, politician, and descendent of Christian ministers Robert G. Ingersoll said back in the nineteenth century: "If there be an infinite Being, he does not need our help—we need not waste our energies in his defense." Spiritual Nonbelievers, High Church Atheists, Non-theists, Brights and all others who understand their religion as an art form may be losing a supernatural Sky Daddy, but they're gaining a Universe of Sublime Mystery, Awe, Beauty and Joy.

Examples of European Spirituality

Dietrich Bonhoeffer, the German Lutheran pastor who paid with his life for resisting the Nazis, coined a term that has an impact similar to "high church atheist." Musing on what had happened in the supposedly Christian nation of Germany, he came up with the image of "religionless Christianity." This provocative notion is clearly open to many possible interpretations (more on this in chapter 2), but for starters I think it reminds us that any religion has the potential to become dangerous. Religion has long been criticized, most harshly of late by Christopher Hitchens and Sam Harris, for playing a major part in fomenting wars, bigotry, and other evils, all in the name of God or faith. (Internet search: "Toxic Faith.") Chris Hedges' call for religious/spiritual people to act instead with courage and compassion was well illustrated in the life of Bonhoeffer. It seems in fact that many folks are drawn to Christianity more for its theological social activism (sometimes called "the social gospel") than for its doctrines.

Spiritual Atheism is another provocative expression similar to High Church Atheism and is, I think, very much in sync also with the notion of "religionless Christianity." But since atheism tends to have a negative connotation as militantly anti-religious, I decided that the less flamboyant expression "Spiritual Nonbeliever" was a better title for the original version of this book. I also toyed briefly with the idea that the ironic and oxymoronic title "Godly Non-theism" would provocatively express how God-talk is always a dicey proposition. This phrase would have called attention to the problems and limitations of God-talk without implying the rejection of any and all "God" imagery. But it could also have come off as confusing or dull (or as just plain moronic). Foregoing the obvious (marketing) advantages of a clever and catchy title for this new incarnation of the book, I have changed the original sub-title into a plain and direct main title: *RELIGION as ART FORM*. If the book were only about Christianity I might well have borrowed from Bonhoeffer and adapted *Religionless Christianity* for a title. But I have opted instead to follow the lead of Stephen Batchelor's 1997 book *Buddhism Without Beliefs* by adding the new subtitle: *Reclaiming Spirituality Without Supernatural Beliefs.* (We will see in chapter 5 that Batchelor is part of a trend toward producing versions of "evidence based" Buddhism where supernatural and superstitious elements are removed or reinterpreted.) This new sub-title is a deliberately plain and straight-forward statement that gives, I think, a very accurate idea of the present book's fundamental message.

The twenty-first century cries out for new approaches to the way we use God-talk (theology). We need religion and theology that can move beyond both beliefs and Gods. The French theologian and scientist Teilhard de Chardin has given us an example of how Christians and others can both artistically and scientifically develop their own religious traditions without the literalistic arrogance of insisting that all their beliefs or doctrines are plain and simple facts. When Chardin speaks of the "mystical or universal Christ" and of "the divine milieu" he challenges us to evolve beyond doctrinaire beliefs to a multi-layered artistic take on religion and Reality.

Those who speak, preach, or teach about God as a character in a story should always find ways to make it explicit that the story is symbolic of something both more and other than it seems to be on the surface. It needs to be made crystal clear that "God" is a personification in a story designed to help us understand important themes and implement these themes in our behavior. Making this clear will defuse some of the extremely harsh images of God that were created by ancient people whose parochial outlook may seem barbaric compared with our own *supposedly* enlightened society (with its genocides, 9/11, the atomic bombing of Japan, etc.).

Richard Dawkins complains that too many clergy and preachers seldom if ever explicitly acknowledge the metaphorical nature of their discourse. If asked about this some will say they assume listeners understand God-talk to be metaphorical, but Dawkins insists that religious leaders need to be much more direct in pointing out the metaphorical and symbolic nature of their theological language. Marcus Borg suggests that religious groups would do well to make it known in various ways that their members differ in the degree to which they understand religious language metaphorically, but that they share a common passion for their spiritual tradition. Rudolf Bultmann would likely endorse this way of promoting spiritual harmony.

All religions must learn to shake up their use of God language so that religion can become a more positive influence in the global village. In addition to the problematic aspects of treating God as a personified character in stories, holy books too often present God as little or nothing more than an authoritarian legislator. Religions have to resist power trips that derive absolute authority from an absolute concept of God or of God's Word. In short, religion has to stop using and misusing "God." The Center for Progressive Christianity which was created in 1994 and the United Religions Initiative (URI), a nonprofit founded in 2000 dedicated to ending religiously motivated violence and war, are both also dedicated to ending "scandals of particularity" in which individual religions claim to have a unique monopoly on truth or on "God"; URI's network has included as many as 120 faith traditions in 70 countries. (Check out both groups on the Internet.)

In his 2008 book *Society Without God*, sociologist Phil Zuckerman tries to understand how Sweden and Denmark can be among "the least religious nations in the world" while at the same time being "above all, moral, stable, humane and deeply good"—ranking highest among nations in literacy, schooling, child welfare, economic equality, standard of living, competitiveness and life expectancy. In fact, European political parties with "Christian" in their names, true to biblical themes, tend to include a broad diversity of members and to embrace aspects of "socialism." By contrast, a study reported in the Times of London on September 27, 2005 found that in countries with a high level of religious belief such as the United States the rates of murder, suicide, sexual promiscuity, and abortion were typically higher than in less religious countries. I find Zuckerman's analysis particularly riveting because I grew up in the Lutheranism that remains the official religion of the Scandinavian countries. (Presbyterians should ponder the fact that the 500th anniversary of John Calvin's birth found his city of Geneva, Switzerland very ho-hum about the occasion and also a place that according to a November 5th 2009 New York Times article is "very secular and doesn't trust whatever has to do with religion.")

Interestingly, most Swedes and Danes do not describe themselves as atheists or non-religious. Zuckerman concluded, as did I on a visit to Norway and Sweden in 2012, that the basic attitude toward religion is one of "benign indifference." Scandinavians tend to think that religion is "nice" but it is essentially a non-issue and private to the point that talking about God at all is—well—embarrassing. (I suspect that this kind of reticence is the reason some of my old friends in Minnesota usually soften "God" to "the Good Lord.") I don't think we should dismiss this phenomenon as mere cultural, nationalistic, or civil religion. It is more akin to the majority of Judaism in Israel which is a happy hybrid of spiritual and secular, free from the power trips of the temple priesthood since 70 AD, emphasizing holidays, rites of passage, and "sacred bonds" related to Golden Rule type empathy, rather than to God, beliefs, or doctrines. (One of the valuable things about churches, synagogues, mosques, etc. is that, unlike "funeral homes" which are associated only with death, they typically are places where all the various rites of passage are celebrated. Birth, death, coming of age, marriage, anniversaries, holidays—the wide variety of such occasions make religious settings more truly holistic/cat*holic* venues for celebrating life with all its joys and sorrows.)

Far from images such as that of the melancholy Dane, Zuckerman found the Scandinavian people he studied to be generally happy, productive and contented folks who understand their own well-being as interdependent with the well-being of others. This attitude no doubt helps to explain why these countries have been among the first to formally recognize gay marriages. In 2009 Eva Brunne was the first lesbian in a registered partnership to be elected bishop of Stockholm—a position once held by my former dean at Harvard Divinity School, Krister Stendahl. Brunne is the first openly lesbian bishop in the world, blazing a trail as has Gene Robinson who was the first openly gay bishop in the Episcopal Church (although he is much more theologically conservative and cautious than his fellow bishop emeritus Jack Spong—which illustrates the diversity within sexual minority communities, and within the Episcopal/Anglican Church). Zuckerman's findings seem to echo a "Non-religious Identification Survey" reported in 2009 by a professor at Grand Valley State University in Allendale, Michigan, which found that "confident nonbelievers" are just as happy and emotionally stable as religious believers.

The most important thing that Zuckerman seems not to take adequately into account is the fact that Lutheranism is still to some degree the official national church in the countries he studied. Churches are supported by taxes. Clergy are in some sense government officials. In the United States churches are voluntary associations—a fact that received much attention from James Luther Adams, professor at Harvard Divinity School (and also a major editor of Tillich's writings). My Lutheran seminary professors in Iowa often lamented the downside of state sponsored religion. State sponsored churches can afford to be (and are!) largely empty on Sunday mornings—major holidays plus weddings and funerals are typical exceptions to this rule (baptisms tend to be rather private affairs). State sponsored preachers may not need to worry about offending people who could take their money and go elsewhere. But in the United States a church is a voluntary association, and people have to like its preacher and programs enough to join and finance it, a fact that immigrants from Europe typically don't understand. Such immigrants swell the ranks of those who do not financially support a church but take it for granted that the church will be there for such things as weddings and funerals.

One clergy acquaintance of mine, upset like many clergy are about this problem, had his parish raise to an almost astronomical amount the fee that would be requested from non-members who had no previous connection with the congregation but who wanted to have their weddings in its beautiful sanctuary. His goal was to cut down on the appeal of the congregation's attractive setting in order to avoid becoming nothing more than the equivalent of a Las Vegas wedding chapel. Of course, he also risked missing opportunities to help people with their spirituality at an important juncture in their lives.

To keep the *church* in high church atheism, many preachers who are not state sponsored will have to learn how to finesse a move toward more metaphorical and less literal religious discourse and practice. A major part of such a transformation would involve substituting forms of meditation, and community "moral support and concern" for the kind of intercessory prayer that appears to be begging "God" for special favors. As Bishop Spong has done in his various books, I will in these pages and in future projects suggest ways in which churches need to change, revise, or eliminate some rituals, liturgies, hymns, architecture, and perhaps even liturgical costumes. (Although there is something to be said in favor of the artistic theatricality of high church pageantry, I have not been a fan of such displays—unless you count the famous ecclesiastical style show in "Fellini's Roma"). We particularly need a reversal of the situation where clergy have tended to preach and teach in a way that caters to fundamentalist and literalist parishioners. "Fundamentalism lite" will not suffice. Bishop Spong is right that "Christianity must change or die." A cue can be taken from the moderate evangelical pastor in Minnesota who had built up a huge congregation of 5000 but then took an ethical stand on some issues that he knew would (and did) cause at least a thousand of those members to leave.

Those who criticize state church situations typically celebrate voluntary church membership as a way to cultivate true believers. But while there may be some problems with state supported religion, "true believers" can also be a problem. We need more folks who do not wear the mantle of hard-line true believers, but who do support churches and preachers who understand religion as a creative art form! We need more preaching and education that gives support to those who understand concepts such as *religionless Christianity* and *high church non-theism*. It is a serious obstacle to the vision I am outlining here that the human "pillars" of many congregations are traditional believers who are still mightily attached to supernatural notions of God. One solution for this problem involves encouraging such folks to gravitate toward church bodies, organizations, or congregations that still support traditional theistic truth claims. To some degree this is clearly happening already, although it must be noted that the traditionalists also find some of their folks moving toward more progressive groups. Another solution would be for clergy and lay leadership to put more effort into finding nonthreatening ways of downplaying the troubling aspects of good old time religion while also implementing the kinds of ideas and changes I am suggesting throughout these pages.

I have no doubt that folks who hold to a worldview or mindset that is two thousand or more years out of date will be a shrinking group in the long run. The challenge now is to build up religious communities that celebrate Divine, Eternal Mystery and serve the many real needs of individuals and of society. I suggest Glide Memorial Church, St. Gregory of Nyssa Episcopal Church, and the eclectic mix of events at Grace Episcopal Cathedral, all in San Francisco, as particularly good and exciting role models.

Karen Armstrong has made *The Case for GOD* at the beginning of the twenty-first century, emphasizing as did Joseph Campbell that religion is about *experiencing* transcendent mystery, not about "believing stuff." Spirituality is more about a universally available transcendent experience of the sacred mystery of life than it is a validation of any specific visionary or supernatural intrusion from "somewhere out there." Reflecting his Baptist heritage, Harvey Cox marked his retirement at Harvard with *The Future of Faith*—faith understood as *experiential* spirituality as over against beliefs or creeds. (I remember not quite grasping what Cox meant when he would talk in our graduate seminar about moving beyond the Christian sin-and-redemption paradigm, but when he invited Jürgen Moltmann to talk to us about the future and his "Theology of Hope" I began to have at least an inkling of what that new paradigm might be.) Elaine Pagels also makes this point about the experience of transcendent Mystery in her 2003 book *Beyond Belief.* Some Pentecostals may lack intellectual, psychological, or theological depth of insight, but their transcendent, ecstatic spiritual experience can still be very real. Philosopher Jacob Needleman's book *What Is God?* describes the "what" as an inner experience.

Two hundred years ago at the beginning of the nineteenth century a young hospital chaplain in Germany with a Protestant background similar to mine, Friedrich Schleiermacher, self-published a book titled *On Religion: Speeches to its Cultured Despisers*. He made many of the same points that I am making here. He decried superstition. He tried to show secular critics of religion that deep religious experience was still possible and valuable even if one did not have any traditional belief in God. Schleiermacher identified "true immortality and eternity" with "golden rule empathy" and he often used words like universe, eternity, and mystery, instead of God. He also saw religion as an antidote to runaway nationalism. "The religious life itself," wrote Schleiermacher, is "the whole soul . . . dissolved in the immediate feeling of the Infinite and the Eternal." He emphasized that true religion and piety "is always full of humility." He promoted simple spirituality as over against detailed religious systems. He linked mysticism and imagination, and described imagination as "the highest and most original faculty in man. All else in the human mind is simply reflection upon it, and is therefore dependent on it. Your imagination creates the world . . ." On the relationship between art, music, and religion he wrote:

> "Religion and art stand together like kindred beings . . . from of old, what is greatest in art has had a religious character. . . . Let the past, the present, and the future surround us with an endless gallery of the sublimest works of art, eternally multiplied by a thousand brilliant mirrors. . . . Were I to compare religion in this respect with anything it would be with music. . . . How often have I struck up the music of my religion . . . there may be a music among the saints that is speech without words, giving most definite and comprehensible expression to the heart. The muse of harmony, the intimate relation of which to religion has been long known . . . breathed out things that definite speech cannot grasp . . . full of the sacred and the infinite."

Words are symbols with great expressive power. But in the musical "My Fair Lady" Eliza Dolittle sings in frustration, "Words, words, words, I'm so sick of words . . . don't talk of love—show me!" Music shows us! It can convey more than words alone express. This is illustrated by the fact that many great pieces of vocal music can be utterly enchanting even when one pays no attention to the words or their meaning. Music and God-talk both are able to touch the mysterious depths of our being. "Bright" Daniel Dennett argues that humankind needs to outgrow religion in many respects. But, like me, Dennett says he can be reduced to a quivering heap of emotion while singing Brahms' *Requiem* or Mendelssohn's *Elijah*. (I was surprised to see Dennett once scoff at practicing clergy who were willing to describe themselves as atheists, since he himself claims to love singing Christmas carols and other great religious music. Apparently Dennett does not see himself as being deficient in his ability to appreciate metaphorical and symbolic thinking, but is lacking in the ability to recognize the potential for such thinking in others.)

Goethe supposedly said that the world was created so Beethoven could write his ninth symphony with its humanistic and spiritual *Ode to Joy*. Music is able to evoke all the joy and sorrow, all the ennui and nostalgia, all the hope and despair, all of the most deeply felt sensibilities of the human heart. Dennett means no disrespect when he says that great composers use clever "tricks" to evoke these sensibilities—there is by definition an artificial aspect in art that in no way diminishes its beauty and power. I think it is significant that so many people develop an increased appreciation for classical music as they grow older. I don't think it is possible to overstate the value and importance of music. The earliest Brahmin mantras in India appear to predate language itself, are apparently based on the imitation of birdsong, and are only transmitted orally from generation to generation. I am dubious about any religion in which music does not play a major role. Introducing his series of interviews with Joseph Campbell, Bill Moyers appropriately acknowledged music by saying "Mythology was to him the song of the universe, music so deeply embedded in our collective unconscious that we dance to it, even when we can't name the tune."

God As Metaphor for Ineffable Mystery

My thesis throughout this book is that theology/religion is primarily an art form. Different religious traditions use a variety of symbols, metaphors and historical or mythological stories to deal with our basic human archetypal issues. (TV's "Lost" and Terrence Malick's film "The Tree of Life" have also pondered Mystery in this way.) Some of these symbols and stories appear to be contradictory and confusing, but this need not bother us if we see them as artistic and literary rather than as purely historical and factual. As Bultmann pointed out, we must never lose sight of the distinction between historical fact and symbolic truth. This distinction is key to avoiding the dangerous forms of fundamentalism that claim a monopoly on truth. Contemporary fundamentalism, says Karen Armstrong in *The Battle for God*, breaks down this distinction between scientific fact and interpretive truth and sees virtually everything in the Bible as plain fact. One of the most basic definitions of myth is *a made-up (non-factual) story that attempts to convey truths greater than any story or words can express*. When we see that within the same religious tradition there are conflicting artistic images, metaphors, and myths (for example, the mixed metaphors of "hell fire" and "outer darkness" or the masculine and feminine images of God) it reminds us to lighten up and enjoy imaginative play with our religious symbols.

I am aware, of course, that the religions based on the Bible are usually called ethical-*historical* monotheism. Much of chapter 2 will be about the ethical aspect of biblical religion. But what about the idea of a God who acts in history? When I was at Harvard Divinity School, G. Ernest Wright, famous for his writing on this subject, was teaching there. I was somewhat surprised to see Harvard's Harvey Cox affirm in 2009 that he still finds it important to stress the idea that the God of the Bible acts in and through human history. Apparently, however, Cox has in mind not a supernatural God, but essentially a "social gospel" linking of spiritual concern with concern for the welfare of this world here and now in terms of justice and peace. It is true that biblical religion tends to have a linear view of history which supposedly sees regular historical time as meaningful in a way that some of the theology of Asia does not. But many biblical theologians can also be said to have taken history way too seriously in the sense that they have taken Bible stories and images of God too literally. They have identified their belief system and symbols too closely with historical fact and have failed adequately to appreciate and/or to articulate the role of artistic myths in biblical literature. For example, I think we have to agree with those who have suggested that the two main strands of material woven together by priestly editors beginning during the Babylonian exile around 586 BC to create the earlier books of the Hebrew Bible (mainly the Torah) can be compared in some ways with the Greek legends and myths in the *Iliad* and the *Odyssey*. Archeologist and art historian John Romer stresses that while the details in Old Testament narratives make these stories appear to be accurate history, such "facts" are better understood as literary "local color," amplified by the nostalgia typically found among exiled captives such as those ancient Israelites in Babylon.

Another of my professors at Harvard, Richard R. Niebuhr, published an expanded version of his Ph.D. thesis *Resurrection and Historical Reason* which I find to be a significant but also somewhat tortured and unconvincing attempt to explain how the resurrection of Jesus can be understood as historical. He uses phrases such as "the resurrection event" but then piles on so much verbiage about reason, nature, historicity, identification, recognition, mystery and the like that it takes on the quality of "he doth protest too much." Niebuhr does recognize the difficulties with his project, at one point using the phrase "the resurrection appearances *if they are historical at all*" (italics mine) and then adding that "the resurrection despite its similarity to all historical events, is an event unlike any other." If something is only "similar to" a historical event can we really call it historical? This kind of reasoning is usually dismissed as "special pleading." We see another vivid example of such pleading when Richard Rhem, summarizing Wolfhart Pannenberg, describes resurrection as an act of God "which is 'more unique' than the uniqueness of historical phenomena in general." Some try to dress up this logic of a "uniquely unique" event as a glorious "scandal of particularity," but I think it actually amounts to little more than a fancy and misleading way of making an absolute claim for the superiority of one's own religion. (In chapter 6 I will return to Niebuhr's book and note some of the worthwhile observations which are made there by this representative of an influential American family of theologians.)

Nicholas Thomas Wright plays the resurrection of Jesus as a kind of trump card—as proof of the special truth of Christianity—similar to the way in which Jehovah's Witnesses use the idea of fulfilled biblical predictions as proof of truth. His analysis of the uniqueness of the New Testament conception of *resurrection* is interesting and insightful. But his notion of resurrection as involving "a new mode of physicality" (St. Paul's "spiritual body") and a non-normal event, neither of which science can either discern or disprove, basically "spiritualizes" the issue of data and evidence out of the picture. Claims can be made about "uniquely unique events," but nothing is proven. N. T. Wright's claim in his dialogues with Borg on *The Meaning of Jesus* (1999) that "entropy [dissolution] does not have the last word, for humans or for the world as a whole," is a corollary of "intelligent design thinking" that imagines a supernatural ("nonspatio-temporal"—Wright) realm to which the God who created the empirical world will eventually return those who are saved. Such thinking fits with his too-casual dismissal of the Enlightenment and of scientific Postmodernism. Like Oscar Cullmann, who we will meet in chapter 4, Wright confuses the "logic" of New Testament literature about resurrection with actual data or evidence about what is or could be ultimately real! I am concerned too that like many Christian writers he seems to ignore the existence of other great religions in the world. Special elevation of one particular religion's unique vision of hope, salvation, and healing for the world is not likely to foster peace on earth.

Some German theologians who talk about *Heilsgeschichte* (Holy or Salvation History) seem to think of their theological interpretations as a matter of clarifying absolute truths. They assume that ancient scriptures reveal "spiritual facts" about the nature of reality that need only to be accurately explained. It is in the nature of religious worldviews to be comprehensive and mutually exclusive to some degree. These compelling worldviews understandably have a missionary mentality and want to share themselves with the world. But the speculative, subjective, or culturally conditioned element in all such worldviews, as well as the multi-faceted and illusive nature of "objective reality," force us to see these worldviews as art rather than as absolute scientific or historical fact.

This issue of art versus fact is a problem even with the evidence-based version of Buddhism that I will be affirming in this book. As much as this view of Buddhism tries to extract itself from the trappings of traditional Indian culture and Buddhist beliefs, and claims to be compatible with good physical and psychological science, its artistic element remains. Matthew Fox has constructed an updated version of biblical theology that also tries to be in harmony with modern science. His ten rules for living in the universe with an authentic spirituality are: extravagance, inner-connectivity, expansion, diversity, creativity, emptiness/solitude, justice, beauty, sacrifice, paradox, and humor. His approach, which I regularly share with my students, melds science (especially ecological and environmental science), art and religion in a way that, like evidence-based Buddhism, affirms a form of spirituality that doesn't make unique factual claims and is not tied to a specific religious culture.

Seeking to be objective and honest about the origin and development of specific myths and metaphors by embracing the historical critical scholarship of a theologian such as Bultmann, helps to keep religion as an art form from becoming overly vague or subjective. Metaphors and symbols, stories and rituals (such as Christian Holy Communion with bread and wine) tend to have a more or less objective and unique history of origin and evolution. This does not mean that they have only one true, specific, objective meaning. Great symbols and great art touch on universal themes, but this universality does not imply that the unique features of specific religious traditions are absolute, objective truths. Religion as a creative art form avoids the undesirable extremes of both rigid absolutism and vague relativism.

Whatever understandings of history, science, or psychology underlie various religious worldviews, these theologies ultimately cannot move beyond the mythic and symbolic nature of any meaningful theologizing. As Paul Tillich said, symbols may "participate in the Realities to which they point"—they must not be described as "mere" symbols—but they cannot totally capture those Realities. Religious truths, including any specific concepts of God, cannot claim to be totally identical with Absolute Reality. Even the versions of spirituality most compatible with science face daunting complexities and paradoxes. Science itself has trouble with Reality. Scientists struggle to reconcile quantum mechanics and relativity theory.

Tillich provocatively and wisely also said, "God does not exist—God *is.*" He meant that God should not be perceived as one being distinct from other beings (not even a Supreme Being), but as the Ground of All Being. God is not a "who" or an "it"—certainly not the literal "Heavenly Father" of Mormon Latter-Day Saint theology or Michelangelo's artistic rendering on the ceiling of the Sistine Chapel. Philosopher Baruch Spinoza implied something similar to Tillich's idea, describing God as another name for the mathematical system which is the Universe. If one calls God "the Mind of the universe" it is still a personification. My own view, again, is that "God" is a succinct artistic/spiritual term for Ultimate Mysterious Reality. Tillich and Spinoza were non-theists who resisted personifying tendencies without intending to be anti-religion. I suggest that Tillich's "Ground of Being" is better expressed in Gordon Kaufman's description of "God" as a symbol expressing our impulse to create "an ultimate point of reference for understanding everything."

Keeping with my emphasis on musical art and on *the empirical, materialist, matter-based notion of reality*, I should mention composer Bela Bartok's objections to ideas of God and the supernatural world as expressed in a letter to Stefi Geyer: "It is not the body that is mortal and the soul that is immortal but the other way around: The soul is transitory and the body (that is, matter) is everlasting!" Tillich also used the phrase "the God-beyond-God" to indicate Sacred Reality beyond all words, concepts, or experiences. When Jesus is pictured as crying out on the cross the psalmist's words "My God, my God, why have you forsaken me" Tillich sees an example of reaching out to the God beyond God, a reminder to all of us that we must ultimately move beyond beliefs or Gods and embrace the spiritual reality of Transcendent Mystery. A famous holocaust story tells of a play put on by Jewish concentration camp prisoners in which God is put on trial for allowing what is happening in the camps, and is sentenced to death. This story makes the "God beyond God" point when, after God is given the death penalty in the play, an actor announces "The play is over; it's time for the prayers."

Feeling At Home in the Mystery—in Eternity

It is understandable that many folks are very attached to personifying God as "Our Father who art in heaven." But I hope it is becoming clear why we must recognize that such language and imagery is symbolic. To put it bluntly, "God" is a metaphor! As Joseph Campbell often said, "God" refers to "the ultimate reality that transcends all categories of thought." "God" means so many different things to folks that Daniel Dennett thinks the word has become a kind of fetish—people simply "believe in believing" regardless of what they mean by "God." Richard Dawkins and others use the word "meme," typically defined as a *unit of cultural inheritance* analogous to a gene, to describe how an idea can thrive and be popular regardless of the actual truth of the idea. As Oscar Wilde said, "Truth, in matters of religion, is simply the opinion that has survived."

I suggest that the depiction of God as Father is basically about *feeling at home in the universe*! Personification is about feeling a personal connection to all of life. Some non-theists insist that the Lord's Prayer or "Our Father" must be abandoned. My view is that one can still use the traditional Lord's Prayer if it is taken in context as an historical and artistic expression of themes that remain meaningful. This is a good example of reclaiming religious traditions and symbols from otherworldly literalism. There is a lot of "*realized eschatology*" in The Lord's Prayer: "*kingdom come . . . on earth . . . this day . . . daily bread . . . forgive us . . . as we forgive our debtors . . . deliver us from temptation and evil.*" As Marcus Borg elaborates in *The Heart of Christianity,* this prayer is mostly about life in the here and now, what Tillich calls *the Eternal Now.* As is explained throughout this book, the *eschaton* (end or goal) of life is to be *realized* and participated in *now*, not in some imagined, future, otherworldly Kingdom. Spirituals about slaves stealing away and servants sitting down in mansions also expressed practical here and now concerns and hopes!

Performers of the Brahms Requiem sing "How lovely are thy dwellings O Lord of Hosts . . . My soul cries out for the living God . . . Blest are they who die in the Lord." The non-theist can understand this to be about feeling comfortable and at home in the universe, in eternity, in the company of all those who have lived and will live. Howard J. Clinebell describes this attitude of trust and relatedness to the universe as a primary feature of any mentally healthy religion. *Requiem Aeternam* means "Rest Eternal" and I have long wondered how eternal *rest* can be eternal *life.* *Requiem Aeternam* suggests *eternal sleep* or *eternal peace*, which seem to be more honest and ecumenical images than eternal *life* (more on this in chapter 6). It calls to mind "sleep in heavenly peace" from the beloved Christmas Carol "Silent Night." What better image of feeling at home in the universe than that of a child safely and peacefully asleep! As Shakespeare puts it: "We are such stuff / As dreams are made on, and our little life / Is rounded with a sleep." (If we see eternal rest/life simply as the opportunity for endless leisurely passive consumption of various pleasures and entertainments, what would that say about our values?)

In his Requiem, Brahms has the chorus virtually screaming defiance at death: "Where is thy sting?" Wagner's Ring operas include laughing at death. In his early movie "Love and Death" Woody Allen jokes about God being an under-achiever. Allen also laughs in the face of death by belittling it as "a good way to cut down on your expenses." In the movie "Death Takes a Holiday" (more recently re-made as "Meet Joe Black" starring Brad Pitt) death is personified in a whimsical way that attempts to soften its impact. When the real issue related to God and death is seen as our desire for comfort and reassurance, then these artful, musical, cinematic, and sometimes satirical ways of coming to terms with Reality may be much more helpful than a naïve reliance on the supernatural "man in the sky" or "pie in the sky" concept so cleverly skewered in the 2009 movie "The Invention of Lying."

Instead of defiantly screaming at or in various ways belittling, softening or romanticizing death, Albert Camus borrowed the classic myth about Sisyphus stubbornly pushing a boulder up a hill only to have it always roll back down. He says we must come to terms with the reality that life is a constant struggle inevitably ending in death. Simplified, his view is that life is an absurd no-win struggle and the only logical thing to do is to kill oneself—but since life is absurd, why do the logical thing? Keep on with the struggle just to be ornery! Life is by definition conflict and struggle. Camus is usually described as an atheistic existentialist. I prefer to see him as a saint of high church atheism similar to Kierkegaard whose advice to overcome our terror of death by leaping past it makes sense with or without God-talk. Rabbi Kushner echoes Camus in *When Bad Things Happen to Good People* where he expresses amazement at the fact that no matter how many terrible things life throws at us we still want more life and the human race manages to survive.

I feel the need to confess here that, like many preachers, I tended earlier in my life to talk about God much too often in a way that gave a "man upstairs" impression. As mentioned, I have old friends who always speak of God as "the Good Lord." We need to become much more conscious of and explicit about the artistic and metaphorical nature of such theological personifications. We need regular reminders of the symbolic nature of God-talk. We also must tone down or even eliminate some of our most taken-for-granted anthropomorphic personifications. The image of God as a celestial score-keeper or bureaucrat making a list and checking it twice is so far from the *Magnum Mysterium* it is laughable. We must never use this Great Mystery to justify or defend parochial, small-minded notions of God. The tendency of church bureaucrats to treat God as little more than a legalistic "authorizer" is a painful example of human projection. The way some folks repeat the word "father" over and over again during prayers can be downright annoying.

Wm. Paul Young's bestselling novel *The Shack* attempts to provide meaningful personifications of the Trinity and other Christian doctrines—especially those having to do with suffering, love, forgiveness, and relationships. But the novel also makes evident the many shortcomings of overly anthropomorphic images of God. He shakes things up nicely with his picture of God—"Papa"—as a typical mythic shape-shifter who can appear as a black woman. But he never breaks out of the mold of portraying God as a Being, an Agent, a "Who," and still more often than not, as a "He." Young takes his personifications too seriously. His God tends to be mysterious only in the typical old-fashioned sense that "He" is seen as the Creator of an amazing universe, and that doctrines about "Him" are typically convoluted and hard to explain. The understanding of God as *Magnum Mysterium*, as *symbolic* of the Ultimate Mystery of Reality, seems barely to enter Young's consciousness. He talks about facing uncertainty, but actually promotes certainty by emphasizing trust in a literal man-upstairs God and a happy afterlife. Young writes as if Christian theology is *the* theology, seeming to ignore the existence of other religions. He seems unaware of the problems with atonement/sacrifice theology that we will consider in the next chapter. His writing is an imaginative and playful take on some Christian themes, but his artistic skill is in service of a fundamentally literalistic theology—a thinly veiled and preachy defense of typical devotional dogma.

Daniel Dennett describes personification as a natural phenomenon and as an essential, original part of religion. From earliest times, humans have populated their world with agents—spirits, devils, and gods. Dennett concludes, however, that these supernatural, personified agents are imaginary projections which, like Santa Claus, need to be de-mythologized—or taken with a grain of salt. He is leery of the idea that we should get rid of religion altogether, because something worse might take its place. We can't afford to risk leaving religion to extremists or lunatics. His prescription is for all people to be educated so they can understand the diversity of world religions. The most toxic thing Dennett sees in religion is the temptation to stop thinking or questioning. Of course, I couldn't agree more about the desirability of encouraging all people to study world religions, to understand their similarities and differences, and then to learn how to approach them as art forms.

The desire to express gratitude for the joy and beauty of life may include a desire to thank *someone*. But, resisting such personification, on Thanksgiving Day a lot of folks simply hold hands around the dinner table and express their gratitude for specific things or blessings. Folks with a keen understanding of Native American religion will thank the turkey whose life has been sacrificed for their benefit. I've read meditations on "the attitude of gratitude" in which any mention of God would have been superfluous. I usually respond to any invitation to say grace at meals by simply saying "grace," a word which in some languages is the same as "thanks," and a word that I with my Lutheran heritage consider to be one of the most important of all theological words. It is enough just to be grateful for life and for spiritual teachings that put unconditional love—grace and compassion—in the center of our consciousness. If we use a classic ancient Psalm as a spiritual expression of thanksgiving, its historical and artistic nature is evident. "O, give thanks to the Lord for he is good, and his mercy endures forever" beautifully affirms sacred values. The themes of gratitude and compassion are central to any true spirituality, ancient or modern, with or without personifications. We can give ourselves credit for being able to use personifications without taking them literally. We don't need to banish either "God" or Santa Claus. Yes Virginia!

To say that we praise and thank God not because God needs it but because we need it, is the equivalent of saying we don't thank God because God exists! Echoing Don Cupitt's sentiments about occasionally "dropping back" into old devotional habits, an Irish poet I heard on the radio wisely said "Every day I thank the God I don't believe in for my wonderful life." The felt need for a personal God doesn't prove that such a God exists. Slave-owners "needed" their slaves but that didn't prove that slavery was either right or necessary.

One of the great things about music is that when we set religious images and metaphors to music their metaphoric and imaginative nature becomes more obvious. Even the most literal minded will admit that many images are clearly metaphorical. How could Jesus be both Good Shepherd and Lamb of God (*Agnus Dei*)? But soon I will be asking the reader to move beyond "lamb" as metaphor to the broader recognition that *all sacrificial interpretations of Jesus' death* are metaphorical and symbolic rather than plain fact. In chapter 2 we will see that there is a serious problem with any religious notion of human sacrifice or even of martyrdom, and we will see that sacrifice imagery was not the only Hebrew theology drawn upon by the New Testament authors to create and interpret the Jesus story.

Some problematic or outlandish metaphors are used in Christian hymns. Consider the popular Easter hymn "Jesus Christ Is Risen Today." One line is "Now above the sky He's King." The image of a king above the sky is incredibly foreign to a twenty-first century sensibility. Many monarchies today are ceremonial and symbolic, however, so "above the sky" is likely more problematic than the king image itself. There are some symbols or images which are so dated, scientifically naïve, or maybe even totalitarian and anti-humanistic, that we should jettison them altogether. Some are so wildly imaginative that we immediately understand them to be symbolically over the top. Matthew Fox uses an image of God as a "manic depressive with limitless capital" when talking about nature's extravagant excesses.

One of the things that has stuck with me from my seminary days and the mentoring of William Weiblen is the observation that the word "name" is the most important word in the following invocation used at the beginning of many Christian worship services: "In the *name* of the Father, and of the Son, and of the Holy Ghost." The point is that a name is a symbol. The expanded meaning of this invocation is: "We are now going to have a religious service in which we will use names, words, symbols, and constructs to express what is ultimately mysterious; don't forget that they are, after all, words and symbols." If we think of these words and constructs as concrete "things"—if we "reify" symbols—we nullify their symbolic depth. Personally, I sometimes prefer the name "Holy Ghost" rather than "Holy Spirit" because such an archaic image makes its symbolic and poetic nature more obvious. The Tao Te Ching begins by reminding us that "The Tao that can be spoken of is not the eternal Tao." Whenever we think we have totally captured in words the Ultimate Reality of The Way Things Are, we are deceived.

Words fail—especially in theology. And even in science! In the sciences words are also constructs or symbols. Words and phrases such as quark, atom, electron or oedipal complex are ways of describing things or the behavior of things that could be named in many other ways. A butterfly has a quite different scientific name. As Freud liked to remind us, however, the symbols and constructs used by science are related to actual, empirical evidence in a way that religious symbols seldom are. Freud admitted that many of his terms and constructs were illusions, but he also insisted that they were better and more functional than religious illusions because they were based on empirical evidence. In a similar way, modern personality profiling is based on solid behavioral evidence in contrast to astrology which relies on arbitrary and supposedly authoritative signs of the Zodiac. The main issue in psychology is what our constructs and ideas enable us to do and what they prevent us from doing. Constructs channel our actions. Religious constructs may not be empirically based, but they can still enable or restrict our actions. Some constructed images of God can actually encourage sadistic and violent behavior, while other constructs can encourage compassionate behavior.

Tillich's insistence that God does not "exist" but *is* "Beingness Itself" was a pivotal twentieth-century blending of a Middle Eastern, biblical, ethical-historical, monotheistic concept of one Supreme Being called God, with Asian, nature-culture, monistic, pantheistic, symbolic-polytheistic concepts of "God." The great religions of Asia teach that Brahman and Tao are not concepts of a being called God, but symbolize rather The Ultimate Reality (Brahman) of The Way Things Are (Tao). "Monistic" is the idea that all Reality is *one,* and "pantheistic" is the idea that all of this one Reality is sacred (divine or "God"). Karen Armstrong similarly stresses that the Christian doctrine of the Trinity or the great "I Am" ("I Will Be Who I Will Be") of the older Semitic tradition are symbols that highlight the ineffability of "God." "Ineffable" is a word that emphasizes the *transcendent* nature of the Ultimate Mystery of all Reality. When Jesus is pictured as saying that we can call this Mystery "abba" (the equivalent of "daddy"), the image reminds us that this Mystery is also *immanent*—it is in us and it *is* us. The word "image" is the root of "imagination," and as long as we understand "daddy" language as an expression of artistic imagination about feeling at home in the universe we will not be opening ourselves up to J. B. Phillip's classic criticism that *Your God Is Too Small.*

In *A History of God*, Karen Armstrong writes: "All three of the monotheistic religions developed a mystical tradition which made their God transcend the personal category [God as "a being"] and become more similar to the impersonal realities of nirvana and Brahman-Atman." Then she notes how prophets raised objections to these mystical, symbolic, seemingly abstract and non-personal identifications of God with nature and culture (Reality), declaring war on mythology and creating a God of history who calls us to be ethical, to do "His" will on earth, rather than being content merely to contemplate divine Majesty and Mystery. There is much to commend, of course, in the prophetic emphasis on justice and compassion here and now. But Armstrong concludes that the overly personalized, monotheistic God imagined by the prophets could be too small, limited by such things as gender and ethnic bias, while in Christianity both mysticism and the Mystery of the Trinity helped to bring back transpersonal and more abstract understandings of "God." *Tolerant* monotheism can be a positive unifying force, but pagan (peasant) polytheism (many gods) can also provide a good model for our pluralistic world. It might even be argued that *spirituality* is by definition *abstract* because it is so open to interpretation!

I used to talk about how God relates to us "in a personal way" but is not "a person," that God is a Spirit—which really tells us only that God is *not* a physical being like us. I give myself an A for effort, but now feel that if we are to personalize anything *we should personalize the Universe as our Home*, not create an idol in our own image and literalize it as God or the Good Lord. In 1928 a fellow St. Paul Minnesotan, Frederick May Eliot, described spirituality as a sense of "being at home in the world." Since the word ecology is based on a Greek word which means house or home, to say "there's no place like home," especially for the holidays/holydays, is actually quite profound. There's a joke about a child who tells his mother that God's name is Art because of the prayer "Our Father Art in heaven." Personalizing "Father in heaven" language can get ridiculous. But a whimsical take on this joke could remind us how "God" truly is "Art" in the sense that theology is an art form.

The Universe does not do us favors or lovingly number the hairs of our heads. But the Universe does a great deal to promote survival. Darwin's natural selection is about what works, what functions. The spiritual song "His eye is on the sparrow" can be understood as a poetic way of saying that the Universe does a lot to help us survive and thrive. Prayer should be about meditating upon and tapping into the positive life force and energy of the universe. The power of prayer and God-language is about caring and mutual encouragement. It is about focusing on healing as over against disease, optimism as over against pessimism, hope over despair. In psychological counseling, clients often discover that what they are doing or thinking is not working for them, that their ways of coping are ineffective or counterproductive. They learn that the problem is not Reality but their interpretation of reality. They learn that the very structure of reality is geared toward positive adaptation and change. They learn the many levels of truth in Reinhold Niebuhr's serenity prayer that help us understand what we can and cannot change. All of these forms of encouragement stand behind what we mean when we say "God bless you," "good luck," or "may the force be with you." Of course, it would be naïve to see the Universe as only positive and encouraging. A worldview that doesn't have a way of dealing with evil, suffering and death would be shallow, or lame—to use a contemporary idiom. In some of the chapters that follow we will give various answers to this question of how both credit for good and blame for evil can be dealt with in religious or God-talk terms. We have already seen how Chris Hedges counsels us to accept the mystery, ambiguity and suffering of life with compassion, wisdom, and humility— and to act in a manner that expresses these same qualities.

Syncretism and Religious Diversity

Tillich, Armstrong, Thich Nhat Hanh (author of *Living Buddha, Living Christ*), and Joseph Campbell are among many others who demonstrate the possibilities of syncretism. Syncretism at its best is the attempt to focus on the commonalities among religions, to blend or even homogenize disparate traditions by the creative development of common themes such as compassion, love, justice, salvation, enlightenment, change, or the symbolic nature of God-talk. But it would be naïve and even dangerous to think that we are ever going to create one single harmonious worldwide religion. In *The Future of Faith* Harvey Cox recounts a meeting with Cardinal Ratzinger, who was to become Pope Benedict XVI, in which the Cardinal said that his primary worry was not liberals in the church, but syncretism, especially the blending of third world customs and superstitions with traditional Roman Catholic beliefs. (I suggest that this kind of blending always takes place and not only in Christianity.) Cox noted a clear Western, European, Greco-Roman bias in the future Pope's concern. I think we must also note with concern the specter of religion causing ever widening wars between competing and often equally myopic and superstitious worldviews with their sometimes noxious beliefs and practices.

The idea that religions are primarily an expression of creative artistic diversity makes it possible for us to celebrate both syncretistic commonalities and the validity of uniquely distinct theologies. Sports imagery can be very helpful for understanding and appreciating religious diversity. One can see each classic religious tradition as a game with its own rules, techniques, and unique approach to the similar elements found in all religion. If you love baseball, you may not have any interest in football, golf, basketball, soccer or tennis—even though every one of these sports uses a ball. In the same way, those who center their religion upon Buddha, Christ, Mohammed, Lao Tzu or any other central figure may simply have neither the time nor the inclination to play around with the symbols and images of the other religions. Campbell similarly uses a computer metaphor, describing each great religion as a kind of computer software program that will work independently of the others. What must be avoided is the idea that only one religious figure, one game, one ball, one program, one set of symbols and metaphors is the only one that is true, beautiful, or meaningful. How ridiculous it would be to spend time arguing about whether golf balls are better than footballs—or whether Russian is better than French! As this book demonstrates, I do think that everyone should make at least some effort to understand other religious traditions. But this doesn't mean that people can't prefer to stick with the "game" (or language) they know and love best.

Some Christians argue for the superiority of Christianity by pointing to its great success in spreading around the globe. Many in Islam do the same. We are currently in a time when these two religions seem to be polarized almost in the way that the United States and the Soviet Union were at loggerheads during the so-called cold war—although my point in this book is that the more significant divide is the one *within* religions between those who have a dangerously literal and supernatural approach to religion and those who do not. When we carefully consider the history of both Christianity and Islam, we see the role played by chance, luck, or simple coincidence. The slightest development having gone differently could have meant a completely different outcome. To say that it was God's plan to have the Roman emperor Constantine begin making Christianity the official religion of his Empire, which led to the church becoming a "holy" version of that Roman empire, is to ignore the many evils accompanying this "success" of Christianity. In *Through The Eye Of A Needle*, historian Peter Brown illustrates how changes in the church's attitude toward wealth were in many ways at odds with central features of the earliest Christian movement. The denigration of "liberation theology" (which takes the side of the poor and huddled masses) by some Christian leaders is embarrassing, to say the least. Self-aggrandizing notions that Christianity is the only way to salvation— "there is no salvation outside of the Roman Catholic Church"—helped turn the Church into another version of the oppressive, wrathful, violent (inqui-sitions, etc.) type of domination system to which the Christian movement, with its suffering and self-giving Messiah, originally intended to offer an alternative! (See, *the Last Week* by Borg and Crossan.)

As Christianity was becoming the official religion of Constantine's empire, the book of Revelation was embraced and reinterpreted by the growing orthodox establishment—especially by the hugely influential Bishop Athanasius, whose 367AD letter contains the first suggestion for a New Testament Scripture to include Revelation, a list identical to our present 27 books. (Many other lists from that period and beyond are also identical, except that they exclude Revelation.) The dubious interpretation of John's Revelation that suited Athanasius and Constantine, and that was eventually adopted by their successors, saw it as opposing, not the Roman Empire, but fellow Christians. The orthodox establishment branded them as heretics or apostates who were deliberately choosing to misinterpret and corrupt the faith. (The term "anti-Christ," which has now become a kind of "religious football" and generalized epithet, never appears in Rev-elation but only in the short letters titled First and Second John.) Elaine Pagels points out that literature of this type frequently enjoys renewed popularity when people feel they are living in unusually turbulent times.

The spread of Islam took place largely through trade, but there were darker sides to its history as well. When we face up to the role that chance and luck play in the world, we also have to recognize the arrogance of claiming that every apparent advance of religion is a matter of God's will or favor toward his chosen! It must be recognized that great good has been done by devoted followers of every religion, but also great evil—"lest any-one should boast." (As I see it, the diversity of religions and of religious holidays being celebrated within a country can help to curb the similarly dark and dangerous arrogance of extreme, virtually idolatrous national-ism that acknowledges and promotes only state holidays.)

Life Before Death

In *A New Christianity for a New World*, and in *Eternal Life: A New Vision*, Bishop Spong says that religion is motivated by the fear of death and the desire for security and certainty. Others have elaborated this theme that our uniquely human reflexive self-consciousness, especially as it relates to death, has made us spiritual beings—that the need to make peace with our mortality is at the core of our spirituality. Sociologist and philosopher of religion Ken Wilber views death as the ultimate or fundamental taboo. Echoing Kierkegaard, he says that the mortal self is essentially terror and trembling. He concludes that we must transcend the self as in Buddhism and resist the urge to create permanent and timeless "immortality symbols that aspire to durability." Greenblatt's Pulitzer Prize winning *The Swerve: How the World Became Modern,* blasts religion for exploiting the fear of death.

Early in my ministerial career I ruffled a few feathers with a sermon focusing on these words from a thirteenth century Spanish hymn: "Were there no heaven to gain, no hell to flee, for what Thou art alone I must love Thee." My point was that while God-talk understandably deals with the question of what might happen after death, the more important issue could be life *before* death! What if spirituality is not basically about life after death? Can we be so heavenly minded that we're no earthly good? What if the point of confronting death is that it makes life here and now all the more important and valuable? What if Sam Harris is right that belief in life after death is dangerous because it encourages suicidal martyrdom or reduces our incentive to improve this world and reduce human misery? What happens to ethics if, again to quote the hymn, our motivation to be good is "not for the hope of glory or reward?" One of my favorite child-hood hymns exhorted us to be "Fervent in spirit, serving the Lord: Not for world's gain or the hope of reward."

Contrasting with my experience where I upset some folks by down-playing the notion of eternal rewards and punishments, in the most recent congregation I served there was a terminally ill but typically upbeat man who wrote me a note expressing his tongue-in-cheek worry that his wife "says I am not the best Christian because I am not too concerned with what happens to me after my death." This gentleman certainly understood that on some levels religion is clearly a matter of life and death. He also seemed to understand, however, that we should not focus on surviving death but should concentrate instead on getting beyond our *fear* of death.

There is a certain irony in the fact that many people spend more time thinking about death on "Happy Easter" Sunday than on any other day of the year. In many ways the great religious traditions of the world make death their ultimate concern. Belief in some version of life after death has always been a fairly universal way to soften the blow of facing the grim reaper. The popular American spiritual that begins with the words "Soon ah will be done ah wit de troubles o' de world" ends with the bold refrain

"I'm goin' to live with God!" Much of this book is about how the idea of "going to live with God" is interpreted in various religions.

Issues of death and immortality will be prominent throughout these pages, but it needs to be kept in mind that the central theme remains understanding religion as a creative art form. The earlier quotes about music from Martin Luther suggest that theology and music are virtually equal as great art forms. Luther's use of the word "queen" in describing music needs to be placed next to the fact that theology was typically referred to as the "queen of the sciences" in Luther's day and during much of early European history. This royal imagery for both music and theology is equally superlative. I've done music therapy with folks in nursing homes and some of them can still sing the old songs when they don't even know their own names! This phenomenon, illustrating the multi-dimensional nature of music, is clearly relevant to the issue of music trumping theology. When my mentally challenged sister died, the point was stressed at the memorial service that theologian Karl Barth famously summarized his massive volumes of dogmatic theology by quoting the simple song "Jesus loves me." My sister loved religious and classical music. She would scarcely have understood a word of Barth's theology—or mine for that matter—but I saw how, for her, the medium (music) could be the message.

I like to frame the question of life after death by asking "What is our individual relationship to eternity?" Many of my students say that religion is about the individual relating to some "power" (or energy) greater or higher than self. Some tend to think of this "something greater or higher" in personified terms as God. If I suggest to them that they might also think of this greater reality simply as Eternity, a few will object that the image of a relationship to eternity is too abstract? But is an overly personalized idea any better? Is it mere wishful thinking? What does "eternal life" mean? Do we live "with" or "in" God in the sense that our individual identity is submerged in some version of Nirvana or the Seamless Whole?

Both eternal death and eternal life can present us with undesirable prospects. Our death involves the grief of saying goodbye to everything and everyone we have ever known. Does anyone in their right mind really believe that death itself is a totally wonderful thing to be celebrated without reservation? But the prospect of eternal life can also appear to be a fearful trap from which there is "No Exit"—to quote the title of Sartre's famous play. Writers such as Jonathan Swift and John Milton have described how everlasting life could itself be a type of horrible death sentence. The "Twilight saga" vampire stories as well as the movie "Tuck Everlasting" and the zombie or Dracula movies paint similar pictures. The novel *Death with Interruptions* by Saramago portrays a horrifying world without death. Would we really want to live forever? A wry poet wrote "Eternal life is something God gives you, and once He gives it to you, you can't get rid of it!" The metaphor of eternal life as an "endless day" in the carol "Lo, How a Rose" is not at all appealing to me. Deep down, when I see quashed road kill, do I really believe this unfortunate raccoon "went somewhere"? Do I really want to spend eternity with my relatives? Both eternal death and eternal life have pros and cons. How do we come to terms with this conundrum? We dread a death sentence, but we could just as well dread a life sentence.

I have come to the conclusion that the most appropriate attitude toward death is one of profound ambivalence. I think Poet Dylan Thomas is right when he admonishes us not to go gentle into that good night but to rage against the dying of the light. I think tears are appropriate. Death can be legitimately characterized as an enemy. There is nothing pretty about death. But death can also be seen as a defeated enemy. We can come to terms and make peace with the reality that if our lives had no limit they would lose their meaning and value. More on this later.

Death and religion both have to do with change. As we shall see in chapter 5, some religious worldviews stress that change itself is the only eternal reality, that change itself is the fundamental feature of life. But it is perhaps more common for people to see religion as the antithesis of change. A popular hymn owes much of its appeal to the line "Change and decay in all around I see; O Thou who changest not abide with me." For many folks the pure and simple staying power of the church is its main strength. Forget relevance and adaptation and reform. "The church don't change and that's what I like about it!" Even the simple idea of living eternally with God could express an unseemly craving for absolute certainty and everlasting security. But this anti-change attitude, for which the dying cardinal archbishop of Milan chastised the Vatican in 2012, has turned many European churches and cathedrals into museums—glorious ones to be sure—reflecting a world long gone. The Vatican Museum, the burial crypt beneath St. Peter's Basilica, and the Basilica itself are now largely reminders of past glory. It is an insightful joke that the seven last words of the church are "We never did it that way before."

In North America many churches have become little more than bastions of very narrowly defined, status quo, middle class, conventional or reactionary values, despite the evident ways in which Jesus is a far from conventional figure (see the 1962 book *The Suburban Captivity of the Churches)*. The problem with narrowly defined conventional values is that they are typically too quick to judge as dysfunctional or maladjusted anyone who is different. This risks driving into destructive, anti-social behavior those who are perfectly functional except that it is in an unusual way. People who are artistic, exceptionally intelligent, dyslexic, creative, gay, transsexual, or who may be struggling to cope with unusual circumstances of various kinds have often turned out to produce some of humankind's most important advances.

It is in the developing world, particularly in the southern hemisphere (the "global south"), that Christianity is still on a growth curve, but I think this mainly reflects the typical enthusiasm of new converts and a legacy from the era of imperialism and colonialism. We often find in those areas a naive faith, accompanied by superstition and outdated prejudice—especially against sexual minorities. The advancing spirituality of the developed world is tending to outgrow this naiveté and these prejudices, but those in the developing world find it difficult to view these kinds of cultural changes in the developed world as progress. They seem more likely to see such changes as another form of cultural imperialism rather than as a sign of progress and development, ignoring the cultural imperialism of reactionary interlopers who jump at the chance to promote traditional prejudices.

Whenever we ignore the New Testament image of a God who says "I make all things new," lively and relevant spirituality is endangered. We need to keep our ears attuned to the broadest possible symbolic implications of: "The trumpet shall sound and we shall be changed!" This theme of change describes Ultimate Reality. Change is our destiny!

Overcoming the Sacred/Secular Dichotomy

Late in the twentieth century the Roman Catholic diocese in San Francisco had to close five large churches because of declining attendance. I think it is appropriate to note that the largest building closed was the impressive stone cathedral-type church, St. Brigid's on Van Ness Avenue, and that this building was eventually sold to the Academy of Art University, an institution with a sprawling complex of locations throughout the city. This University will preserve St. Brigid's as an historic and artistic treasure while also utilizing its space for many artistic purposes. A large Congregational Church building in the heart of downtown San Francisco was also sold to the Academy of Art. I sang in many concerts and rehearsals at both of these church buildings. The closing of St. Brigid's was a sad and troubling experience for many folks. Protests were mounted. But in a longer-term perspective this transformation from religion to art, this confluence of religion and art, can be seen as progress. Other churches in San Francisco are known for the concert series they sponsor as part of their service to the community. Whatever strengthens the tie between religious and artistic endeavors bodes well for the future, it seems to me.

In this book I am arguing that traditional, literalist, supernatural religion can actually be dangerous in our increasingly interconnected world. A case in point is the polarization we find in various parts of the globe between somewhat progressive secular governments and relatively extremist religious groups. The Iraq war and the uprisings related to the so-called "Arab spring" led to the ouster of a few dictators and in some places the replacement of mildly progressive secular governments with more rigid religious governments. Other countries seem poised on the brink of similar developments. A few more or less progressive secular governments in the region, such as Turkey, have tried with varying degrees of success to promote the separation of religion and state. In Egypt, various minorities and progressive secularists are rightfully worried about a backward movement to "strict Islamist" rule now that a long-time dictatorial regime has ended. We can sympathize with those who are struggling to escape from a history of dictators and colonial imperialism. But those among them who want to live in a postmodern secular world (a cultural milieu in which science and spirituality are valued equally) have reason to fear that their "revolutions" may amount to jumping from the frying pan into the fire. It is one thing for individuals in a society to have a religious worldview that relates to every aspect of life. But it is quite another to live under a literalistic, authoritarian, rigid theocracy where, for example, every sin can also be a crime. The more desirable alternative is a society that combines the best of secular postmodern values with a deep appreciation of religion and spirituality *as an art form*.

The word "religion" comes from a root that means "to tie, bind or link." During an orientation when I arrived at Harvard Divinity School, Richard Niebuhr described theology as a field in which one could specialize in not specializing. Religion binds us together in communities and relationships, it links us to great traditions, it restrains our harmful behavior (morality), and it ties everything in life together for us, providing a pervasive artistic worldview. In Gordon Kaufman's words, again, "God" is our imagining of an ultimate reference point for understanding every-thing. I suggest that fewer churches would close, and each religion could continue to celebrate its spiritual heritage, if the faithful would come to better appreciate the bond between religion and art—particularly music. This bond also links spirituality with humanism (with arts and humani-ties). The separation of church and state does not necessarily imply hostil-ity between spirituality and what is often pejoratively described as secular humanism. The "spiritual humanism" I envision is not an oxymoron. Its blend of artistic spirituality (religion) and postmodern secularity (scien-tific worldview) could be our salvation!

On many levels, spirituality can transcend the sacred/secular split. Churches, temples, museums and concert halls can all embody a spiritual dimension. A pervasive theme of much progressive spirituality these days is the metaphor of depth. As Bishop Spong would say, we most truly meet divinity precisely when we delve most deeply into our humanity. Religion based on compassion and empathy is self-validating because it challenges us to treat every human life as sacred, to overcome artificial boundaries and destructive hostility between people. We need no abstract or external reason to be spiritual, just as we need no external, supernatural reason to be moral, to promote the flourishing and well-being of each other and of our ecological home—Mother Earth and the wider Universe.

Much art that is not explicitly sacred nevertheless has a deep, spiri-tual, "wholistic" dimension and can put us in touch with Absolute, Eternal Mystery (God). Martin Luther recognized a distinction between sacred and secular, calling them the Two Kingdoms. He was wise to say that both realms belong to God—that "God is interested in a lot of things besides religion"—and to defend his adaptation of secular melodies for hymns by joking "why should the devil have all the good tunes?" But an overall thesis in this book is that the idea of two separate realms, the empirical/natural realm and the spiritual/supernatural realm, *underestimates the Mystery, depth, and splendor of the One Natural World, our one and only home—the Universe.* As Bernard Meland, professor of theology at the University of Chicago wrote in the 1930s ". . . religion is a fine art with cosmic content."

Coming Hereafter

The following chapters will focus on the artistic nature and insights of ma-jor religious traditions, particularly their theological perspectives on the relationship of human beings to reality and to eternity (to space and time).

I once heard noted Lutheran theologian Joseph Sittler give a series of lectures on eternal life. His fundamental conclusion was that while we may believe in it, we have no idea what it means to "live eternally with God."

Chapter 2 will focus on ideas about final judgment and eternal salvation. Have I been good enough? Will I go to heaven or hell? Here the issue of one's relationship to eternity is seen in terms of ethics, sin and redemption—being saved from sin and guilt. Bruce Bawer presents an excellent critique of the over-individualized version of this perspective in his 1997 book *Stealing Jesus: How Fundamentalism Betrays Christianity*. In his 2003 book *The Heart of Christianity*, Marcus Borg also notes the individualistic and self-centered mindset of "Blessed Assurance, Jesus is *mine!*" and its obsessive focus on afterlife. Beyond their folksy quality, the popularity of many sentimental gospel hymns makes perfect sense if Christianity is understood exclusively in terms of going to heaven when you die. The proliferation of personal pronouns (I, me, my, mine), along with serene images found in songs such as "In the Garden," have given Christianity much of its appeal. The criticism of sentimental piety focused on afterlife is nevertheless valid. The relationship between ethics and religion has many dimensions that both individuals and society at large would do well to understand. Would Christians still be concerned about ethics if ethics had nothing to do with getting to heaven? Do believers have better reasons than nonbelievers to be moral? What are the social justice implications here and now of the fact that Jesus was crucified because he challenged oppressive traditions and systems? How can a person have a sense of moral urgency about issues without becoming a fanatic? How might a sense of humor relate to all this?

Another perspective (chapter 3) is also concerned with ethics, but the focus is on fairness. Belief in reincarnation did not originally center on the issue of life after death but on the obvious unfairness of life. Innocent children die and evildoers live to a ripe and rich old age. How can one possibly believe that life (or God) is just and fair unless you believe that the soul lives many lifetimes and in the end what goes around comes around (karma)? But if fairness can only be achieved in a next life, what motivation is there to make life in the present as fair and fulfilling as possible? We will be exploring how, in classic Indian thought, reincarnation is seen as a treadmill-like continuation of suffering, a punishment for not letting go of the illusion of "self." Nirvana means "to extinguish the flame" of ego and of self-centered *ignorant craving* (for things like fairness or immortality!) *which is the main cause of suffering.* Escape from reincarnation equals the end of suffering! This version of the ultimate goal for our lives has often been imagined as a single water drop being absorbed by the ocean, or more provocatively, as the whole ocean being absorbed by a single drop.

Moving beyond the ethical dimension of salvation, in chapter 4 we ask whether there is any solid, empirical *evidence* for life after death. Recent trends in biblical theology have seriously called into question whether resurrection theology should be taken literally either as it applies to the historical Jesus or to those who believe in him. There are questions about science and reality, literal Bible interpretation, miracles and the supernatural. Some scientists now speak of "multiverse" instead of "universe" and contemplate parallel universes, string theory, and big bang theories with worlds spontaneously exploding into existence from a tiny speck in a split second. Could the phrase "with God anything is possible" be close to having a scientific equivalent without resorting to the notion of the supernatural? There are various ideas about how we might survive death. The concept of the immortality of the soul usually reflects a dualist notion that the body is evil or unreal and dies, while the good and real immortal soul lives on. (This dualism is often called *Manichaean*—Mani was an ancient Persian dualist.) New Testament resurrection theology tends to see this dualism as a false dichotomy between soul and body which fails to recognize that there may be at least something of eternal significance in that category of reality which we describe with terms such as body, form, material, physical, shape, substance, and identity. The Hebrew Scriptures speak of Sheol as "the place of the dead," a kind of limbo between being and non-being. Some speculate that souls are "entities" who travel within time and space (experiencing past and future lives) or beyond time and space, busily trying to explain themselves to the rest of us through "trance channeling" mediums. Wayne Dyer sees us as "infinite spiritual beings having a temporary human experience" and others understand their place in the universe by thinking of themselves as "a thought in the Divine Mind." Some see immortality not in the soul but in their DNA living on in their offspring. Many believe that the way to have a connection with eternity is to make a positive difference—to change the world for the better.

Another perspective on one's relationship to "eternal reality" could make chapter 5 the most provocative chapter for some readers. This viewpoint is expressed in the Hindu/Buddhist concepts of emptiness, contingency, "no-self," or in Western process philosophy. Here the thought is that everything in the universe (even God, however defined) is in process. Just as you can never step into the same river twice because it is always flowing and changing, so likewise you also are not really the same person as time goes by. What we humans call "self" is so much in process that there really is no such thing as a static self. Since I have no concrete self in the first place, why should I fret over this non-existent self's demise or relationship to eternity? This outlook has been described as particularly compatible with a scientific, psychological worldview because it doesn't require belief in some sort of afterlife for which there is no real evidence. (Critics may see this view as little more than a sugar-coated version of "when you're dead, you're dead; get used to it!") These traditions also talk about eternity as a matter of experiencing "the eternal now," "the Seamless Whole," or the "contingent" interconnectedness of reality where time and space are transcended and the question of how long anything lasts becomes irrelevant. "Everlasting" refers to time that never ends. "Eternal" suggests an experienced reality that goes beyond the very categories of time and space. One of the most profound Buddhist ways of expressing this sense of "the eternal now" is for each individual to say: "I am the universe happening." *Carpe diem* (seize the day) because life is now or never!

Chapter 6 concludes that the best way of looking at the question of one's relationship to eternity is to contemplate what it means *to feel comfortably at home in the Eternal Mystery of Ultimate Reality*. While some, like Albert Camus, take a rather cynical view of life as a struggle doomed ultimately to failure, I suggest that it makes more sense to adopt an upbeat, hope-springs-eternal, serene, open-ended, loving attitude toward life—and death. To embrace spirituality and various images of God is to embrace an essentially artistic, poetic, and musical approach to, and celebration of, love, life, and relationships. The very process of creating purposes, meanings, and living relationships becomes the ultimate expression of what life is. This capstone chapter summarizes how the theme of religion as an art form, and the theme of coming to terms with death, blend into a vision for the future of religion, of humanity, and of each sacred individual.

Our uniquely human, reflexive self-consciousness has made us "the religious animal." People put their faith in an amazing variety of worldviews and belief systems in order to make sense of life. Many have a powerful need to believe that a superior being or universal mind intended things to happen a certain way. Some commit suicide to follow a comet to Heaven's Gate. Some cobble together unusual combinations such as Judaism and feng shui (Fung Schway). Others believe that every event recorded in the Bible is a straightforward historical fact and that these cumulative historical events (often seen as having been accurately predicted) prove their beliefs to be true. Many find comfort in visualizing their deceased loved ones as looking down lovingly on them from heaven or contacting them from beyond the grave. Political, psychological and other kinds of creeds also provide quasi-religious belief systems.

It's clear to me that folks believe whatever they want or need to believe about the meaning, purpose, or eternal destiny of their lives, without really having any substantial evidence for their beliefs. Up to a point this probably is as it should be, since the purpose of life can be seen as the very process itself of searching for meaning and purpose in life! However, even if we aren't chasing comets, there are other ways in which it can be dangerous to reify (concretize) our religious/poetic imaginings. When we treat metaphorical images, mental constructs, or clever rationalizations as literal fact, we can appear as confused and ridiculous as did Gracie Allen in the comedy of Burns and Allen when she would take literally a phrase such as "pie in the sky." Rabbi Kushner's *When Bad Things Happen to Good People* describes the spiritual and psychological damage done if we buy into literal notions that everything happens for a reason or is God's will and plan—notions better construed simply as about making the best of unfortunate situations!

As previously noted, a spiritual worldview is sometimes pictured as a game with its own specific rules. This is a helpful analogy, but understanding a religious worldview as artistic is a much more nuanced approach. Rather than searching for the one best portrait of the way things are, or the ultimate, authentic spirituality, I think that for the foreseeable future we should be content to admire and appreciate the artistry and insights of various spiritual worldviews. No doubt limited by their assumptions and historical settings, these artistic portraits are nevertheless among the better and more meaningful intimations of Truth that we have. Do we have to make value judgments about whether Rembrandt is better than Dali? A big part of the beauty and value of the artistic approach is that it allows the various spiritual traditions to get along much better with each other. Seeing Religion as an Art Form is the antidote to the poison of warring absolutes.

Can any of the religious answers to questions regarding spirituality, death and eternity be proven with some kind of scientific evidence? An important aspect of scientific reliance on solid evidence is that the ongoing quest for evidence keeps science flexible and open-ended. Science does come up with solid, reliable and useful truths, but always within the context of the possibility that the discovery of further evidence will require modifications. The empirical and technical language of advanced theoretical physics often ends up sounding as much like philosophical and even theological discourse as it sounds like scientific analysis. Therefore, it seems to me that the scientific, empirical (natural as opposed to supernatural) worldview can reasonably affirm a similar philosophical contemplation of the cumulative wisdom of the world's religions regarding our spiritual relationship to reality and to eternity.

What is the nature of religious wisdom if it is not based on supernatural, divine, "special revelation"—a source of knowledge beyond the scope of empirical evidence? I am convinced that religion is the ultimate artistic endeavor that aims to harmonize intellectual, social, and emotional intelligence. The imaginative creation of symbols and metaphors is a way of visualizing and comprehending our situation in the universe. Religion is not about imagining supernatural "realities" into existence. Spiritual imagination is about gaining insight into what is truly real and meaningful.

Chapter 2

Beyond Heaven and Hell

Many Interpretations of Jesus, Atonement, and Salvation

In the middle of the twentieth century, Swedish theologian Gustav Aulen published his now classic book *Christus Victor* in which he outlined three main types of Christian atonement theology. The "satisfaction or substitution theory," most famously codified by St. Anselm, sees the life and death of Jesus as a sacrifice vicariously satisfying God's demand for righteousness and for the punishment of Sin. The "moral influence" approach emphasizes how the story of Jesus brings us into a very personal relationship/reconciliation with God, demonstrating both God's loving compassion and human sinfulness in an emotional way that makes us want to stop hurting God with our immoral behavior. The "Christus Victor" theology, seen by Aulen as the earliest version of atonement, is a mythological (artistic/poetic!) approach to understanding the death and resurrection of Jesus as the story of God's ultimate victory in a cosmic battle between elemental forces, but also between the more down-to-earth powers of evil and good, bondage and liberation, death and life.

Aulen saw a need to move beyond atonement ideas that focused exclusively on viewing the sacrificial crucifixion and death of Jesus as a legalistic transaction which saves mankind from death and hell, thus providing eternal life with God in heaven. This "saved from judgment and wrath" version of atonement theology is dramatically portrayed in the text and music of Giuseppe Verdi's operatic Requiem:

> Deliver me, O Lord, from eternal death
> on that dreadful day
> when heaven and earth shall be moved,
> and Thou shalt come to judge the world by fire.

> I am seized with fear and trembling
> when I reflect upon the judgment
> and the wrath to come.
> When the heavens and the earth shall be moved.
> That day of wrath, of wasting and of misery,
> Eternal rest grant unto them, O Lord,
> and let perpetual light shine upon them.

This "Dies Irae" (Day of Wrath) imagery is used in many famous Requiems and has been dubbed the greatest pop song of the Christian Middle Ages. The people who built the great cathedrals of Europe took all of this angst about death, suffering, and judgment very seriously and very literally. When Martin Luther was a young man he was terrified of Christ the righteous judge. His rediscovery of God's grace did not eliminate the issue of sin, wrath and fear, but it did bring some balance back into beliefs about God's judgment and mercy. A major shortcoming of the emphasis on sin and forgiveness is that Christian ethical life can become little more than a cyclical revolving door of groveling confessions about "my own most grievous fault" coupled with routine declarations of forgiveness. A better model for Christian ethical life would be to focus on a proactive process of bringing ever more compassion and justice into our lives personally, politically, and economically.

Many twenty-first century folks, for whom I am writing this book, find it difficult to take seriously all this angst about judgment, sin, impurity, wrath, guilt, and fear. We tend to feel enlightened in comparison with those benighted souls who suffered under the oppressive power of the medieval church. (While cathedrals and churches gave these souls a glimpse of glory, frightening images of the damned were also plentiful.) Greenblatt's The Swerve makes a compelling case for avoiding such guilt trips. Best-selling author Rabbi Harold Kushner takes up the issue of runaway guilt and shame in his book, How Good Do We Have To Be? One of his main themes is that not all mistakes are sins; in fact, we cannot learn and grow if we are too afraid of making mistakes.

When Harvard professor Harvey Cox wrote his 1977 book Turning East: Why Americans Look To The Orient For Spirituality—And What That Search Can Mean To The West, he was addressing a growing tendency in Western culture to be turned off by all the sin and guilt of biblical religion. The philosophies of India impress many as offering a more positive spirituality of higher consciousness, meditation, personal fulfillment, and serenity. But even such supposedly positive spirituality does not eliminate the ethical aspect (both personal and social) that is bound to be present in all spirituality. Ethical concerns are a central feature of our humanity; we have a sense of responsibility to enhance life and resist evil. Part of the genius of biblical theology is the way in which it takes both human failings (sin) and divine grace (forgiveness/mercy) very seriously. William James noted that all religions see "something wrong" in the world (social oppression and personal sin). Sound biblical theology avoids using this awareness as a club to browbeat people into submission.

Much traditional Christian theology sees the ethical dimension of life as the central core of what is called "salvation history." A simple, literalistic version of "God's plan of salvation" goes like this: God, the Supernatural Creator, is also a righteous judge who expects moral perfection from human beings. But human beings have "sinned" by "missing the mark" of perfection, and "the wages of sin is death." Fortunately, however, God is also merciful and has provided a method to satisfy the requirements of both righteousness and mercy. God arranges a vicarious atonement in which He sends his supernatural, divine/human Son into the world to live a perfect life, and then, sinless, to suffer the punishment for sin (death and hell) on behalf of all people. The reason that this supernatural savior must be both human and divine is so that his perfect life and innocent death will acquire infinite merit, enough to "pay for" the sins of all mankind. (As an individual human being, Jesus would only have been able to die as a substitute for one other person.) By accepting in faith what God's Son has done for them, human beings can come into a personal relationship with God through his Son, a relationship that continues into the next life (salvation to heaven). This is no doubt the most well-known version of atonement theology. (As we will see, much of its "popularity" may actually have more to do with psychology than with theology.)

This *substitution or satisfaction interpretation of atonement,* most systematically delineated by St. Anselm in the twelfth century, presents numerous theological difficulties. Jesus here is a supernatural "Christ" (Greek for the Hebrew *title* "Messiah," a royal image meaning "anointed one"), sent to earth by God his Father with a job description. His "work" is basically a legalistic transaction in which, on behalf of all mankind, he lives a perfect life and then pays the death penalty for sin by dying as a vicarious substitute, sacrificial lamb or scapegoat who "takes away the sin of the world." But the Jewish Messiah/Christ was always understood to be a human being, not a supernatural divine being. (The Hebrews had other images for special divine beings, such as angels and the apocalyptic "Son of man" who was typically seen as the ultimate judge.) Furthermore, to whom is this penalty paid? To God, so God's sense of righteousness can be satisfied? To the Devil, because the devil has power over God and can force God to kill Himself in the form of His only begotten Son? Another problem is that if the "wages of sin" is eternal death in hell, how can it be said that "God in Christ" suffered this eternal hell if he is raised from death after less than three days? (Some versions of the Apostles' Creed try to sidestep this issue by saying that Jesus Christ "tasted death to the full" rather than that he "descended into hell"—more about hell later.)

The greatest problem with this entire scenario is the idea of Jesus as a fundamentally supernatural being who knows exactly why he is here and what he has to accomplish. In addition to begging the question of how this supernatural person could possibly be fully human (described by Luther in his famous hymn "A Mighty Fortress" as "the man of God's own choosing"), the idea of an all-knowing Jesus suggests that there is only one true theology in the entire New Testament and only one true Christian Church. It lays the groundwork for an inevitably authoritarian domination system or mindset controlled by authoritarian personality types, with rigid rules, orthodoxy, and potentially violent tendencies.

Bishop Spong insists that the theology of blood atonement through human sacrifice is grotesque. Bultmann called it a "hotch-potch of sacrificial analogies" untenable for us today. It is not surprising, however, that the New Testament uses Old Testament sacrifice/atonement theology to make sense of the crucifixion of Jesus. The New Testament book of Hebrews uses mixed metaphors of Jesus both as the sacrificial Lamb of God (*Agnus Dei*) and as the High Priest offering the sacrifice. But contradictory metaphors such as these make it obvious that we are dealing with symbols rather than facts. The theology of Hebrews, like the theology of the New Testament in general, is best understood as an artistic interpretation of the possible meaning of historical events! The only undisputed factual event on which the theology of the New Testament Gospels is based is that, just as earlier they had been brutalized, killed, and dragged into exile by the Babylonians (around 586 BCE), the Jewish people (including those who are creating the New Testament) are now being virtually wiped out by Imperial Rome (between 70 and 90 CE). The Jesus stories are based on this historical fact of the crucifixion of many Jews and, in effect, the crucifixion of the Jewish people as a whole.

The four Gospels were written after the city of Jerusalem and the temple had already been destroyed by the Romans—some 40 years after the likely date of the crucifixion of Jesus. Many crucifixions were indeed historical events, but as we shall see, there is significant debate about the historical nature of the specific accounts of the crucifixion of the Jesus who is pictured in the New Testament. Whatever the facts about Jesus might be, the creators of these Jesus stories clearly were drawing on almost every theological image, metaphor, or theme the Hebrew Scriptures ever had in order to deal with this horrific period of violent oppression and destruction. That sacrifice would be one of these themes (but only one!) is no surprise.

Midrash—The Tradition of Constant Reinterpretation

The New Testament is clearly a *Midrash* (reinterpretation), most specifically of the Jewish Messiah/Christ (Anointed One) concept, using the story of Jesus to create a revised meaning of "Messiah." Hebrew kings were anointed with holy oil rather than being crowned. As their greatest ever anointed one, King David is the Hebrew prototype for later heroic figures. The first person in the Bible to be honored specifically as a hero Messiah is the Persian king Cyrus, who defeats the Babylonians and "saves" the exiled Jews, allowing them to return from Babylon to Jerusalem around 537 BCE, where they rebuild the city and their ancient temple. The next major messianic figure is the military leader Judas Maccabaeus, who puts together an army that drives the Syrian/Greek occupation out of Judea around 164 BCE, making possible a rededication (Hanukkah) of the desecrated temple. So Messiahs had been human beings—political, royal, or military heroes.

But drawing especially on the "suffering servant" poetry of Isaiah in the Hebrew Scriptures (Old Testament), the writings eventually chosen to be included in the Christian New Testament Scriptures create the revolutionary concept of a Spirit-filled, serving, suffering, and even humiliated Messiah—we might even say "a non-messiah Messiah" who is not a hero but a teacher and prophetic messenger calling people to a new way of living based on justice, peace and compassion. This interpretation of the Messiah as a suffering servant and prophet was quite a stretch, although Cyrus had also been an unlikely Messiah since he was not even Jewish.

Midrash is the Jewish term for artistic, theological, sermonic reinterpretations or revisions of classic themes and stories—a common practice also in Hinduism (see *The Hindus: An Alternative History*). In *From Metaphysics to Midrash* (2008), Shaul Magid writes that midrash "deepened biblical myth by embellishing it and extending it to include new vistas of imaginative thinking." To what degree the stories about Jesus reflect an actual "historical Jesus" and to what extent these stories are creative reinterpretations of themes in the Hebrew Scriptures is a matter of ongoing debate. A few scholars doubt whether Jesus ever existed at all as an actual historical figure. They suspect that the various versions of his life story are essentially artistic, midrashic fabrications, based on earlier rabbinic sayings and homiletical (sermonic) traditions, on stories or motifs from the Hebrew Bible, and on issues that reflected later developments in the Jesus Movement. (Check out the documentary "The God Who Wasn't There" and its DVD extras.) Others suggest that Jesus may be a composite character representing many Jews of that time who were crucified. If one does see iconic religious figures such as Jesus, Moses, or Mohammed as actual historical persons, one must also see them as persons who themselves engaged in midrash—in the process of interpreting and reinterpreting traditions.

Although Mohammed is perhaps less disputably an actual historical person, partly because he lived from about 571 to 632CE (closer to the present day than Jesus by six hundred years), some of what has been said about him is increasingly disputed. Was he really illiterate? The idea that the prophet was illiterate is used to bolster the supernatural revelation to him of the Qur'an, which he is said to have spoken (perhaps in a trance-like state) while others wrote it down—a hint at least of multiple authors. But there are quite a few reasons to doubt that he could not read or write, including that fact that he worked with his older first wife Kadisha who was a successful business woman. Of what little there is of his life story in the Qur'an itself, the famous account of his miraculous "Night Journey" from Mecca to Jerusalem where he ascends to heaven for a "conference" with Allah is understood by most credible Islamic scholars to be a visionary experience or dream rather than an actual, physical trip. (The key words *miraculous* and *night* suggest its mystical, dream-like nature.) The imaginary aspect of this story is most obvious in the interpretation which claims that the angel Gabriel brought the entire city of Jerusalem to Mohammed!

The main record of Mohammed's sayings and activities is called *Hadith* (narrative traditions), and these have more or less officially been divided into three categories: things that he actually said and did, narratives whose historicity is questionable, and narratives that are edifying but almost certainly not things he actually said or did. As we move into the twenty-first century, the kind of historical-critical methods that have been used in biblical studies for well over two hundred years are just beginning to be employed to analyze the Qur'an, revealing for starters that its history is more checkered than has been traditionally believed. I think the one indisputable fact about Mohammed that is most relevant for contemporary theology is that his mission was in large part driven by his concern about the growing gap between rich and poor within his own tribe that dominated the city of Mecca. The parallel with Jesus who was concerned about the economic and political situation of his people under Roman occupation is dramatic and, I think, normative for our theologizing today!

There is a clear consensus among biblical scholars that we must read the gospels as artistic "theological portraits" rather than as biographies. We should consistently use the expression "Jesus *is pictured as saying*" rather than the broad generalization "*Jesus says*" when we discuss and interpret these Gospels. It is also very important to realize, as New Testament scholar Walter Bauer described in 1934, that there are multiple theologies in the New Testament gospels and epistles. This is why Gustav Aulen describes various "theories" or versions of atonement rather than one consistent doctrine. This diversity also means that forgiveness, non-violent resistance, service, "new creation," or other themes besides atonement provide a way to approach the Jesus stories. The theology of Paul predates the written gospels. The notion that Paul turned the simple religion *of* Jesus into a complicated theology *about* Jesus is misleading because we now understand that the gospels from Mark through John are increasingly exaggerated, legendary and imaginative portraits rather than objective biographies of Jesus—and are *no less theological than the letters of Paul*!

Bishop Spong, Marcus Borg, and I are among those who contend that there almost certainly was an impressive and charismatic historical Jesus who was more a catalyst for than a creator of a *Jesus Movement* led by those who had experienced this amazing person. Spong, however, rightly emphasizes that the imaginative stories and theology about Jesus were created by this movement using massive artistic, midrashic, poetic license— quite possibly structuring these stories for use as liturgical readings in the synagogues which were the early meeting places of the Jesus movement. Some of the different versions of his life story and sayings are most likely the result of various oral traditions being imperfectly remembered. It is also likely that Jesus could have said similar things in different ways on various occasions. But there is also no doubt that many and perhaps even most of the differences in the stories about Jesus are the result of deliberate midrash and artistic theological license on the part of the writers who, we must remember, were all by then writing in Greek rather than in the Aramaic dialect that Jesus spoke.

If we ask which came first, Jesus or the Christian movement, the answer would have to make a strong case for both views. It can be said that Jesus came first as founder of the movement to the degree that his impressive personality and behavior was at the very least a catalyst without which there might not have been such a movement. (The phrase "followers of The Way" seems to have been most commonly used to describe this movement before the term "Christian" was coined.) On the other hand, many if not most sayings of and stories about Jesus were created by the developing Christian movement based on sources that in large part both pre-dated and post-dated the actual lifetime of Jesus. So there is a sense in which the movement comes first because elements of it were in place before Jesus, and because the later movement created most of the stories about him as the Christ many decades after his crucifixion.

The developing Christian movement created strikingly different and at times even troubling versions of Jesus—violent in Luke 19:27 and 45, divisive in Matthew 10:34–37, or bizarre in the non-canonical *Infancy Gospel of Thomas* where a young Jesus strikes playmates dead and cripples a teacher. (The latter writer's ill-considered intent may have been to emphasize how Jesus' specialness was evident even as a child.) A tiny Coptic fourth-century papyrus fragment which appears to have Jesus using the words "my wife" suggests at most only that one Christian group may eventually have pictured him as married. Borg sees the historical Jesus as an intelligent, charismatic, Spirit-filled prophet (somewhat like Mohammed, perhaps). Spong points out how the earliest Gospel Mark is completely unaware of supernatural birth stories about Jesus and connects the Spirit with his baptism rather than with a miraculous conception.

When we look at the books of the New Testament in the order in which they were written we see the specialness of Jesus being pushed earlier into his life. In the very first writings, the letters of Paul, Jesus is special mainly because of his crucifixion by the Romans and vindication/resurrection by God. Then the Mark Gospel pictures him as becoming special at his baptism. Next, Luke sees Jesus as special in his childhood (at age 12 confounding the experts in the temple), and also in his birth and conception. Matthew has nothing about his youth, but also imagines his special conception and birth. Then the John Gospel seems to suggest a much earlier pre-existence of Jesus "in the beginning with God." This process could also be described by saying that in the synoptic gospels Jesus *becomes* the Christ, whereas by the time the John Gospel is written Jesus *is* the Christ. It can also be said that the progression is from Mark's *theology of the cross* to John's *theology of glory*. The last words of Jesus on the cross also show a progression from "Why have you forsaken me?" in Mark to ever more calm and confident words in the later gospels. During this same late first-century period of development we also get the striking metaphorical images of Jesus in the book of Hebrews and in the Revelation of John of Patmos.

When it comes to atonement theology, those who still read the Gospels as biographies of Jesus rather than as imaginative, creative Midrash also tend to see atonement quite exclusively in terms of God sending an essentially supernatural Jesus to pay for our sins by dying as our substitute. They view this particular *interpretation* as the fundamental *fact* and they resist any suggestion that the political and social context of Judaism during this period is the core fact—a fact that can be interpreted using something other and actually much better than this sacrificial-substitute-for-us notion of atonement.

This better and still clearly biblical interpretation of the crucifixion of Jesus, which maintains a more intrinsic and down-to-earth relationship with the factual situation at the time of Jesus, sees the New Testament Scriptures as being about a good man (and his nation!) being destroyed by a violent, powerful, oppressive empire/kingdom/system! It sees Jesus as a new type of Messiah whose life is "for our benefit" as expressed by the foot-washing example of humble service in the John Gospel. It sees Jesus as Isaiah's "suffering servant" whose death is "sacrificial" in that Jesus, like people such as Ghandi and Martin Luther King Jr., took great risks which exposed the dark side of violent, oppressive systems of domination while also inspiring us to find what Paul calls "the more excellent way" of justice, reconciliation, peace, compassion and love. (Some Christians use especially gruesome crucifix images not because of a martyr complex, but because they live under particularly violent and oppressive systems themselves, and they find it comforting to feel that Jesus—representing God's compassion—suffered more than they do.)

Judaism started out as a theocracy, a religious coalition of tribes. Therefore, social/political issues and religion are necessarily intertwined in biblical theology! But in a theocracy God is typically seen as a divine monarch whose agents run the world according to strict laws. Far removed from the perception of God as Ultimate Mystery, theocratic notions of the Kingdom of God are both simplistic and arrogant. I use the term "romantic literalism" to describe views of God as authoritarian ruler and literal author of every word in scripture—"romantic" because it involves naïve, wishful thinking that true believers have clear, absolute authority and information directly from God. A much better approach to social/political/moral issues views the role of religion as offering general guiding principles rather than specifics. Theologian Thomas Sheehan says that the New Testament "Kingdom of God" is not about a specific blueprint for human society but is about humanity being empowered here and now to commit to (to believe in) a way of thinking and acting based on justice, mercy, compassion—and I would add, grace.

Bishop Spong is certainly right to point out that we get a very troubling image of God as a perpetrator of human sacrifice—the ultimate child abuser—when sacrifice theology is seen as literal fact rather than as an artistic and imaginative (although problematic) reinterpretation of various sacrifice themes and images in Hebrew theology. *It is seldom sufficiently noted that the condemnation of human sacrifice, specifically in the form of child sacrifice, is a central formative feature of Hebrew theology!* We see this condemnation perhaps most clearly in Leviticus 20:1–5 (Cursed be those who sacrifice their children to Molech, aka Melek and sometimes Baal) and in Micah 6:7–8 (Do not give the fruit of your body for the sin of your soul but instead "do justice, love kindness and walk humbly with God"). The history of biblical sacrifice themes runs from fertility religion involving child sacrifice, to animal and cereal offerings, to the end of temple sacrifice "once for all" with Jesus as both metaphorical sacrificial lamb and high priest, to a little wine and bread in the Eucharist. I think this theological development of the sacrifice motif must be seen as a fortunate, sophisticated, artistic development of symbolic thinking. (I think it is to Islam's credit that it has traditionally rejected the notion of "blood atonement," although I would argue that the nuanced Christian theological approach to ethics that I will discuss later in this chapter offers insights that tend to be missing in the Qur'an's sometimes moralistic and heavy-handed reward/punishment approach to ethics.)

It clearly makes absolutely no sense that a God who begins by demonizing the child sacrifice aspect of fertility religion would end up trying to save the world by orchestrating the ultimate child sacrifice of His only begotten Son! To make this idea the one primary meaning of the crucifixion story is to suggest that it was actually God who wrote the sadistic screenplay for Mel Gibson's gruesome movie "The Passion of the Christ." Only if we see Hebrew sacrifice imagery as just one of many ways in which the early Christian movement struggled to make sense of this first century version of a Jewish holocaust will this imagery be helpful. The evils behind this holocaust were typical examples of human sinfulness—military oppression, political intrigue, injustice, greed, violence, brutality, prejudice, bigotry, lack of empathy and compassion, etc. Those who continue the compassionate struggle against such evils need not be self-denying ascetics, but they often do make great sacrifices to promote the well-being of others. Gordon Kaufman, reflecting his Mennonite heritage, puts it this way in his book *God, Mystery, Diversity*: "The powerful Christian incentives toward self-giving, toward service of the weak, the poor, the unfortunate, toward self-sacrifice for others' well-being, which have always been central to the Christian ethic, are all expressions of this motif—symbolized by the cross—of the value and meaning of suffering for others." In this same spirit/Spirit, Dietrich Bonhoeffer described Jesus as "the man for others."

One particularly unfortunate result of too much focus on the idea that God sacrifices His only Son has been "spare the rod and spoil the child" ideas about child rearing. Psychologist and Christian fundamentalist founder of the group Focus on the Family, James Dobson, has been a fierce advocate of a kind of anti-Dr. Spock notion of child discipline that is virtually sadomasochistic. Parents—fathers in particular—are encouraged by Dobson and his ilk to be strict authoritarians, to spank or beat children whenever necessary, but then, immediately after the beating, to hug them and assure them they are loved. This fits the classic model of sadomasochism seen in the 2009 movie "The White Ribbon," and it fits the model of God as both torturing and loving his Son. It also reminds me of what some critics have said regarding both the story itself and the various artistic renderings of Abraham about to stab and sacrifice his no-doubt traumatized son Isaac. The criticism is that these religious images have provided an influential cultural underpinning for child and spousal abuse. The point is not at all far-fetched. The attempt to downplay the horrendous aspects of this scene by describing it merely as the "binding" of Isaac actually seems to me to highlight its grisly outrageousness.

I think it is beyond dispute that the original reason this particular story appears in the Hebrew Bible had to do with the developing sense that God would not want child sacrifice. All other interpretations, including the stated notion that God wanted to test Abraham's faith and loyalty, must be seen in light of the final result—God stops this particular child sacrifice! How in the world does it make any sense that this God would end up being himself the ultimate child sacrificer, the ultimate sadomasochistic parent? I think that male circumcision, which now is increasingly argued to be (like "female circumcision/mutilation") a form of child abuse, is quite possibly a holdover from fertility rituals, the most drastic of which was actual child sacrifice. (I support replacing routine circumcision with a symbolic ritual.)

We will soon take note of the Judas Gospel that includes a scathing criticism of the then-typical Christian glorification of gruesome martyrdom. This non-canonical Gospel saw the encouragement of martyrdom as a form of child abuse in the sense that generations of Christians were being taught to see this particular kind of suffering for God's sake as especially meritorious. We see the tragic results of this martyr mindset now among Islamic suicide bombers. We also saw it in the fanatical suicide dives of Japanese kamikaze pilots into U.S. ships during the Second World War, in misguided devotion to a supposedly-divine emperor.

Despite its major theological difficulties, I think the "sacrifice" understanding of atonement has been so widely embraced largely because of its psychological ramifications. Accompanied by the appealing altruistic themes of laying down your life for those you love and of self-sacrificing, non-violent resistance to evil, it has offered people a way of doing something that we all must do in one way or another. Lutheran minister's son, psychologist Carl Jung, recast sin as the shadowy dark side of our lives. We all need a way to face the not-so-nice side of ourselves without being destroyed by this confrontation with our "shadow side," our inner Darth Vader. A huge theme of Christian hymnody is that I'm a terrible sinner but God loves me anyway. (God loves me "Just as I am." "Chief of sinners though I be, Jesus shed his blood for me.") Sacrifice and satisfaction theology has allowed people to look honestly at themselves without being destroyed by what they see, and to move forward unencumbered by guilt about past failings. Many if not all of us harbor a deep-seated fear that people (not to mention God!) would reject us if they knew what we were really like—a theme that I see running through the HBO cable TV award-winning series "Girls." But this version of atonement tells us we are loved no matter what! Forget the theological problems—this is good pop psychology! What else can explain, in America's self-confident and increasingly secularized culture, the popular appeal of the song "Amazing grace . . . that saved a wretch like me"? (The hymn writer was referring at the time to his former wretched support of the slave trade, which he had come to bitterly regret.)

Instead of focusing on the problems of traditional literalistic Christian theology, I am going to outline here an approach to biblical themes that can speak to twenty-first century folks who tend to describe themselves as spiritual rather than religious. I do this in the spirit of Dietrich Bonhoeffer's "religionless Christianity," and in the spirit of Bishop Spong who writes about "A New Christianity for a New World." We will see that the core insights of Christian theology can still offer serenity and hope as we face concerns about ethics, death, and eternity.

Romantic literalists argue that reading the Bible mainly in terms of its themes and metaphors is too vague and unreal. They insist that theological interpretations must be seen as solid facts. But the real truths of theology are found precisely in the big thematic pictures. Major themes, far from being reductions, are the real meat and potatoes of theology. Romantic literalists have the classic problem of not being able to see the forest (the big picture) because they are too busy staring at individual trees (specific Bible passages). They fail to understand the larger context. They also get lost in the woods trying to explain away the myriad contradictions or textual and translation problems in the Bible. The better approach is to use "systematic theology" to sort out the meaningful themes in all of these textual complexities.

Gustav Aulen's three distinctive artistic/theological interpretations of atonement theology remind us that we can take the Bible seriously without taking every word or story literally as fact. There is virtually unanimous consensus among mainstream biblical scholars that every individual word of the Bible should not be viewed as literally the Word of God. The words of the Bible do, however, convey fairly consistent messages and themes. Interpreters differ, understandably, on the way in which they might see these messages and themes as sacred or inspired. A popular hymn (reflecting the John Gospel) pictures Jesus as "the Living Word . . . beyond the sacred page." This theme that a living human person embodies and exemplifies existential (personal and in-the-moment) Divine Truth, as opposed to the notion that words on a page have absolute authority, is related to the idea that "the medium is the message." This existential understanding, that a person like Jesus allows us to see and experience what "divinity in humanity" is like, has been emphasized by many as one of the more profound insights of Christian theology. The variety of artistic theological viewpoints in the New Testament helps us flesh out the various aspects and dimensions of this Living Word beyond the sacred page.

The romantic view that sees the Bible as written by "entranced stenographers"—that is, by "God Himself"—ignores all that has been learned about the complicated human process that produced the Bible. The Bible is a very human book. It contains very human and not always flattering images of its characters, including God as one of those characters. We see much literary and poetic imagination at work in its pages. That this kind of creative writing can be seen as bringing us revelatory, even divine insight is viewed by some as an aspect of the great mystery of spirituality. Those who object to "holy books" because they reject the idea of authoritarian and arbitrary sources of knowledge and rules, inevitably find a receptive audience in this scientific age. But if the real power of sacred literature is seen primarily in the artistry, creativity, and insight of its themes, then holy books can offer us inspiration and freedom rather than the letter of the law and authoritarian mind control.

The first five books of the Hebrew Bible are called Torah which is usually translated as meaning "law," but Torah is about much more than law; it includes instruction, poetry, legend, myth, epic, saga, origin (etiological) stories, rituals, records, and stories about relationships. The bottom line is that *literature is ultimately an art form*—to author is to be creative—and since most religion is based on literature of one kind or another, it bears repeating that religion itself is also clearly an art form.

A striking example of contemporary biblical analysis will be helpful here before we return to our consideration of atonement theology. As we have seen, following in the tradition of midrash, the New Testament is mainly an attempt to create a dramatically new interpretation of the Messiah concept in Judaism—a suffering and martyred Messiah! By the time of the writing of the four canonical Gospels (approximately 70 to 100 CE when the city of Jerusalem has already been destroyed by the Romans) it is quite clear that there has not been and is not going to be a miraculous political or military Messiah to save the Jews from the Romans, such as Cyrus who saved the Jews from the Babylonians or the Maccabee brothers who had liberated them from the Assyrian Greek occupation. But in an effort to show that Jesus (the name means "God saves, delivers, liberates, or heals") is indeed a new type of Messiah, the Matthew and Luke Gospels want to bolster his relationship to King David, the ultimate source of Messianic credentials. One way to do this would be to show Jesus as a descendent of King David, born in Bethlehem, the birthplace of David.

The Matthew Gospel does this partly by creating a father for Jesus named Joseph and also a Davidic genealogy for Joseph—a genealogy that problematically contradicts the notion of virgin birth! Some scholars think the virgin birth element in Matthew must have been ineptly edited in later. Spong suggests that the inclusion in the Matthew genealogy of women pictured in the Hebrew Scriptures as having tarnished reputations (Tamar and Rahab) could be a sly hint that although Mary might possibly have had an unsavory reputation as an unwed mother, she was still worthy to be the mother of the Messiah. There is no birth story in the Mark Gospel, and while the mother and brothers of Jesus are mentioned, there is no mention of a father. But an episode in Mark chapter 6 suggests a slur against Mary's reputation when a hostile character calls Jesus "the son of Mary." To call a grown man the son of his mother in that society was most likely a clear insult to both mother and son. There is wide agreement that the Matthew quote from Isaiah refers to a "young woman" living in Isaiah's own times, and that when it is used in Matthew to describe the mother of Jesus it also should be translated as "young woman" rather than as "virgin." (The translation of the Hebrew Scriptures into Greek called the Septuagint is likely responsible for this mix-up.)

To keep this brief, I will concentrate on the ways in which both Matthew and Luke try to explain how a man consistently described as Jesus of Nazareth could have been born in David's city of Bethlehem in Judea near Jerusalem. The glaring problem is that—relying on sources of information about which we can only speculate and writing with little or no knowledge of each other—the authors of these Gospels come up with totally contradictory ways of explaining how Jesus could have been born in Bethlehem.

In the Luke Gospel, Mary and Joseph live in Nazareth but are required to travel south to Bethlehem for a census. While in Bethlehem, Mary gives birth to Jesus in a stable because there is no room for them in the inn. Some of the many problems with this scenario are: 1) this kind of census taking is logistically implausible—and nowhere in the extensive records from the reign of Caesar Augustus is there any mention of such a census; 2) the time-frame regarding Herod, Quirinious, and Augustus is problematic (part of the reason scholars now think Jesus might have been born in 4 BC); and 3) one has to wonder what husband in his right mind would take a nine months pregnant woman on an almost 100 mile trek through difficult terrain, whether on foot or by donkey (the story never specifies the mode of travel). Luke has the holy family staying for approximately thirty days at some unspecified place in the south for the circumcision of Jesus and the ritual "purification" of Mary in Jerusalem (no mention of a trip to Egypt!), and then they return to their home in Nazareth. Luke does say that the family returned to Jerusalem every year for the Passover (Luke 2:41), hence the unique story of Jesus at age 12 in the temple. But that the family's home was always in Nazareth is abundantly clear in Luke's story.

By contrast, in the Matthew Gospel it is clearly assumed that Mary and Joseph *live* in Bethlehem—in a house! Bethlehem is their home at the time of Jesus' birth and early childhood. The wise men (*magus,* in Greek) come following a star (there is no star over the stable in Luke's story); King Herod hopes to eliminate Jesus (who is repeatedly described not as an infant but as a child) by killing every boy two years old and under in Bethlehem. Implausibly, this "slaughter of the innocents" is not mentioned in any other historical records. The reference to boys as old as two implies that Jesus might have been close to three years old at the time. The holy family escapes to Egypt, and when Herod is dead they return, not to Bethlehem, but way up north to Nazareth where they will presumably be safe from the new King Herod.

Could we harmonize the two stories by guessing that the holy family of the Luke Gospel moved back to Bethlehem from Nazareth in time to be living in Bethlehem when Matthew's wise men arrived, or that the wise men showed up during the approximately thirty days that the couple and their new baby lingered in the south? The answer is no. This kind of guesswork has zero credibility. It is based on presupposing that the Bible cannot possibly contain any contradictions and on wishing to harmonize the stories, not on any shred of real or plausible evidence.

Based on this discrepancy between the stories in Matthew and Luke, whose authors were almost certainly doing their midrashic imaginings independently of each other, many scholars have concluded that Jesus was more likely born in Nazareth. A name like "Jesus of Nazareth" would probably mean to contemporaries that the person was born in Nazareth. Because it is trying to match Jesus up with as many references in the Hebrew Bible as possible, the Matthew Gospel also affirms that Jesus is a Nazarene—supposedly fulfilling a reference in the Hebrew Scriptures (a reference not clearly specified, see Matthew 2:23)—in no way intending to deny, of course, that Jesus was born and lived briefly as a child in Bethlehem. The creators of the John Gospel portray the critics of Jesus asking "can anything good come out of Nazareth?"—a recognition of Nazareth as Jesus' home town, but also a scene no doubt intended to highlight the difficulty of winning folks over to the unusual notion of a suffering Messiah, crucified by the oppressive Roman superpower.

The difference in the birth stories is one of the most obvious pieces of evidence for the fact that the Gospels are to a large extent midrashic reinterpretations of themes from the Hebrew Scriptures. In the culture of that time these stories would not have been seen as lies. They were expressions of theological/artistic license—poetic license! Mary's hymn of praise (the Magnificat) is a midrash on the song of Samuel's mother Hannah in the Old Testament book of First Samuel. It is nothing short of ridiculous to think that this wonderfully crafted poetic song was spontaneously uttered on the spot as Luke's story suggests. Many other things in Luke's account parallel the story of Samuel.

The Matthew Gospel pictures the young Jesus as escaping the slaughter of the innocents in a way that parallels the first Passover story in Egypt; next, as coming out of Egypt like Moses and acting as lawgiver on the mountain (Sermon on the Mount)—again like Moses. It is also the Matthew Gospel that most likely first created the character Joseph as the father of Jesus. Joseph is never mentioned anywhere else in the New Testament except briefly in the Luke and John Gospels. He basically disappears beyond the birth stories, although legends understandably proliferated in non-canonical literature, some suggesting that he was much older than Mary (which could explain his disappearance and imply that the siblings of Jesus mentioned in the New Testament were Joseph's children from a previous relationship). Matthew's Joseph is a son of Jacob, goes to Egypt, has and interprets significant dreams related to the salvation of his people, and experiences turbulent relationships with kings—all similar to the ancient Hebrew Joseph of Genesis and Exodus. We do not know who wrote Matthew (such titles were added later), but we do know that this gospel is directed specifically at a Jewish audience to convince them that this new concept of Messiah makes sense and is congruent with many things in the Hebrew Scriptures. The transfiguration story, where a shimmering and glorified Jesus is joined on a mountain by the figures of Moses and Elijah, is a dramatic way of giving Jesus, this new Messiah, further credentials as both ultimate lawgiver and prophet. (The Mark Gospel clearly uses the description of Elijah in 2 Kings 1:8 to depict John the Baptist.)

The German theologian Joachim Jeremias is one of many who try to detect authentic words of the historical Jesus in the parables. He argues forcefully that the relative uniqueness of these parables suggests that an original personality produced them. However, there are aspects of various parables and other sayings attributed to Jesus that reflect developments within the Christian movement which only became major conflicts significantly after the lifetime of Jesus. Some parables and saying, like a number of those in Matthew 21, show the growing tension between the early Christian movement and the Jews who opposed it. When we see that parables and sayings reflect issues and situations from the late first century time period in which these Gospels were written, or that others mirror sources and images predating the lifetime of Jesus, we have evidence that at least some of these narratives do not come from the historical Jesus.

Those scholars who question whether the Jesus of the New Testament is an actual historical person suggest that the various gospels were constructed solely out of stories, themes, and images from earlier rabbinic sayings and from the Hebrew Scriptures—the Psalms, the Suffering Servant poems of Second Isaiah, the Lamentations of Jeremiah—"Surely he has borne our griefs and carried our sorrows . . . he was wounded for our transgressions . . . and the Lord has laid on him the iniquity of us all . . . . like a lamb who is led to the slaughter. . . . Is it nothing to you, all you who pass by?" The "I AM" sayings in the John Gospel echo the voice of God from the burning bush. These scholars see "The Greatest Story Ever Told" as just that—the Jesus stories are first and foremost literary creations, the product of impressive theological imagination on the part of the early Christian movement. The very fact that Jesus is pictured as a teller of made-up tales (parables) can be seen as lending some credibility to this notion that much of his life-story itself might be such a tale.

Whether or not one accepts the extreme view that there never was an historical Jesus of Nazareth, the fact remains that the New Testament is not primarily based on predictions miraculously coming true. When the gospel writers describe Scripture as being fulfilled, we must instead see them as *deliberately shoehorning their depictions of Jesus as the Christ into the Hebrew Scriptures and rabbinic traditions.* Elaine Pagels thinks that there was an historical Jesus who might well have accurately predicted the destruction of the Jerusalem temple. But although, like contemporary pundits, biblical prophets who "spoke for" God did occasionally prognosticate about the future, the larger reality is that the gospel writers more often created Jesus stories by *borrowing* words, ideas and images from the Hebrew Scriptures. They attempted to show that their "revisionist" understanding of who and what the Messiah should be was in sync with many things in their ancient Scriptures. To put it another way, almost every idea, honorary title, or theme in the Hebrew Scriptures eventually gets applied to Jesus (*Yeshua*/Joshua, the successor of Moses!) or is used to create his messianic story. Perhaps the most important thing to realize is that Resurrection/Easter was almost certainly not an isolated event, but rather a *process* of creating the "post-Easter Jesus"—the "biblical Christ"!

Midrash can involve conflicting, selective, and even some rather farfetched revisionist theologizing, such as Paul's characterization of Abraham's "justification by faith" in Romans chapter 4. Despite very apparent differences between Peter and Paul (not to mention between Paul and the author of Revelation) on issues such as the Jewish or Gentile orientation of the Jesus Movement, the authors of First and Second Peter (writing what Ehrman bluntly calls forgeries) "spin" the story to make Peter and Paul appear to be in substantial agreement on these issues—all the while warning against those who twist their interpretations of scripture! The New Testament is full of different and developing interpretations of how soon or late resurrection, salvation, or the (second) coming (*parousia*) of Christ might occur. It seems clear that by the time the John Gospel is written, earlier ideas about the second coming of Christ have given way to the idea of Jesus sending the Holy Spirit "in his name" as "another counselor." I think the fact that this kind of theologizing has been going on from the beginning of the Christian movement, and permeates the entire New Testament, validates our own later-day revised and selective theologizing! I do not think it validates all novel or bizarre later-day spins on Christian themes, but it certainly does allow us (like Aulen) to parse out the variety of ways in which themes such as atonement can be understood and developed. This includes playing down some themes and favoring others, as when the Christ-died-for-our-sins interpretation of crucifixion and resurrection is subordinated to or even replaced by an emphasis on the theme of God's reign (Kingdom) of compassion and distributive justice as the way to peace on earth.

Let me be clear and blunt. In this postmodern world we absolutely must recognize that some interpretations of the Jesus stories, however prominent they may have been, no longer work—are no longer meaningful to people in the way they once were. They need to be regarded as at best historical but outdated expressions of Christian faith. These interpretations, images, and metaphors need to be given a limited place in Christian theology and practice while other interpretations of biblical themes take their place. To put it another way, we have no choice but to be *intelligently selective* as we deal with the multitude of ideas, images, and metaphors in biblical theology. The three great Christian Creeds have long been understood by theologians mainly as historical documents reflecting the language and ways of thinking that belong to bygone times. The Nicene and Athanasian Creeds were written to settle specific debates going on in specific historical circumstances. (How many today know what "proceedeth from" means in the Nicene Creed, or could read parts of the Athanasian Creed without laughing at some of the rather convoluted language?) We honor these creeds, but we express ourselves differently today. While catchy new music and the use of other instruments besides the organ is all well and good, such efforts can be somewhat like rearranging deck chairs on the Titanic. If the content of a faith message no longer conveys intellectually compelling good news to people, how can that message have any spiritual impact or meaning in their lives?

A further ramification of midrash is that Christian proselytizers need to refrain from using the simplistic argument that Jesus was either right or crazy when he claimed to be the Messiah. Bart Ehrman thinks the actual historical Jesus did claim to be some kind of Messiah, but only secretly to his closest followers, and it was this secret that Judas disclosed to the authorities—as some have suggested, to force Jesus into taking dramatic action against the Roman occupation. But even if we assume that Jesus of Nazareth is an actual historical person whose life we can consistently outline, most scholars think it more likely that he never did claim to be the Messiah, the Christ. It was his followers and the gospel writers who began a process of creating the "post-Easter Jesus" as a new kind of Messiah. The "messianic Secret" in the Gospels where Jesus tells his followers not to tell anyone that he is the Messiah (see Mark 8, Matthew 16, Luke 9) is part of the evidence indicating that, even if there was a historical Jesus, he probably did not make the kind of claims that are attributed to him, especially the frequent and dramatic claims in the John Gospel. When Jesus is pictured as urging his disciples not to tell anyone that he is the Messiah, the storytellers may reflect a concern that contemporaries of Jesus who were still alive might insist they never heard him (because he never did!) make such claims. Or, they may simply be reflecting the general difficulty of "selling" the idea of a crucified Messiah—a difficulty the storytellers often expressed by picturing his disciples as misunderstanding or questioning those claims. Since it is, however, very debatable whether the historical Jesus claimed titles such as Messiah, Lord, or Son of God, to confront potential converts with a stark choice between Jesus as either right or crazy is exposed as a crass attempt to manipulate or embarrass folks into "accepting Christ." On the other hand, it does not invalidate everything

Jesus represents if we concede that he could have been wrong about some things. Only those who see Jesus as the supernatural God incarnate are unwilling to admit that he could be mistaken about something.

The Problem with Biblical Inerrancy, Infallibility, and Authority

Biblical literalists like to quote 2 Peter 1:16: "For we did not follow cleverly devised myths when we made known to you the power and coming of our Lord Jesus Christ, but we were eye-witnesses of his Majesty." However, this short New Testament book almost certainly (for many reasons well documented by Bart Ehrman in his book *Forged*) was not written by eye-witnesses, and seems to date from as late as 140 AD, which would make it the very last of all New Testament writings. The reference to myths likely is not a broadside against all mythology or creative storytelling in general, but is directed specifically at the Gnostic Gospels which had appeared by this time. Elaine Pagels' 1979 *The Gnostic Gospels* elucidates the diversity of Gnostic notions about secret knowledge, which included Buddhist-style understandings of consciousness and divine truth within the self, but also supernatural ideas about gaining access to the realm of the spirit. By the time Second Peter was written, the dubious process of establishing an institutional orthodoxy was well underway, and its defenders inevitably claimed that opposing views were the result of clever twisting and spinning run rampant.

Pagels points out that some Gnostics put greater emphasis on feminine symbolism and on the role of women in Christianity, and it remains obvious yet today that orthodoxy has often quashed such tendencies. It is also true, however, that the Gnostic gospels, in particular the Thomas Gospel, occasionally reflect a rather negative and condescending attitude toward women. Karen Armstrong has said that the Sufi mystics brought a feminine dimension to Islam, and I would add that the whirling dervish poet Rumi seems perhaps even to have celebrated same sex love. Islamic orthodoxy has tended to think of Sufism as heretical and has ignored or sometimes condemned feminine-positive themes. Rumi, generally considered to be the founder of the Islamic Sufi movement, was a master of metaphor and simile. His translator Coleman Barks has described him as one for whom "love is the religion and the universe is the book, that experience as we're living it [each moment] is the sacred text that we study."

The delay of a second coming (*parousia*) of Christ was becoming a hot-button issue as well by 140 AD. This caused many believers to be confused or defensive. So in spite of "any day now" hints elsewhere in the New Testament, the writer of Second Peter is at pains to explain that "soon" in God's timetable is not the same as "soon" in ours. The growing retreat on the notion of "soon" is another of the significant things that become crystal clear when we look at the books of the New Testament in the order in which they were written.

A recently found Gospel of Judas (see *Reading Judas* by Elaine Pagels and Karen L. King—2007) reflects a period in which controversy had arisen among early Christians over the desirability of martyrdom. This Gospel's striking image of Jesus deliberately asking Judas to help him die was actually part of a theology that quite early on rejected the "human sacrifice" motif found in some canonical New Testament writings. The Judas Gospel also rejected the understanding of the Eucharist (Mass) as a reenacted sacrifice. The version of Jesus offered in this Gospel reflects both Manichaean and Gnostic ideas about the death of the physical body as the gateway to "life in the spirit." Jesus' death is seen not as a sacrifice demanded by God to pay for the sins of the world, but as a way for Jesus to proclaim a completely otherworldly spiritual kingdom in comparison with which any physical suffering is as nothing. The "martyr complex" is said to be wrong because it is based on two mistaken ideas: 1) that a good and loving God would require and encourage human sacrifice, and 2) that the reward for suffering a physically painful martyr's death would be a physical resurrection of the flesh. Greenblatt's *The Swerve* goes all out to show how much Christianity promoted physical pain, suffering, torture, and actual hatred of pleasure! Consider this verse from a popular hymn: "And blest would be their children's fate, if they, like them, should die for thee: Faith of our fathers, holy faith!"

In chapter 4 we will more specifically look into the issue of "physical" versus "spiritual" ways of interpreting resurrection, salvation, and "the world to come." The most important thing we need to notice here is that from the earliest days of the Christian movement there were those who strenuously objected to any human sacrifice theology as a way of understanding the death of Jesus. The Judas Gospel goes so far as to condemn the other eleven disciples and many leaders in the early church as "murderers" because they promoted pain, martyrdom and human sacrifice.

The early theological diversity, brilliantly revealed in Walter Bauer's 1934 classic *Orthodoxy and Heresy in Earliest Christianity*, exposes the fatal flaw in notions of biblical inerrancy and infallibility, or of pristine theological orthodoxy. When we understand how the process of theological, artistic license (midrash), textual revisions, redactions, and other changes over time resulted in contradictions and inconsistencies, ideas of biblical inerrancy and infallibility appear absurd—as do those who insist that they do not interpret the Bible selectively. All biblical interpretation is inevitably selective! No sane person, for example, would insist on literal adherence to all of the Torah death penalty laws. Everyone interprets the Bible and "Christian tradition" selectively in one way or another! The real issue is how much discernment, knowledge and honesty is brought to the process.

Perhaps most problematical of all for the "inerrancy and infallible" idea was the process involved in producing copies and translations of Bibles both before and after the canon of Scripture was established. Bart Ehrman has elucidated this process in his 2005 book *Misquoting Jesus: The Story Behind Who Changed the Bible and Why*. Ehrman argues that even if one believed that God controlled the original writing and collection of the Bible, one would have to admit that God clearly did not control the much longer process of copying and reproducing (not to mention translating) Bibles. (Salmon Rushdie, with sardonic glee that got him into some pretty hot water, makes the same point about the Qur'an in his novel *The Satanic Verses*.)

Ehrman describes some of the thousands of mistakes or deliberate changes that were made by copiers before the invention of the printing press. A classic example of a deliberate change is that it was almost certainly a later editor who inserted bits about women being silent in church into St. Paul's letters, clearly counter to Paul's own close working relationships with women and his clear insistence that "there is neither male nor female for we are all one in Christ Jesus." (There is at least one instance in which a female name was altered to make it male, most likely in order to hide the fact that Paul could affirm the work of a female apostle. See also John Dominic Crossan's 2004 *In Search of Paul* for his discussion of Thecla.) So while it *might* remain reasonable to say that the major themes of the Bible are "inerrant and infallible" *in their ability to convey a "divinely inspired" message,* I frankly think we should drop such terminology altogether, because it harbors an absolutist, supernatural mindset and ignores the monumental problems and issues associated with manuscript transmission and translation.

Biblical literalists are hung up on the authority of Scripture. They have tended to understand this authority in abstract, legalistic terms as if God were simply an ultimate, controlling bureaucrat. But when Martin Luther said that "whatever leads us to Christ" is the norm for determining which parts of Scripture are central as opposed to peripheral, he was also making a more basic overall point, namely, that we must develop interpretive principles (hermeneutics) for determining the relative merit of scriptural material. Luther lambasted the New Testament book of James as worthless because it seemed to lack "grace alone" (and perhaps because it was awfully hard on the rich). "Whatever leads us to Christ" (whatever highlights the revised, existential, humanistic, compassionate Messiah theme) is but one example of an interpretive principle. The wider ramification of Luther's reliance on an interpretive principle is that the *author*ity of Scripture is about its authors creating (authoring) various themes that can be interpretive principles! This point about interpretive selectivity has traditionally been made by saying that "Scripture interprets Scripture."

The biblical themes which can function as interpretive principles may have developed over time with a variety of nuances, but they are nevertheless quite evident and consistent. One major theme is none other than reinterpretation (Midrash) itself. Midrash is about multiple perspectives and constant analysis. This helps to explain why Jews are often seen as being both thoughtful and argumentative (see Deuteronomy 6:6–7, which mandates constant discussion and reconsideration of ethical and theological issues). Other consistent themes are Mystery, Eternity, God, Awe, Grace, Love, Truth, Creation, Justice, Morality, Law, Service, Struggle, Life, Compassion, Discipline, Unity, Diversity, Forgiveness, Reconciliation, Spirit, Wisdom, Faith, Hope, Joy, and Peace. Isolated or idiosyncratic statements, attitudes, and beliefs that are culturally outdated or scientifically inaccurate cannot be interpretive principles. The idea that Scriptural authority is all-or-nothing (that every word in the Bible is of equal value as *God's Word!*) can force one into defending the indefensible, as when Luther himself mistakenly defended a geocentric universe against the heliocentric universe of Copernicus. An all-or-nothing approach to biblical authority exposes an inappropriate desire for absolute certainty—and can make its defenders seem ridiculous, or worse.

Misguided use of "Scriptural Authority"

As I was working on this manuscript, the Evangelical Lutheran Church in America (ELCA—the largest Lutheran Church Body in the United States) passed resolutions at its national assembly by a substantial majority vote allowing local congregations and jurisdictions the option of deciding whether or not to bless same-sex unions or to allow pastors in such unions to be ordained. The caveat was that to maintain unity in the church the "bound consciences" of those on any side of the debate would be respected. I am frequently asked what I think of this development. My answer puts the focus on the way we use Scripture. I can't imagine that today we would go out of our way to respect the "bound conscience" of someone who quoted the Bible about the curse of Noah's son Ham or about "hewers of wood and drawers of water" (Joshua 9) to promote racist views or to justify slavery. Yet this is exactly what we do if we validate those who quote the Bible to condemn and insult the love shared by same-sex couples. Those harboring racist or pro-slavery views are no longer seen as providing only a legitimate and balancing alternative view. The theological concept of *status confessionis* means that some moral issues are so clear that there is no balancing "other side." There is, for example, no justification for apartheid or Nazi ideology.

In my view, the ELCA must actively support the "reconciling work" of unbinding prejudiced consciences. Attitudes or beliefs which are culturally conditioned, scientifically inaccurate, and prejudiced cannot be legitimized or promoted based on a misguided, naïve, and indiscriminate "the Bible says" view of Scriptural authority. Ironically, many Jewish, Christian, and Muslim proponents of such notions of biblical authority complain that those who affirm same-sex relationships are caving in to cultural relativism, while it is actually they who are stubbornly clinging to dated, culturally biased attitudes that go back at least two or three thousand years!

One of the things that should alert us to the problem with romantic literalism or other naïve attitudes toward Scripture is the fact that the episodes and narratives in the Bible as a whole tend to be highly stylized. They do not work as screen-plays. The dialogue is typically too stiff, too flowery, too obviously the product of artistic, literary manipulation. The words put in Jesus' mouth probably are seldom the actual words of the historical Jesus, especially if we also consider the issue of translation. (One of the most hilarious—but also disturbing—bumper stickers I ever saw proclaimed "If it ain't King James, It ain't Bible!") However stylized the language of Scripture might be, *the message intended by the biblical authors* can still be an accurate reflection of the spirit of this new movement and its "greatest story ever told."

In addition to the issue of stylized language, we must be alert to the problem with taking narratives literally at face value, or interpreting them by psychologizing the feelings and motivations of the characters. We must resist the urge to psychoanalyze literary characters. You can psychoanalyze Charles Dickens, perhaps, but you would look silly trying to read the mind of Ebenezer Scrooge. If we try to take a mind-reading approach to gospel stories we can miss the real import of the narrative. Taken as straight-forward reporting of actual events, biblical stories can at times make God or Jesus appear to be downright cruel. For example, there is a prominent story in the Mark and Matthew Gospels where Jesus is pictured as insulting a non-Jewish woman by comparing her to a dog when she asks him to cure her daughter. The Matthew author clarifies Mark's version by having Jesus say that he was "sent only to the lost sheep of the house of Israel." Taken at face value, this episode makes Jesus seem heartless and mean. Comparing a person to a dog is still an especially terrible insult in the Middle East. But if we focus—as we should!—on the artistic literary *intent of the storyteller* we discover that what we have here is an attempt to finesse a very difficult issue in the early church.

Many early Christians were "Judaizers" (also called Ebionites) who felt strongly that Jesus was a Messiah only for the Jews or those willing to become Jews. The Matthew Gospel is intended particularly for this kind of Jewish audience, so it depicts Jesus himself as sympathetic to this view, having him tell the woman he is only here for Jews. But then, when she responds to Jesus' insult by saying "yes Lord, but even the dogs eat the crumbs that fall from their master's table," the *author* of Matthew portrays Jesus as changing his mind, saying "Woman, great is your faith; let it be as you ask." When the story stresses that her daughter is healed instantly, the *author's* point to readers is that if Jesus can change his mind about his relationship to non-Jews, so can they! (Bart Ehrman's analysis of the Matthew Gospel in *Jesus Interrupted* lacks this focus on the author's purpose.) Led by St. Paul the early Christian movement increasingly rejected the Judaizers' attitude and embraced an inclusive faith open to Jews and Gentiles alike—open to all!

One more example will colorfully illustrate how the Scriptural morality and worldview of thousands of years ago can be applied today only if we are extremely careful and thoughtful. The stories of Onan, Tamar, and Judah in Genesis 38 describe practices and behaviors that we would certainly not want to emulate. But one of the underlying principles in the Onan story of "levirate marriage"—a rule which required a man to marry his widowed sister-in-law even if he already had a wife—is that we should make provisions to care for the weaker and more vulnerable members of society. Caring for widows and orphans is used regularly in the Bible as a symbol of genuine morality and true religion. The principle of caring for the weaker and more vulnerable members of society is still valid today and applies, for instance, to the issue of paying taxes to support what we call the social safety net. It is a tragic irony that the story of Onan has been turned upside down and misused to make children, who are always uniquely vulnerable, feel unnecessarily guilty about masturbation (wrongly described as "onanism" in English dictionaries) because in the story Onan is condemned and "slain" by God for "spilling the seed!" This reference to spilling the seed is actually about *coitus interruptus*, not masturbation. (Masturbation is never mentioned in the Bible!) It is about Onan's selfish refusal to follow through on his moral obligation under the levirate marriage law to impregnate his dead brother's widow, which would have provided her with protected status, and his deceased brother with an heir who could rival Onan's claim to an inheritance.

Many stories from the Bible remind us that two or three thousand years ago human sexuality and gender were not understood as they are today. The Hebrews had no idea of the 50/50 genetics of sperm and egg. Ritual purity laws forbade fertility rites such as child sacrifice and cult prostitution. Such laws have often been misunderstood by subsequent generations—some have been seen, for example, as general condemnations of homosexuality when they were actually about cult prostitution (sex as a form of worship) and had nothing to do with sexual orientation as we understand it today. The Ten Commandments assume that women can be treated as property, like cows, houses and servants. Today we have scientific sexology that must be taken into account when we talk about sexual morality. To uphold rules that stubbornly ignore what we now know to be true about the realities of sexuality is, in itself, a form of immorality because accurate knowledge must always be a major part of the equation when we formulate sexual ethics.

The underlying point of these examples is that the Bible presents us with literary and theological artistry as opposed to straight facts, history, or science. We must read the Bible as a literary art form and view the religion based on this literature as likewise an art form. These stories and theological ideas can be loved and celebrated for the meaning and guidance which we derive from them. Christians can, without apology, give particular importance to the stories of Jesus as an activist, compassionate, reconciling, suffering Messiah (Christ) who "is divine," not in the sense that he is literally or physically "of one substance" with a "Man Upstairs version of God the Father," but in the sense that he embodies the best divine and/or human qualities we can imagine. The stories in Scriptures can be embraced without being defensive or arrogant about the question of whether they are factual or not. If all religious people would do this with their stories, humankind as a whole would be much the better for it. Taliban-type fundamentalism is dangerous in any religion.

Jesus is often pictured as one who taught with authority—not like the Scribes and Pharisees who promoted scrupulous adherence to the letter of the law as handed down from Scripture and tradition. Unfortunately many Christians have made what they think of as the "new rules" from Jesus into just another set of rigid laws. But the unique authority illustrated by Jesus was precisely about his willingness to question the authority handed down from earlier times. So we may not necessarily say or do exactly the same things that Jesus said and did, but we can say and do *similar kinds of things*! Jesus is an exemplar of the authority to question old ways of doing things, to challenge hide-bound rules and traditions. It would be a mistake to turn all of his purported sayings about morality into just another set of absolute rules. It seems quite clear that, assuming there was a historical Jesus, he was a person who understood the ways in which rules are made to be broken, as when he is pictured as saying that "the Sabbath was made for man, not man for the Sabbath." Jesus may have been associated with the "liberal wing of the Pharisaic Party" which emphasized the spirit of the law rather than the letter of the law. The validity, applicability and authority of principles, laws and rules must be open to constant reassessment if they are to serve as true guides to our humanization.

Original Blessing and Original Sin

Before we return to other interpretations of atonement, the notions of "Original Sin" and "Original Blessing" need to be clarified. Moving beyond an idea of "inherited" sin where one is blamed for things over which one has no control, we need to understand that the insight behind these terms is about life having a dual quality. Life is a wonderful opportunity to be celebrated (the Genesis "original blessing"—"God saw that all was good"). But at the same time life is also a predicament, an endless series of problems. "Original Sin" points to the dark or shadow side of human nature. While human beings are capable of wonderful kindness based on innate empathy, we are also capable of monstrous evil. Even when we want to do the right thing we discover that "the road to hell is paved with good intentions."

This duality is also expressed in our use of terms like "awesome" and "awful." In much of world mythology it is expressed by picturing the woman (whose womb brings us into the world) either as Madonna or as whore/temptress. We bless our mothers and the gift of life—the woman is Madonna. But if we focus on the fact that the minute we come out of the womb we start that inevitable (tragic) march to the tomb, the woman is temptress or even the devil, as in the movie "The Ninth Gate" where the Johnny Depp character is having intense sex with a beautiful woman, not realizing that she is actually the devil in disguise. Sex itself is a most wonderful gift, but it can also seem at times to be the ultimate temptation. The sexual "F word" is used both positively to express erotic passion and negatively to express violent contempt. The notion that sex is mainly about women tempting men is one of the reasons that women in some cultures are forced to cover their bodies so completely when they are out in public, or are required to worship separately from men.

The language in the Psalm about "I was born in sin and in sin did my mother conceive me" does not mean that sex *per se* is sinful; it means rather that life is a predicament from the outset. Another aspect of this predicament character of life is that life feeds on life—everything we eat dies so that we can live. Creatures would still be killed during the process of growing our food even if we were all to become vegetarians or vegans. The dark side of life is also evident in the fact that even our empathy can become distorted so that we lavish all our compassion on ourselves and ignore the suffering of others. We see this also in "innocent" children, who can be incredibly cruel and insensitive to each other because of their self-centered preoccupations. Nietzsche saw life as necessarily both Dionysian/tragic and Apollonian/pleasant.

These dark sides of life have been portrayed in many provocative films such as "Through A Glass Darkly" by Ingmar Bergman, "Lord of the Flies," "the horror" of "Apocalypse Now," and the 2009 film "Antichrist" by Lars von Trier, where the cruelty we find in nature is summed up by a character who says "Nature is the devil's church." This film ends with a scene that for me conjures up artistic portrayals either of the damned or of Hitler's holocaust victims. (I would only recommend von Trier's version of

"Antichrist" to someone who has a profound understanding of psychology and mythology—and who also has a strong enough stomach to endure the most violent and sadistic horror movies such as the "Saw" films and Mel Gibson's "The Passion of the Christ.")

The duality of "original blessing" and "original sin" reflects a paradoxical (or dialectical) perspective on life. Any truly insightful theology is often going to require that we struggle to synthesize apparently contradictory experiences and perceptions. (In chapter 5 we will see how this struggle occurs in Buddhism.) The theme that a "wretch like me" is saved from the predicament of life by the overwhelming power of God's amazing grace (Ephesians 2:8–9), stands in paradoxical contrast with the theme of my personal ethical responsibility to "work out my own salvation with fear and trembling" (Philippians 2:12), or with Matthew's Jesus who says that only those who do the will of God will "enter the kingdom." The Reformation in the 1500s was largely a struggle over this paradox—as will soon be explained in more detail.

More Midrash on the Theology of the Cross

We turn now to the other two versions of atonement theology outlined by Aulen which are not so legalistic or business-like as the satisfaction theory, elaborated by St. Anselm (described at the beginning of this chapter), in which Jesus dies as a vicarious substitute to pay the penalty for our sins—to satisfy God's demand for ethical perfection and for righteous (retributive "get what you deserve") justice. These other versions involve a more clearly symbolic and paradoxical understanding of the tension between opposite themes.

The so-called *"moral influence" theory of atonement*, associated with Peter Abelard who lived in the thirteenth century, emphasizes that the story of the crucifixion of Jesus has an emotional impact that should make us want to do God's will—to be moral. Our motivation comes from seeing the contrast between human sin and God's love in this story. We see that we ourselves are involved in the kinds of social and economic oppression, bigotry, self-righteousness, and fearful collaboration with violent domination that killed Jesus, who represents divine love and peace. Seeing this motivates (influences) us to "stop that!" A typical sermon along these lines would stress how we drive nails into Jesus or pierce the heart of God every time we sin. American poet Edwin Arlington Robinson in his poem

"Calvary" put it this way: "How long, O Lord, how long are we to keep Christ writhing on the cross."

Atonement here is not a transaction in which Jesus pays a penalty. It is a revelation, a "teachable moment" similar to the way that *holocaust* stories are about saying "never again!" The crucifixion of Jesus is not the result of a theological script written by God as part of a deliberate plan. The crucifixion of Jesus is about the crucifixion of the whole Jewish people by the Romans, a basic fact of history similar to the Hitler holocaust (burnt offering) or the Babylonian conquest. *Much theology is about interpreting the meanings we find in such events after the fact!* The "moral influence" interpretation is about an emotional/spiritual "at-one-ment" with each other, with the universe, with God/Mystery. At-one-ment is not an etymologically correct parsing of the term, but it does accurately express how the world needs reconciliation (consider the Truth and Reconciliation Commission in South Africa). At-one-ment is personal: "God is faithful and just to forgive" (1 John 1:9)—because it would be unjust of any God to demand unachievable perfection and then condemn us for not achieving it. At-one-ment is social and political: "God was in Christ reconciling the (whole) world . . ." (2 Cor. 5:19).

Supernatural images and ideas can sometimes remain useful and meaningful. In our postmodern world, however, we generally need to look past such images and myths to see both the metaphoric/symbolic and the practical down-to-earth meaning of it all. We have seen, in particular, how one of the most compelling ways to understand the continuing practical relevance of the New Testament "Kingdom of God" and "Jesus as Messiah/ Christ" theologies is *to focus on envisioning alternatives to any systems, like that of the Roman Empire, which involve violent domination, oppression, and various forms of injustice.*

Much theology is also about psychology—coming to terms with our most intense emotions. A major aspect of the biblical notion of reconciliation is the idea that God takes both credit and blame for the world being the way it is. God is pictured as suffering along with us, showing compassion like a loving father rather than demanding punishment like a judge, and allowing us to be angry about the dark side of life. In his cantata "The Crucifixion," Sir John Stainer puts it this way: "Very God Himself is bearing all the sufferings of time." The mythology of God losing a son through crucifixion has been a powerful way to say that our grief, sense of loss, and even anger when we come face to face with suffering and death (especially untimely or violent death) is understood and validated. For the spiritual nonbeliever, this image does not mean that there actually is a Supreme Being out there somewhere who sympathizes with us. The story of God losing his son can mean simply that compassion is like a law of the universe, and that there is great solace in empathy.

Death and dying expert, psychiatrist Dr. Elizabeth Kübler-Ross, would tell people facing death and grief: "It's okay to be angry with God. It's God's job to deal with your anger. God can take it!" The idea that God, in the form of Jesus, takes the sins of the world onto himself must not be taken literally as meaning that our personal sin and guilt is vicariously transferred onto Jesus in a transaction that makes divine forgiveness possible. The image of God bearing all the sin, guilt, suffering, and anger in the universe needs to be understood in the sense that we can allow ourselves to challenge and question Reality (God) as to why life is such a conundrum—so bittersweet with its mixture of sorrow and joy, tragedy and comedy, suffering and pleasure, good intentions and failed performance. To say "Lord, have mercy!" is to say "ouch!" Having questioned and complained, we then learn to accept the world as it really is! Think of it this way: Reality (God) encourages us to face the evil and suffering in the world, and yet at the same time encourages us to focus mainly on Reality (God) as a source of healing, wholeness, justice, and victory over evil and suffering. I remember a rough time in my own life when a friend greatly encouraged me simply by saying "Reality is very supportive!"

Aulen's third "Christus Victor" approach to atonement theology uses the grand mythological image of a cosmic battle between God and Satan—Good and Evil—in which the Christ-figure (Jesus) both loses and wins, is both humiliated and exalted on the cross. The idea is that human beings struggle with "principalities and evil powers." We are not totally helpless creatures, but we are sometimes nevertheless victims of forces beyond our control. Life is indeed such a bittersweet conundrum! One aspect of the paradox in this mythical, symbolic formulation of atonement theology is that human beings are both responsible and not responsible for their sinfulness, and by the same token are both responsible and not responsible for their salvation. "Forgive them, for they know not what they do" also expresses the paradox of responsible but not responsible. (The traditional Roman Catholic version of this poetic paradox turns it into something more like a mechanical transaction in which, just as we "inherit" original sin over which we had no control, so we are forgiven of this sin when we are baptized as infants who also are neither in control nor responsible.)

Other interpreters of this mythological, symbolic approach to atonement theology see it as basically about optimism versus pessimism. You believe either that the universe is basically good or that it is basically evil. Which attitude you adopt will make all the difference in your life. Many see this issue of attitude to be also the main theme of the Mark Gospel with its focus on casting out demons and replacing them with something better, and its stories of Jesus miraculously feeding people in the desert or calming storms at sea—the exact places, as Bultmann's myth-busting showed, where evil spirits were thought to have the most power. A classic example of a hopeful optimistic attitude comes to us from The Diary of Anne Frank where she writes: "In spite of everything, I think people are basically good at heart."

In their book *The First Paul,* Marcus Borg and John Dominic Crossan argue that for St. Paul the themes of "Christ crucified," "Jesus is Lord," and "the new creation" reveal the contrast between the *Roman Way* of pacification using violent, oppressive domination, and the optimistic, hopeful *Christian Way* of bringing about true peace on earth through compassion (sometimes in the form of non-violent resistance), love, and efforts toward the establishment of distributive justice. Opposition to the Roman Way is a major theme in this book, but Jesus also in some ways opposed groups within Judaism such as the Sadducees, Pharisees, and the "temple business." Jesus opposed misguided religion and morality. The repenting (*metanoia*) called for in the beginning of the Mark Gospel is about changing a way of thinking. The gospels do not view the Messiah as a conquering hero. Thomas Sheehan says that this means focusing more on the message than on the messenger. He describes Jesus as a non-messiah Messiah who is about a new way of thinking and living here and now, who is about "empowering ordinary people to stake their lives on justice, mercy, compassion and peace." The poetic Christ-hymn in Philippians 2 suggests to me that resurrection is not a supernatural event but is, rather, the vindication and exaltation of the *values* to which Jesus was committed. What survives is not Jesus but his Name, his Message—his Living Word about how to live *now.*

The Art of Paradox

Some criticize Christianity for its paradoxes. But it bears repeating that, given any type of depth analysis, *life itself always seems to include exquisitely paradoxical tensions!* Therefore, any worldview or system of belief that doesn't take paradoxical experience and perception into account is ultimately shallow and unsatisfying. (Philosopher and mathematician Bertrand Russell observed that it wasn't until he came to terms with the problem of non-contradiction that he understood anything. The cutting edge physics of quantum and relativity theory involves a struggle between two apparently contradictory—paradoxical—models of how the universe/ multiverse works.) To think about paradox is to struggle with the rules of logic and critical thinking. A major problem with logic is that if you take an idea all the way to its extreme logical conclusion you are likely to find that you have come full circle to its opposite. You find yourself asserting, for example, that there absolutely are no absolutes! Or, if you go far enough to the political left you end up in the kind of totalitarianism that is just like right wing fascism. Or, you struggle with the issue of tolerating intolerance. These examples cannot be dismissed as mere semantics, nor do they show that logic is bad. Coming to terms with paradoxical perspectives is not about short-circuiting logic as some do in the name of faith, using the incomprehensibility of God as a weak excuse for their illogical ramblings or doctrinaire pronouncements. Rather, when we view life in paradoxical mode we confront a *dialectic* that brings us to a new level of understanding, a more poetic and artistic level.

A paradoxical perspective is about holding apparently contradictory notions in mind *as if* both are true, with the goal of maintaining our equilibrium between opposite and legitimately competing ideas or attitudes. Practically speaking, a paradoxical outlook is about the process of determining situation-appropriate behavior. Some prefer to use the term *dialectical* rather than *paradoxical*. Either term is appropriate, in my opinion, but I prefer "paradoxical" because it hints at the mysterious aspect of life and the limitations of mere logic. Many who have a problem with paradox tend to be forgetting that the word is defined as an *apparent* or *seeming* contradiction!

Most great thinkers usually wrestle with paradox in one way or another. F. Scott Fitzgerald famously asserted that "the test of a first-rate intelligence is the ability to hold two opposed ideas in the mind at the same time, and still retain the ability to function." German reformer Martin Luther was a monk, a priest, and a professor of philosophy. His collected writings are voluminous. Like other great thinkers he often took his arguments to an extreme. His most extreme teaching was "sola gratia"- Grace Alone! As have many Bible scholars before and since, Luther came to the conclusion that the most unique theme of the Bible and of the New

Testament in particular is *radical grace*—God's *unconditional love* for the world. People need this unconditional love, said Luther, because they are totally trapped in sin and the power of evil. To put it in familiar religious terms, Luther believed that none of us could ever be good enough to earn our way into heaven (to become "right with God")—or to make this world into a perfect paradise. In Luther's time, salvation was primarily focused on getting to heaven and avoiding hell or purgatory, but he also put great emphasis on ethics, compassionate service, freedom and liberation. Karen Armstrong and Dennis Hinkle criticize Luther for being too pessimistic about the bondage of the human will to sin and evil. I suggest rather that we see Luther as just being realistic about the *potential* for evil both in human nature and in a pursuit of moral perfection. Hannah Arendt's observation about the "banality of evil" reminds us that even the most ordinary person can be capable of monstrous evil.

Luther's extreme (radical) understanding of both human sinfulness and of our corresponding need for God's radical (unconditional) grace led him into paradox. One of the most obvious places where this paradox shows up is in his Small Catechism's explanation to the third article of the Apostles' Creed: "I believe that I cannot by my own reason or strength believe in Jesus Christ my Lord or come to Him. But the Holy Spirit has called me by the gospel . . . ." The paradox is obvious when we leave out just a few words. Luther is saying "I believe that I cannot . . . believe!" To the simplistic logical mind this is nonsense. But Luther had a paradoxical understanding of faith. At times he describes faith as the best "good work" a person can do that has ultimate value—to have faith *(trust in)* Jesus Christ. But Luther also insisted that faith is purely a "gift" of God's unconditional love. "Unconditional" means that there are no ifs, ands, or buts. "By grace are you saved, through faith; it is a gift of God, not of works, lest anyone should boast." (Ephesians 2:8–9) *By* grace *through* faith puts the focus on grace, not on a set of required correct beliefs. Compassionate faith cannot be a requirement. It is a path to follow.

Luther had a similarly paradoxical understanding of grace. The Roman Catholic Church of his day distinguished between two types of God's grace. One was "active grace" and this grace is reflected in Luther's statement that faith is the greatest good work a person can do. Active grace is the power God gives human beings to do good works and to have faith. God graces us with this power, but the bottom line is that *we* must do the difficult work and "keep the faith." Borg and Crossans' *The First Paul* considers how "fixing the world" requires this kind of empowering grace. The other type of grace was called "prevenient grace" by the Roman Church. "Prevenient" means "to come before the meeting of any requirements" and this is the kind of grace that Luther emphasized with the phrase "*sola gratia.*" Luther felt very strongly that the Church of his day had lost the message of God's prevenient, unconditional love and grace—that too much emphasis was being put on the perfectionist notion that salvation, justification, and justice is up to us. Humorless and ungraceful pursuit of perfection, excellence, and success can be sadly counterproductive! Michael Sherer calls it "achievement morality run amuck."

Whether we call it the paradox of faith or the paradox of grace, what this paradox means in our lives can be stated in a number of helpful ways. Near the end of the twentieth century, Lutherans and Roman Catholics signed a formal statement on "the doctrine of Justification (Salvation) by Grace Alone." They were in basic agreement that active grace and passive (prevenient) grace are both equally important notions. I am concerned about how well anyone, Christian or not, truly comprehends the paradoxical nature of this insight. That Roman Catholics can and do understand it is illustrated by the fact that one of the best formulations of the paradox comes from Ignatius Loyola, the founder of the Jesuit order: "Work to do your best and to make the world a better place as if everything depends on you, but pray and trust God as if everything depends on God!" The double use of the phrase "as if" expresses the paradox. We are to live "as if" two totally opposite things are both true.

The story is told that when the outstretched arms of an altar statue of Jesus were blown off by bombs during World War II, instead of repairing the statue, the congregation put a new sign under it reading "He has no hands but our hands." This is a wonderfully meaningful and poetic anecdote—and President Kennedy turned it into "here on earth God's work must truly be our own" in his inaugural address. Michael Sherer has put it this way: "Don't sit around waiting for a miracle. Be the miracle!" But the opposite sentiment is equally meaningful, and can be expressed in a similar metaphor by imagining God as having "the whole world in His hands." In non-religious terms the paradox or dialectic here is basically about taking ourselves both seriously and not too seriously as we struggle to lead an ethical and compassionate life.

Another classic way of stating the paradox of faith or grace is to say that "good works" are both necessary and unnecessary for salvation. Without going into the logic of "necessary cause" and "sufficient cause," let it suffice to say that the intent of a paradoxical perspective is to have us do "good works" because we want to, not because we have to. Christian ethics are just as concerned with motivation as with outcome! Good works are a "necessary"—in the sense of— *inevitable response* to the message of divine unconditional love, but they must never be seen as a necessary cause of, or prerequisite for, God's grace and love. "Unconditional" means that there are absolutely no requirements that must "necessarily" be met before a person can be "saved" or "right with God." (We will see that there are many nuances to this issue of "saved by grace" versus "salvation based on law"— a conflict some view as a discrepancy between the Pauline epistles and the Matthew Gospel.)

One reason we must go so deeply into this topic is that the typical Christian claim to uniqueness (and superiority!) is that Jesus is the one and only savior of the world. Many Christians tend to see all the other religions of the world as do-it-yourself-religions in which each individual's standing with God is basically that individual's responsibility. Orthodox doctrine developed the theme that no human being could ever be good enough "to get right with God." It was proclaimed that the only way to be saved was by God's grace. Whenever Christian theologians compromised on the theme of God's absolutely unconditional love and grace, they were said to be involved in the heresy called "synergism." Synergism means "cooperating energies." It suggests that humans have to do their part, to cooperate with God when it comes to getting right with God or being "saved." If it is said, for example, that God does ninety-nine percent of the work of salvation and the human only does one percent by accepting the gift of faith and salvation, the notion of Christianity's uniqueness is compromised. Even that one percent cooperation means that salvation is still, finally, up to the individual—in which case Christianity is just another do-it-yourself religion. All it has left as a unique claim is not the paradox of grace but only special pleading such as "Our Jesus is better than your Buddha or your Mohammed" or "Our beliefs are better than yours beliefs."

By the way, this type of debate about saved by grace and synergism is also sometimes found in Hinduism. "Salvation by the cat-hold" parallels "grace alone"—the image is of the mother cat picking the kitten up in its mouth with no cooperation from the kitten, whereas "salvation by the monkey hold" depicts the synergistic image of the baby monkey cooperating by grabbing onto its mother as she picks it up.

Remembering that a paradox is defined as an *apparent* contradiction, when we talk about acting "as if" opposite things are both true, we are not suggesting that Reality is absolutely contradictory. Such a claim would be nonsense. Paradox is about the moment-by-moment experience of opposites *seeming* or *appearing* to be true. For example, I find it profoundly meaningful to hold these two thoughts simultaneously in mind: I will live each day as if it were my last *and* live each day as if it were the first day of the rest of my life. These kinds of paradoxes are emotional and artistic in nature. They are experienced. As fact, they are nonsense. It makes no sense to say that Reality is actually contradictory. But when understood from a poetic, metaphorical, artistic, theological and experiential perspective, paradoxical (*as if*) awareness makes perfect sense. My feeling of profound ambivalence about death is another example of this kind of paradox. We rage against the dying of the light as if death were our worst enemy, and yet we can face death as if it is a defeated enemy and we can be serene.

Does Jesus Save?

Before we look at more facets of this paradoxical understanding of "salvation," we need to re-focus on the role that Jesus plays in this. The type of traditional theology that seems to make Jesus into little more than a magic lucky charm, having to do almost exclusively with getting into heaven, has outlived whatever usefulness it may have had! The first Project Greenlight film, "Stolen Summer," produced with the sponsorship of Ben Affleck and Matt Damon, was a very touching portrayal of this issue and, happily, the young boy at the center of the film comes to a gracious understanding that he does not have to worry about whether or not his dying non-Christian playmate will go to heaven—will be "saved."

A lot of rethinking needs to be done regarding what it means to believe in Jesus. Religious language about salvation must take the symbolic meaning of the name Jesus very seriously. To exalt the name of Jesus (a Greek version of the name Yeshua in Aramaic and Joshua in Hebrew) above every name is to exalt what this name means. It means "God saves!" To say that there is salvation in no other *name*, which on the surface sounds very arrogant and exclusive, needs to be understood as saying that the only way to be saved is by God—not by the church, not by the pope or by Billy Graham, not by Christianity. Salvation *only in the name of Jesus* means/symbolizes that salvation is ultimately up to God—and we cannot put limits on God's saving grace! Furthermore, since "God" in this context is a symbol for ultimate grace (and not some version of "Superman to the rescue"), and since salvation can also mean healing or deliverance (including the salvation and healing of planet earth which is our home), we cannot assume that salvation is necessarily about going to another world when we die. The idea that "God" (Ultimate Grace) alone is in charge of "salvation" suggests that anyone can be healed/liberated/saved, and I think this dovetails nicely with Bonhoeffer's religionless Christianity. It suggests that the prospect of getting to a supernatural next life is over-rated—that our life in this world needs to be much more highly valued! It means that we should stop focusing on or worrying about our destiny after death and put more effort into caring for the one world we have here and now! To paraphrase the Sermon on the Mount: "Take no thought for a next life; whatever that may or may not be will take care of itself."

The name of Jesus is, for Christians, the ultimate symbol of unconditional, limitless love and grace—which the New Testament often describes with the Greek word *agape*. "If I have all faith so as to remove mountains, and have not compassion/love (*agape*), it profits me nothing." Paul Tillich described Jesus as a symbol for "the New Being" with "The Courage To Be" in "the eternal now"—a model for humanity and not just a ticket to heaven. For Tillich, religion is more about us (humanity) than it is about some objective thing called God. Unconditional love, saving grace, justice-seeking compassion, courage, cooperation, Mystery and spirituality—all of these experienced realities express ultimate sacred values! The paradoxical doctrine of Christ as both fully/perfectly human and fully/ perfectly divine *is also symbolic of humanism as the ultimate criterion of value!* Many thoughtful Christians such as Gordon Kaufman have said that in the Jesus stories we are "called to be human" while at the same time called to acknowledge "the irreducible mystery of things" that transcends everything human. In *God, Mystery, Diversity,* Kaufman writes that, as symbols, God and Jesus can help focus devotion and commitment on "that which can draw us beyond what we presently are toward an existence more truly humane and better attuned to our environment." Thomas Sheehan expresses similar themes when he describes how a focus on Jesus, the Christ as the messenger has obscured the message of this "man for others." He says that we need to avoid what amounts to a personality cult, and keep the focus on Jesus as a symbol of grace and bringer of a message about the empowerment of ordinary people who "bet their lives *now*" on the way of justice, compassion, and peace.

Some feel that this version of believing in Jesus as having to do with the interplay of paradoxical themes discredits what they see as the atoning "work" of Jesus, his deliberate martyr sacrifice. But in our pluralistic and increasingly interconnected world, Christians need paradoxical insights more than ever in order to keep their faith from drifting into cultic narrow-mindedness, holier-than-thou-ism, or practical irrelevance. *It must be emphasized again that the themes, metaphors, images, and doctrines of religion are interpretations, not facts! They are artistic perspectives.* It is not a fact that Jesus "died for the sins of the world." Although it may have multiple levels of meaning, this phrase is just one (frequently misused) interpretation of the Jesus story—a story which itself is not purely factual. The struggle to establish orthodox dogmas and doctrines has tended to be seen as a matter of getting the facts straight. But it needs to be seen more as a process of trying to determine whether some interpretations or perspectives are simply "too far out"—too far afield of the basic themes of scriptural tradition. Sometimes it can be demonstrated that far-out interpretations distort these themes and cause people to act in destructive ways, flunking the test of "by their fruits you shall know them."

For myself, when it comes to the question of my eternal destiny, I take the paradoxical theme of salvation by grace alone to mean that *I am freed not only from worry about whether I will be saved—but freed even from concern about whether there actually is any such thing as eternal salvation!* The idea of trusting in the unconditional, saving, justifying love of God means simply that *I can relax about my relationship to eternity!* Whatever that destiny, if any, I *imagine* it as in the hands of a gracious Divinity. I can in a sense forget about religion, and live spiritually in the eternal now! This is the outlook that I derive from my Lutheran/Christian heritage, and I value it as a unique route to becoming a spiritual nonbeliever. This outlook reflects the spiritual serenity that should be at the heart of all true religious experience. The thirteenth century Spanish hymn I mentioned earlier expresses it well by affirming how we should play down the thought of heaven to gain and hell to flee—play down the logic of eternal reward and punishment as our reason for being ethical.

Bart Ehrman insists that becoming an agnostic has made him a more ethical person rather than diminishing his ethical concern. When we contemplate the likelihood that this life here and now is all we humans have, if we are at all wise we become exquisitely aware of the need to make the most of it. (In the concluding sections of this chapter we will be addressing the issue of those who would use this as an excuse to misbehave.) In *The End of Faith*, Sam Harris insists that belief in life after death is downright dangerous because it keeps us from taking this life seriously enough. I think he has a good point. But as I have tried to describe, we can affirm a positive relationship to eternity and recognize some value in metaphorical religious language (including some "God stories") without necessarily becoming any less concerned with, or committed to, the life we have now. Somewhat ironically, many of the folks who are officially declared saints after their deaths are people who really knew how to make the most of life in the here and now.

Since in Hebrew the same word can mean salvation, deliverance, liberation, freedom, or healing, consider the healing and liberating power of humor. Both serious studies and anecdotal stories have demonstrated how humor can contribute to our physical and emotional well-being. Relating humor to ethics, the paradoxical understanding of divine grace can be put in non-religious terms by saying that it helps us *to combine a sense of moral urgency about making ourselves and the world better with a sense of humor that doesn't take our efforts too seriously.* Those who take their religion (or their politics) too seriously can be very dangerous, as we have seen all too clearly at the dawn of the twenty-first Century. September 11, 2001 (9/11) has become a symbol of mythic proportions for the evil of fanaticism. But we can also err in the direction of not trying hard enough to improve this world. Borg and Crossan say that Christians should participate wholeheartedly in bringing God's "justification" (distributive justice) to the world. But they also note how St. Paul counseled sly caution and non-violence in relating to Rome so as to avoid futile martyrdom. On the other hand, many great moral icons of history such as Paul himself and, in more recent times, suffragette leaders Alice Paul and Lucy Burns, Dietrich Bonhoeffer, Vaclav Havel, Nelson Mandela, Martin Luther King Jr. and many other civil rights activists took enormous risks and spent significant time in jail to advance the cause of "liberty and justice for all." Jesus himself, of course, was briefly a prisoner and was executed as a criminal!

Greenblatt in *The Swerve* slams the idea of a God who demands absolute perfection because it has been used to make people feel powerless and guilty. The grace of humor is an antidote to perfectionism. We need the paradoxical ability to take our efforts at righting the wrongs of the world both very seriously yet not too seriously. This is not just about "balance," because at one time or another we may need to go very far in the direction either of moral urgency or of humorous detachment. The point is not to go off the deep end in either direction. As opposed to striving for balance, the better image is of maintaining *equilibrium*, moving back and forth with situational appropriateness between times when we are very serious, times when we are deliciously into our sense of humor, and times when our senses of seriousness and of humor are more or less in balance. This equilibrium and *paradoxical* (!) combination of seriousness and humor can help to prevent or to heal the kind of wounds that too often have been caused by fanatical or utopian religion, politics, or any other kind of perfectionist pipe dreams.

Motivation and Guidance for Morality

Another aspect of paradoxical theology concerns our motives for being moral. What is the spirit in which we go about trying to be good and to improve the world? While much of this discussion will seem to focus on our individual moral attitudes and behavior, it should be clear that efforts to "make the world a better place" are always understood to be a major part of the equation as well.

Few people are psychopaths, without any conscience, without the ability to empathize, without any commitment to the good. Does religious faith make one different ethically? One traditional Christian way of talking about this has been to say that no good work is really worth anything if it is done by someone who doesn't have faith in Jesus. Speaking in this way can suggest that Christians are some kind of morally superior species, which runs counter to the pervasive biblical theme of walking humbly with God. When he was a candidate for vice president of the United States, Senator Joseph Lieberman, an orthodox Jew, got into hot water for appearing to suggest that non-religious people might tend to be less ethical than religious people. There is, in fact, an etymological link between the words "god" and "good" in the history of the English language, but it is a rather tenuous relationship at best.

Richard Dawkins, Daniel Dennett, Greg Epstein (*Good without God*), and Sam Harris (*The Moral Landscape: How Science Can Determine Human Values*) have argued, convincingly in my opinion, that ethical behavior is an innate, pre-religious feature of our humanity. As Dr. Hinkle says, "People don't need religion in order to feel empathy and compassion for others." Rabbi Kushner contends that the Hebrew phrase "fear of God" is better translated as "innate sense of morality." Dennett acknowledges that religious institutions have often been the most effective organizers of moral teamwork, for example, the movement against slavery in the United States and, I would add, the amazing work done by the church-sponsored hospital ship Africa Mercy now serving the area from which many slaves had originally been abducted. This organizing potential in religion is part of my rationale for emphasizing the church in "high church atheist." Religion has frequently led the way in harnessing moral energy in productive ways, as author Alain de Botton illustrates in *Religion for Atheists*. While effective school teachers, counselors, parents and the like can foster empathy and compassion, religious communities can indeed be an important partner in these efforts. The biggest danger Dennett sees in religious morality is its tendency to settle for authoritarian, simplistic answers to complicated questions. It's worth noting again that since he has embraced agnosticism regarding God and has focused on life *before* death, Bart Ehrman feels he has even more reason to be ethical (partly, I suspect, because he is not sitting around waiting for miracles).

An important aspect of Christian paradoxical theology is the way in which it motivates us to strive for the highest ethical goals while recognizing from the outset that even our best (if we manage to do it) is not going to be good enough, is not going to achieve total perfection or utopia. (A comparable Muslim view is that only God/Allah is perfect.) During my life as a Lutheran pastor I spent sad times sitting at the bedside of dying people who were trying to convince me (and themselves) that they had done their best and were worthy of going to heaven. I hope this book might help to prevent such sad scenes. The combination of a sense of moral urgency with a sense of humor gives us what I call a "struggle and relax mentality." This mentality keeps people safe from the twin dangers of perfectionism or fanaticism on the one hand, and despair or dilettantism on the other. This struggle and relax attitude could even be imagined as perhaps having helped Jesus and St. Paul cope with the non-arrival of the perfect Reign of God. Love does ultimately trump even hope!

The objection is regularly raised that an over-emphasis on the unconditional love of God and any hint of moral relaxation leads to ethical relativism, shallow religious universalism, or both. There is indeed a danger that unconditional "radical grace" can become what Bonhoeffer called "cheap grace." A love-is-the-only-rule situational ethic could give some unprincipled people a way to rationalize their druthers. The so-called new morality of the 1960s and 70s was sometimes dubbed "the old immorality condoned." But in ethics we must come to terms with the paradoxical truth that our desire for moral absolutes and our intuitive awareness of ethical relativity are both valid. Our *desire for absolutes* is about the need for firm principles and guidelines. Our *awareness of ethical relativity* is about realizing that "situations alter cases." An ethic of specific and rigid absolutes can be difficult to follow when it says we must act in a certain way whether we feel like it or not. But this absolutism can also become a way to avoid making any real ethical decisions—one just follows the rules without any struggle or deliberation. A relativistic ethic, on the other hand, is difficult because it requires the making of arbitrary decisions in ambiguous situations, without using the decision process merely to selfishly rationalize doing what we personally would rather do.

Those whose lives have become totally dysfunctional in multiple ways may latch onto a strict religion of absolutes as a means of learning to live within limits. Many religious groups focus precisely on reaching out to such folks, offering a kind of refuge to lost souls. Comedians Cheech and Chong lampooned this phenomenon by portraying a character who says "I used to be all messed up on drugs, but now since I met the Lord, I'm all messed up on the Lord." It could be argued that a life within strict limits is better than a life gone wild, but bouncing from one extreme to the other is not the only option. The initial effort to overcome extreme behavioral dysfunction may require strict limits or some intense alternative commitment, but the eventual goal should be to enter the healthy give and take of personal decision-making. Neither pathological conventionality nor cult-like fanaticism is a desirable alternative to life on the wild side. Buddhist wisdom understands that living in the moment and making thoughtful ethical decisions is by definition situational and relative. If it can be said that Buddhism has an absolute moral precept it would be *to act with compassion in all situations*. However, what compassion might mean, especially in complex situations (dealing with convicted serial killers or terrorists, for example) could be hard to determine. The many books that came out in the 1960s dealing with "situation ethics" tended to emphasize love as the only absolute ethical principle. The typical criticism of this idea has been that love is not specific enough to serve as a meaningful ethical guideline. It is true that many other values and concerns inevitably come into play, but I contend that love, empathy, and compassion certainly do provide a solid bottom line for any ethical decisions we might make.

The reality is that a truly ethical person cannot avoid the struggle between doing what a law or rule says, and doing what one feels is right after weighing as many factors as possible. I think Bart Ehrman misreads the Matthew Gospel, when he sees its Jesus as a purely law-oriented Jew who felt salvation was achieved by following the law. Matthew bends over backwards to respect Jewish reverence for the law, mainly because he is writing specifically for Jewish followers of Jesus. But when Matthew's Jesus says that those who take a more flexible attitude toward law will be "least in the kingdom of heaven," Ehrman apparently fails to note that they are still *in* the kingdom! Matthew's Jesus doesn't tighten the *letter* of the law.

He emphasizes the *spirit* of the law, the "weightier matters" of the law. He lambasts those whose morality strains out gnats and swallows camels. In stories where Jesus has to choose between a person and a rule, he always chooses the person. (In Luke-Acts, supposedly impure Samaritans and eunuchs become good role models!) The beauty of the internalized ethical motivation that grace theology produces is that it frees us from the kind of conventional, oppressive, authoritarian religion that Joseph Campbell caricatured by comparing early images of Yahweh to the God of his computer as having "a lot of rules and no mercy." One of my favorite illustrations of the tension between absolute and relativist ethics contrasts the rigid strength of the oak tree which might break in a storm with the flexible strength of the willow tree that bends with the wind.

In his book *Psychoanalysis and Religion*, Psychologist Erich Fromm contrasts authoritarian religion with humanistic religion. He uses the story where Abraham argues with God about the ethics of destroying innocent people along with the guilty in the cities of Sodom and Gomorrah to illustrate how Jewish morality sets the tone for social and ethical criticism—for speaking truth to power. (By the way, the Hebrew of Genesis 19:4 makes it clear that the entire town of Sodom including women and children surrounded Lot's house, making it probable that the basic sin of the townspeople in this story was—as clearly stated elsewhere in the Bible—inhospitality to strangers, not homosexual rape. Even if homosexual rape were being condemned here, it would not necessarily imply a condemnation of all homosexuality!) Of course, stories where God destroys the whole world with a flood, or entire cities with fire and brimstone, present us with a very troubling image of God, to put it mildly. Some see this God as a monster. But we must remind ourselves that in virtually all early religion the Gods are typically presented as characters in a story who act in much the same way as their human creators acted. If we aim to be fair, we must sift through these ancient theologies to find whatever of value remains. For example, the image of humans as "having dominion over the earth" can be read as meaning ecologically sensitive care for the earth, and the warrior God of the Hebrews can be seen in a favorable light as always on the side of the oppressed! The ancients' use of at times egregious and disturbing personifications can help us recognize counterproductive ideas and beliefs of our own that need to be modified or eliminated.

The expression "what would Jesus do?" is also about making ethical decisions. The difficulty of using this question as an ethical guideline becomes especially apparent when we realize that if we were all to be celibate as Jesus or St. Paul supposedly were, the human race would die out.

Assuming the historical Jesus did expect the imminent arrival of God's Kingdom of justice and peace, it seems that if we similarly were to expect an imminent arrival of God's reign, we would likewise be disappointed. A better framing of the question asks "what *kinds of things* did Jesus, Mohammed or the Buddha do?" They embodied compassion for the poor, the sick, and for oppressed victims of social, political, and economic injustice. But, as noted before, the words or actions attributed to them cannot be turned into absolute rules for all times and situations. We can do the kinds of things they did, but we won't necessarily do exactly the same things.

Martin Luther made a strong statement about the limitations of the laws of Moses which James Russell Lowell later expressed as "new occasions teach new duties, time makes ancient good uncouth." Yet Luther himself was totally wrong when, based on the biblical story about Joshua making the sun stand still, he condemned Copernicus. If we ask "What would Luther do?" it becomes apparent we would not want to emulate his prejudiced diatribes against Jews and peasants or his occasional harsh anti-intellectual condemnations of reason. Good ethical decision making, like good science, requires attention and openness to accurate and timely information.

The word "condone" is problematical. It suggests that we absolutely know what is right and then we cave in to relativism—we bend the rules. But to start our moral deliberations with the premise of an absolute or one-size-fits-all ethic is a mistake. For example, at first glance it may seem obvious that the absolute ideal family is an intact nuclear family of mother, father and children. But the reality is that not all such families are very functional (to put it mildly), and that other types of families can function very well. Gay families, extended families, single-parent families, various forms of mixed marriage—all suggest that a better ethical model for families is one that honors diversity. To prepare children to live in a world of diversity is the better model for success because it is based on reality. Gay marriage is indeed partly about sex, and the resistance to it demonstrates that many people still have a hard time dealing with the diversity of human sexuality. But gay marriage is far more about the validation of love and family than it is about sex. This is what the misguided and absolutist defenders of heterosexual marriage fail to understand.

Absolute ethical perfectionism turns out to cause more problems than it solves. Abstinence-only safe sex idealism illustrates the failure of moral absolutism. The frequently documented, dramatic failure rate of abstinence-only sex education is far higher than the failure rate either of condoms in particular or of comprehensive sex education in general. Many forms of religion clearly have been too uptight about sex. When Christians came to the "Indians" in both Asia and the Americas, they imposed rigid understandings of sexuality on cultures that, with the advantage of hindsight, now seem to have been in some ways more sane and healthy than Christian culture. The *Kama Sutra* makes the biblical Solomon's *Song of Songs* seem tame by comparison. The "two spirit" understanding in Navajo culture made room for four genders—male, female, feminine male and masculine female. The basics of sexual morality are the same for everyone—responsibility, honesty, integrity, non-exploitation, consent, safety. The so-called missionary mentality which allows only the heterosexual "missionary position" for sexual acts is absurd and ridiculous. The counter-productive damage wrought by uptight religious sexual morality has been incalculable. A glaring example is the sexual abuse scandal among Roman Catholic clergy. The sexual drive is simply too powerful to be forced into the narrow channels so often prescribed for it by religion.

Hell Fire and Outer Darkness

But is not relativism the same thing as that proverbial road to hell paved with good intentions? Doesn't the Bible say that there is a very real hell of fire from which we need to be saved? Aren't those who don't accept Jesus as their personal savior going to hell for all eternity? The theme of moral responsibility, judgment, and damnation does appear in the Bible, along with the theme of unconditional love, mercy, grace, compassion, and forgiveness. Can we ignore the condemning and judgmental theme in the Bible?

First of all it must be repeated that many self-described Christians tend to be very selective in a way that distorts the "good news" when they hammer away at the theme of judgment and damnation while the theme of love and compassion gets short shrift. Many are eager to place the Ten Commandments in public places, but not the Beatitudes ("Blessed are the merciful"), the Magnificat ("the rich he has sent empty away"), or the empathetic and compassionate Golden Rule ("Do unto others as you would have them do unto you"). Some inconsistently deny communion to those who are pro-choice on abortion but not to those who support the death penalty! I've seen bumper stickers that say, "Read your Bible. It'll scare the hell out of you." The fact is that neither images of hell nor death penalties have proven to be effective forms of behavior control.

Second, we need to remind ourselves of the metaphorical/artistic nature of religious language. To say something is metaphorical is to be aware of the limitations of language and concepts. Jesus is pictured as using many figures of speech. Hell fire is one of them. So is "outer darkness with weeping and gnashing of teeth." Have you ever wondered how hell can be outer darkness if there is all that fire? After all, a huge fire-ball, the sun, is synonymous with light. (Ironically, the German word "hell" means bright or light.) Mixed metaphors remind us not to take symbolic language too literally. (The wildly imaginative New Testament book of Revelation is full of mixed metaphors describing Jesus, often using the phrase "something like" to pile metaphor upon metaphor, midrash upon midrash—a virtual smorgasbord of reinterpretations.) The English word "hell" is a translation of the Greek word "*gehenna*." This word has associations with the practice of child sacrifice in the Valley of Hinnom, which became the city dump outside Jerusalem and hence the images of evil and of a constant smoky fire. Gehenna is a metaphor for life ending up on the junk heap—life wasted.

The main place where hell appears in the Bible is in the parables told by Jesus in the Matthew Gospel. It never appears in the Hebrew Scriptures but shows up seven times in Matthew, three times in Mark, and once each in Luke, James and Second Peter. St. Paul talks about eternal death but never mentions hell. A major principle of interpreting parables is that they generally have only one main point. We are likely to miss that point entirely if we assume that every element in a story is of equal value as a Word of God. So in the story where a wicked servant does not learn an extremely obvious lesson of forgiveness and is deemed worthy of being thrown into "outer darkness where there will be weeping and gnashing of teeth," we do not have proof that a place called hell actually exists. We do not even have a scare tactic. What we have is a shock tactic, like the punch line of a joke, in which the obvious point about forgiveness is intended to hit like a thunderbolt. It is also clear that anyone who would not get the point of the story is perhaps so far gone that any attempt to explain it further would be as ridiculous as explaining a joke and expecting laughter. So perhaps the *gehenna* image of a wasted life ending up in the junk pile quite accurately describes the situation of a person being so out of it, unresponsive, dense, or stubborn that not even infinite divine mercy and unconditional love would seem capable of saving or reclaiming such a person.

The various images of "hell" are best understood as figures of speech, shock tactics, and not as the last word on the destiny of a vast number of human beings who fail to accept certain religious doctrines about Jesus. At the very least this means that Christian theologians must give the benefit of the doubt to the theme of God's unconditional love. They may not feel qualified to endorse the classic Unitarian/Universalist doctrine that God saves and redeems everything and everyone, because they feel that such grand conclusions and final judgments are not for human beings to make. But they certainly can agree with "judge not lest ye be judged!" In addition to many similar non-judgmental themes and specific passages in the Bible, Christian theologians would seem obligated to come to terms with the affirmation that ultimately "God will unite all things in Christ, things in heaven and things on earth." (Ephesians 1:10) This theme of universal divine grace is not about evildoers getting off scot free. The theme of judgment is not about punishment, getting even, revenge—not about scaring people into behaving themselves. Both grace and judgment are about being motivated to do all we can in the eternal now to promote love, compassion, peace, and better lives for all of humankind.

The harm done by fire and brimstone preaching is chillingly described by Robert Ingersoll: "The doctrine of eternal punishment is in perfect harmony with the savagery of the men who made the orthodox creeds. It is in harmony with torture, with flaying alive, and with burnings. The men who burned their fellow-men for a moment, believed that God would burn his enemies forever." Clubbing people over the head with a threat of divine judgment is no way to promote meaningful morality. Comedian George Carlin had a routine in which he described a God who could allow you to spend eternity writhing and screaming in agony, but then Carlin would cock his head and say with an ironic and devilish grin—"But he loves you." Since the theme of God's unconditional love, grace, and compassion must certainly trump the theme of judgment and punishment, individuals can find amazing spiritual serenity (salvation, healing) in this "good news" (gospel) of Christ. I am reminded of the metaphorical vision of heaven adapted from the book of Revelation into the popular religious song "The Holy City" where "all who would might enter and no one was denied." While it may be appropriately humble to avoid making doctrinaire pronouncements to the effect that universal salvation or redemption for all humanity is a sure thing, it certainly is equally appropriate to center our own individual lives on the assured reality of divine empathy, compassion, and love. I think it is also appropriate to mention here that in Western culture, when the worst criminals have been sentenced to death, it became standard procedure for the judge announcing the sentence to finish by saying: "May God have mercy on your soul."

The Attitude of Gratitude, Empathy, and Compassion

One typical reaction to the theme of God's unconditional love is: If everyone is going to be saved, I might as well cheat, lie, murder and steal, because we will all be redeemed and go to heaven regardless. A Dostoyevsky character says: "If there is no God, everything is permitted." The main problem with this "logic" is that the entire thrust of Christian grace theology is about interior rather than exterior motivation. It is about our attitude! Grace theology is about doing what is good and right out of gratitude for the good-news-theme of unconditional love. It is not about coercion, requirements, or punishing evildoers. It is about striving for excellence, but always in the context of understanding that perfectionism is an impossible and dangerous tendency. The "I can do anything because I'll be saved regardless" attitude is based on shallow reward and punishment logic. This is the self-destructive mentality of a child who only eats healthy food or uses a toothbrush when a parent is watching. It is a mentality that refuses to get the joke—that needs to have the punch line explained. This is the real meaning of works (ethics) without faith (insightful motivation). Moral denseness along these lines is about failure to participate in the artistry of living well.

Helping us see that getting into heaven should not be our main concern, Lutheran Bishop Robert Rimbo of the Metropolitan New York Synod has written that if we focus on gratitude, our living and dying "won't be distorted by our craving for immortality." An artistic reading of grace theology means that if there were a literal Father-type God, unconditional love would be His nature. Grace, however, is the true reality—not "Him." The same is true for the Qur'an where almost every chapter (sura) begins by describing Allah as "the Merciful, the Compassionate!"

I copied the following from a poster that caught my eye: "Attitude is more important than facts, than education, money, circumstances, failures, success, than what others say and do—more important than appearances, giftedness or skill. It will make or break a company, a church, a school, a home." An instructive example of bad attitude is Pascal's famous wager. The short version is that it would be better to believe in God and be wrong than not to believe and be wrong—and, therefore, damned. The main problem is that this kind of "belief" would be insincere pretense.

Would not God presumably value integrity and be more impressed with honest skepticism than with this kind of bet-hedging? Richard Dawkins suggests that Pascal was joking when he proposed this wager. The attitude it suggests would be beneath the contempt of any righteous God. It would be a transparently craven attempt to latch onto immortality in a totally hypocritical and inauthentic manner. Furthermore, as discussed in chapter 1, great things of value are lost if one is acting out of legalistic obedience to the demands of a rigid, authoritarian God, as opposed to acting out of sincere gratitude, *as if* to a loving benefactor. I suspect that many rigid, legalistic and bet-hedging believers envy the freedom of honest non-believers to think, to question, to grow, and to otherwise expand their horizons.

Thinking in terms of religionless Christianity and religion as an art form means that we can express many of the above ideas in non-theological language. For instance, the paradox of judgment and compassion takes psychological and sociological form in the realization that all humans are both perpetrators and victims of evil. As perpetrators we understand the necessity of owning up to the consequences of our actions or of our failures to act. But as victims we understand the need for compassion and mercy. The exclamations "mercy!" or "mercy me!" effectively restate *Kyrie eleison* (Lord, have mercy). Infant baptism interpreted in non-religious terms is about realizing that we have been produced by the universe and have a right to self-esteem, a right to feel good about ourselves and what we are capable of accomplishing. The value of each person must be recognized, no matter how damaged or deranged. The religious language about being unconditionally loved by God, saved by grace, and a full member of the church, all spoken over a helpless infant who doesn't yet realize what it all means, also illustrates the importance of creating trusting relationships. The fundamental message inherent in this theology about unconditional love and intrinsic worth is closely related to the Buddhist perspective of "I am the universe happening" which will be considered in greater depth in chapter 5.

Salvation can be understood in religionless Christianity terms simply as spiritual serenity. Paul Tillich put "grace alone" in paradoxical terms by talking about "accepting our acceptance." When Christians "accept Christ" it is about having a sense of being already accepted and loved unconditionally (by "God")—meaning that if I see my entire life, every moment, as pure gift, I will know the art of living well. Harvard theologian Arthur McGill expressed a similar thought by describing "the gospel of our common human neediness," according to which compassion eliminates any form of holier-than-thou condescension as we relate to one another, sometimes giving and sometimes receiving help. The theme of God's unconditional love also enables religious folks to be comfortable with not having all the answers, comfortable with Mystery and with the Reality that there is no such thing as certainty. "Let go and let God" is a popular figure of speech that some use to expresses this kind of serenity.

Rick Warren, founding pastor of the Saddleback Church in southern California, who was the controversial choice to give the invocation at Barack Obama's 2009 first inauguration as President, has made a big splash with his "purpose-driven" approach to Christianity. He has said that his main goal is "to get as many people as possible into heaven." My question is: If your main purpose in this life is to get to the next life, what will your purpose be when you arrive at that next life? To put it another way, what makes you think you will be able to appreciate a permanent, eternal, future life (or is it rest?) after death, if you haven't been able to participate wholeheartedly and find purpose or meaning in this life here and now? Fortunately, the purpose Warren talks about also has to do with avoiding self-centeredness by loving and serving others as a way of serving God. While he tends toward a reactionary and overly narrow version of traditional values, and as I see it does not promote the kind of changes in our political and economic system that would lead to a more equitable society, he does promote positive projects to serve people's needs. He has been described as representing a new and softer face of evangelical Christianity.

My main concern about the more hard-line evangelicals, of course, is that they do not have enough appreciation for the artistic nature of the words and symbols they use. They see the Bible as an authoritative textbook and too often allow individual proof texts to trump major themes. Even Warren is like many who allow a few highly debatable passages about sexuality to over-ride much broader themes of love, compassion, non-judgmentalism, inclusiveness, hospitality, truth, and integrity as they relate to the issue of sexual orientation. Dennis Hinkle wearies of any God-talk and asks "Why not serve others for their own sake, simply because you have empathy and compassion?" It's a point well taken, but many folks find the support of a spiritual community to be an important asset in their efforts to promote compassion, justice, and peace.

The word "evangelical" in its various forms is made up of two Greek words, "eu" meaning "good" ("eu" morphed into "ev") and "angel" meaning "message" or "messenger." In those parts of the Hebrew Bible not influenced by Persian religion, angels were envisioned as walking around like human beings and serving as messengers from God (see Genesis 17 and following). Their role was similar to that of the prophets as spokespersons for God. Somehow the Greek "evangel" morphed into "Godspell" in old English and eventually into "Gospel." Hence evangelism or preaching the gospel is about bringing a good message—good news! The angels in Luke's Christmas story say that they bring "good news of great joy which shall be to all people." So evangelism has to be about much more than (and other than!) saving individual souls and getting as many of them as possible into heaven. Christian faith is about "peace on earth," well-being ("good will to all"), justice (especially distributive and economic)—sharing all the good things of life and our common human values not in a spirit of condescension and paternalism, but in the Spirit of mutuality, empathy, and compassion.

In these early years of the twenty-first century, prophetic voices are calling attention to growing income and wealth inequality in the super-power United States. It is also being pointed out how United States military spending is greater than that of many other countries combined, most of which are allies of the United States. How does this imbalance correlate with the gospel's concern for the poor and warnings to the rich—with the United States as a "Christian country" where good news is preached? Compassion, justice, love and grace must not be mere abstractions and pious platitudes! Efforts to insure a more just and equitable society here and now, to "promote the general welfare," must not be condescendingly characterized and dismissed as the promotion of lazy dependency. If there is a "safety net" for big banks and corporations, why not for individuals and families who have tried and failed or who have simply been unlucky! Too many Christian sermons and hymns ("Come ye disconsolate . . .Earth has no sorrow that heaven cannot heal") seem to ignore the welfare of "the least of these" and to promote life-after-death as the only safety net about which Christians need to be concerned. I think we in the developed world need to focus more energy on learning how to temper capitalist avarice with compassion!

Christians proclaim that *for them* the good news of divine unconditional love is most clearly seen in the various New Testament "Jesus theologies." The paradox of Jesus as both human and divine is not that a human being was also "physically" (ontologically) God, but that Jesus is presented and understood as showing us what "God" and divine compassion are all about. Bishop Spong says that behind the Jesus stories lies "the Jesus experience"—Jesus experienced as embodying divine compassion and love, *an experience that non-Christians may find elsewhere!* (We should note that compassion is a better term than mercy because mercy implies condescension of one who is superior to one who is inferior, while compassion implies a thoroughly mutual relationship.) In the Luke Gospel Jesus talks about not judging others in the same context where he also says "Be compassionate as your Father is compassionate" (the use of Father instead of God softens the superior tone and in light of the larger context strongly suggests that "compassionate" is a more accurate translation than "merciful"). The fact that the closest parallel to this saying in the Matthew Gospel comes in the context of exhortations to love everyone including enemies, suggests that the translation "You, therefore, must be perfect, as your heavenly Father is perfect" is more about *perfect compassion* than it is about some legalistic notion of moral purity.

According to the Jesus theology of the apostle St. Paul, the Spirit of God and the Spirit of Christ are the same (Romans 8:9), and the test of true religion and authentic spirituality in this world is whether it produces the fruits of the spirit, especially love, compassion, peace, and justice (distributive justice in particular). Real love is more about action than it is about emotion or sentiment. True love and compassion involves the ability to understand and on some level empathize with even those we do not necessarily like, or with those whose psychopathic and anti-social actions we may deplore. Love is able to forgive enemies "for they know not what they do." To paraphrase the New Testament book of James: "faith without love and compassion is dead." While the Greek word *agape* has been translated as both charity and love, if I limit myself to translating it with only one word I prefer to use compassion. "If I have prophetic powers, and understand all mysteries and all knowledge, *and if I have all faith, so as to remove mountains, but have not compassion, I am nothing.*" (1 Corinthians 13, italics mine)

CHAPTER 3

Past Lives—Future Lives

Reincarnation—Immortality as Recycling

ANOTHER WELL-KNOWN VERSION OF life after death also puts the focus on ethics. This idea of reincarnation into another life (*samsara*—wandering across) according to one's *karma* (action) was not originally developed, however, out of a desire to live forever. It was created primarily in order to deal with the obvious unfairness of life! This belief system is associated mostly with southern Asia—with India. In her 2012 book *Revelations*, Elaine Pagels explains that whenever people face extreme social, political, or existential crises, they desperately want and need to believe that there will be some ultimate ethical accounting, some Judgment Day when all will be made right. Human beings struggle to find some hope or meaning in the midst of horror and despair. The apocalyptic literature found in both the Hebrew and Christian Scriptures typically imagines this kind of hope. Reincarnation offers hope for ultimate justice in the idea that we all live many lifetimes.

It has been argued that reincarnation as a version of life after death appears in the Bible. While the Bible does have consistent themes of judgment and vindication, there is no explicit imagery that corresponds to typical ideas of reincarnation. There is the theme of Emmanuel (God with us) and the Incarnation of "God in Christ," but no idea of Re-incarnation. Some have tried to read the idea of reincarnation into the story of the prophet Elijah who is taken up to heaven in a fiery chariot. But the Jewish expectation of Elijah's later return (as acted out in the Seder Meal during the observance of Passover) was based on the notion that he had never died. This is quite different from the usual understanding of reincarnation found in India. Israelite theology had a very this-worldly, here and now approach to issues of justice and righteousness. Micah wrote that religion was about doing justice, loving-kindness and walking humbly with God. Amos cried out for justice to roll down like waters and righteousness like an ever-living stream. Unfortunately, like many people who take up the banner of justice today, the ancient Hebrews often expressed much more concern about their own suffering than about the injustice and hurt suffered by others. Wars and punishments were typically brutal, and Yahweh (The Lord) of the Hebrews has sometimes been excoriated as "a serial killer of women and children."

But Hebrew theology was also noticeably humane in comparison with other cultures of its time and place. One central tenet came to be that "as we were unjustly treated as slaves, we ourselves should avoid treating others (strangers) unfairly." Such progressive notions as giving even slaves and animals a day of rest on the Sabbath has led to other progressive changes, one of which has been the eventual abolition of slavery itself. (It also has to be said that before we castigate the brutality of that day and age, we must come to terms with the fact that the increasingly secularized twentieth century was the bloodiest in human history!) It is also important to note again that although The Lord (*Yahweh*) was sometimes described as a "man of war," this God was always thought to be on the side of justice for the oppressed and for the outsider.

In some cultures, beliefs that seem to involve a form of reincarnation are mainly about continuity in a society. The rituals surrounding death confirm the values of the tribe. Some rituals involve the commingling of the ashes from cremated members of the tribe—a kind of tea is made from these ashes which every person in the group then drinks, as portrayed in the movie "The Emerald Forest." All previous members of the group are both physically and symbolically reincarnated in those who are still living. Such an approach is somewhat analogous to those who now see their connection to eternity in their own DNA as it is carried forward by their offspring into future generations. In contemporary society a few people are having some cremated remains of loved ones made into jewelry that they can wear. In other cultures a new leader is seen as the reincarnation of the previous leader, as is the case with the Dalai Lama, for example, and hence a tradition is carried forward. Other more scientifically oriented people see reincarnation in terms of the physics which says that matter is neither created nor destroyed—a notion which some choose to see as corresponding with the belief that souls are limited in number and are recycled as opposed to endlessly coming into being as completely new creations.

The Indian understanding of reincarnation according to one's karma originated with the idea that the only way we can believe life is fair is to believe that we all live many lifetimes and will eventually get what we deserve. Other interpreters of this belief see it as referring to the idea that we live many lifetimes before we learn all the lessons of what it means to live a truly human life—as illustrated by Scrooge in "A Christmas Carol" or by Bill Murray's character in the movie "Groundhog Day." It seems to me that this kind of artistic/poetic portrayal of reincarnation or past lives as being a matter of learning life lessons is the more practical approach to what in Sanskrit is called *karma/samsara*. I see this version of past and/or future lives functioning something like an imaginative object lesson. It is not a real fact of life, but it helps us approach every day as a new chance to learn, grow, and improve. It reminds me of St. Paul's New Testament language about daily dying and rising to new life.

Just Desserts

The idea of getting what one deserves seems like a good thing at first glance. But on further reflection a number of problems come into view. Who really deserves anything, particularly anything better or worse than anyone else? How could it possibly be determined who deserves what? When thoughtful people ask "why me?" they often find themselves answering "why not me?" It has been wisely said that if we could actually know what some of the people we envy were experiencing, we would not want to change places with them no matter how well off they might appear to be. Knowing how to make the best of what you have is far more useful than envying the supposed advantages of others.

Perhaps the greatest problem with *karma/samsara* is the kind of conclusions that could be drawn from the idea that everyone's lot in this life is deserved or pre-determined. Why should I have compassion for a person who lost his legs when he stepped on a land mine since he must have done something in a past life to deserve such a fate? "Just desserts" may not be all they're cracked up to be. Life is best understood as a gift, and gifts are not thought of as being connected to earning or deserving. The New Testament does not try to envision a scheme in which we all get only what we deserve. The evangelical good news moves beyond the simple logic of reward and punishment. "By grace are you saved, through faith, it is a gift of God, not of works [not deserved!], lest anyone should boast" (Ephesians 2:8–9). This statement was penned after the time of St. Paul, but it is one of the most direct and concise summaries of the Pauline theme of radical divine grace to be found anywhere in the New Testament. This theme of divine unconditional love leads to the paradox of grace (as discussed in chapter 2) in which notions of earning or deserving are replaced by a simple attitude of gratitude for the gifts of life and love.

The wisdom of emphasizing that the most important thing about God or life is unconditional love and grace becomes more apparent when we contemplate the many problems that come with trying to prove that all people get or should get what they deserve. Logically, absolute justice would require that everyone's life be exactly the same—same length, same quality, same talents, same everything. The reality is that some people may lead fuller lives in ten or twenty years than others do in eighty or more years. Equal opportunity for all people is a reasonable goal, but a guaranteed equal outcome or equal success is not. Such a world would be unbelievably boring. The image of a God who would totally determine everything that happens in order to ensure absolute equality (a type of predestination) would not give us a "best of all possible worlds" scenario. When Jesus is pictured as saying "the poor you have always with you" it should not be seen as justifying apathy toward a lopsided and unfair distribution of wealth. It is best understood as a simple recognition of the variety of the human condition at any given moment in time. The parable attributed to Jesus in which all the workers receive the same pay regardless of how long or hard they worked seems to promote an injustice. But what the parable is really saying is that there always come times when love must trump justice because all the forms of justice are at best only relative. If we seek any absolute uniformity in life, let it be the uniformity of unconditional love, the unconditional valuing of every person's unique life.

In *When Bad Things Happen to Good People,* Rabbi Kushner describes how quite a few of the ideas we might suggest to make for a better world actually would make things far worse. Would we want a world in which a capricious God constantly interferes with the laws of nature or provides favors for certain people? Would we want a world in which everyone's life is basically and predictably the same? Would we really want to eliminate the huge role that chance and luck play in life? The 2009 movie "500 Days of Summer" is a "non-love story" that very cleverly contrasts the fatalistic notion of "meant to be" with the realization that contingency, coincidence, and chance play major roles in our lives.

Everything does not happen for a preordained reason, and if we act as if everything that happens is meant to be, we are likely to miss out on many opportunities because of our lack of openness to multiple perspectives and contingent possibilities. Instead of fatalistically saying that everything happens for a reason, a better approach is to initiate creative action and look for ways to bring something good out of tragedy or misfortune. When folks say it was meant to be or is God's will, they are often deep in the situation of struggling to accept something unacceptable such as the tragic accidental death of a child. We should give folks some credit for being able to use this kind of initial coping mechanism without taking their expressions literally. Another form of such resignation is to say "It is what it is." A common problem occurring here involves outsiders to a situation imposing the "meant to be" or "God's will" explanation in a way that doesn't take seriously enough the degree to which others are suffering.

Important as fairness and justice are, love is ultimately of greater value and importance. The age at which or the circumstances under which we die are not as important as the sense of being surrounded by love and compassion when we die. We are better off if we live in an awareness that life simply is not and cannot be totally fair in any quantitative sense of the term. We should never use this realization as an excuse for not trying to make the world as fair and just as possible, in the same way as we should not use the cliché that "God helps those who help themselves" as an excuse for not helping others. When we see life as a gift it can seem very petty to complain bitterly about the size of that gift.

It is said that the world doesn't owe us a living. The lesson is that we should appreciate the precious, pleasurable moments of life, no matter how many or few of them come to us. The awareness of the inevitable unfairness of life is actually very important, because being in touch with Reality is a good thing. If we go through life expecting it to be something it simply cannot be, we are bound to be miserable. That is part of what is meant when Buddhism tells us to avoid ignorant desires, desires that fly in the face of the way things are. It bears repeating that just because we want or think we need something, such as total and absolute fairness or a literal Father in Heaven, does not make it so.

One of the major problems that I have with common views of both heaven and reincarnation is that they envision any future life as basically more of the same. They smack of extreme wishful thinking. Reality is not created by mere wishful thinking. What we might like to have and what we can actually have can be totally different things. We want to be with our loved ones again, or to take care of unfinished business with the deceased (a valid concern addressed in the otherwise superstitious movie "The Sixth

Sense"). The emotional appeal of reunion or past life/future life thinking is easy to understand. It offers the prospect of eternal life in more or less the same world that we already know. When folks talk about who they were in a past life it seems clear that they are uncomfortable with the thought either of leaving or of being buried in this earth. They want to live and act forever upon its stage—not strut briefly upon it as Shakespeare described our sojourn here. We can't be blamed for entertaining such images, but alas, wishing doth not make it so. I see Buddhism as telling us that to wish for rebirth in another life or for an afterlife is to prolong suffering. It is better that we learn how to live with joy and grace in the eternal now.

The HBO television series "Big Love" portrayed an independent polygamous family in which the husband devoutly believes in the Mormon concept of celestial marriage. He believes that marriages and families can be "sealed for eternity" and that when it comes to marriage and children "the more the merrier." This husband is played by actor Bill Paxton. When Paxton was asked during an interview if he didn't think this belief system was a little crazy, he responded by suggesting that it was just as valid as any other religious belief system. But in the same interview he also mentioned a 2002 movie he had directed and starred in titled "Frailty." In this horror movie he plays a devout young widower who wakes up one night believing that God has chosen him to go around killing ordinary people whose bodies have been taken over by demons. He even forces his two young boys to help with this, and when one of them objects the plot gets very dark indeed.

Polygamy or polyandry may work well for some people in some cultures. But if such practices are based only on beliefs about the afterlife, is that a sensible way to make such major life decisions? Should people be encouraged to make big decisions based on dreams or hallucinations? The book and film "Prayers for Bobby" tells the heartrending story of a mother whose version of Christian beliefs caused such conflict with her gay son that he killed himself at age 20 by jumping off a freeway overpass into the path of an 18-wheel truck. She came to the conclusion (with which, sadly, I concur) that it was her misguided religious beliefs that killed her son.

The classic problem with religion is that there are in most respects no real standards of evidence for the beliefs. We give ourselves *carte blanche* to believe whatever we wish or whatever religious authority figures tell us. It is frequently said that you can prove anything with the Bible, and this is particularly true when every single word and sentence is seen as an equally authoritative Word of God. The situation is improved when Bible scholars make use of historical, archaeological, literary, and other critical methods to understand the human side of the holy book, and when they develop reasonably consistent principles of interpretation. But whenever there is a notion abroad that people can prove anything with the Holy Bible, the Bible loses all credibility. When it proves everything, it proves nothing. The same can apply to any literature deemed as sacred.

My students tend to agree with me when I suggest that people should be able to believe whatever they want to believe, as long as it works for them, as long as they are sincere, *and as long as their belief system in practice is good for humanity and the world as a whole.* But what if a belief is sincerely mistaken? What if we are kidding ourselves with wishful thinking? What if our beliefs do more harm than good? I have heard it said that religion is not so much Marx's opiate of the people as it is a placebo. Believing can sometimes seem to "make it so," but placebos tend to be of very limited value and can cause great harm when they are relied upon in place of modalities of treatment that have been scientifically proven to be effective. (Steve Jobs is reported to have regretted his forays into alternative medicine.)

A common hope for the next life is not only that it should be as much as possible like this one, but that it should also be totally perfect. But like absolute uniformity, absolute perfection would be unbelievably boring! The joke about two old duffers playing golf in heaven is worth repeating. One says to the other "You get a hole in one; I get a hole in one; you get a hole in one; I get a hole in one; WHAT'S THE POINT?!" I do a lot of fishing. Part of what makes fishing exciting is exactly what many people do not like about fishing—the sometimes long periods of waiting. But it is precisely the anticipation and waiting that makes the eventual "I got one!" exciting. There are at least two versions of the so-called Chinese curse: "Those whom the god's would punish, they grant their desires" and "Be careful what you wish for; you may get it."

In "Candide," Voltaire's reflections on "the best of all possible worlds" demonstrate what is wrong with abstract ideas of perfection. Similarly, Rabbi Kushner sees God as telling the biblical character Job how various notions of a more perfect world wouldn't work. If God exercised more control, what would happen to freedom? If God constantly exercised supernatural interference with the laws of nature, what would happen to the predictability of nature on which our sciences depend? One way or another, any truly desirable image of eternal bliss would have to somehow include elements of conflict, struggle, and challenge. As a movie buff I have played with the notion that heaven might be a place where painful versions of such conflicts would be like movies—all imaginary and entertaining rather than real. But this, too, still amounts to imagining a future life that would be more or less similar to the life we already know.

Hindu philosophy, by and large, does not view *karma/samsara* as something to be celebrated. In Hinduism this physical world is generally viewed as *maya*—illusion. Some would say that a fairly negative attitude toward life on earth is inevitable in the crowded, impoverished place that much of the Indian subcontinent has been during its history. A negative attitude toward any and all human desire pervades much of Hindu thinking. For example, consider this from the Maitri Upanishad Scripture: "In this foul-smelling, unsubstantial body, a conglomerate of bone, skin, muscle, flesh, semen, blood, mucus, tears, rheum, feces, urine, wind, bile, and phlegm, what is the good of the enjoyment of desires? In this body which is afflicted with desire, anger, covetousness, delusion, fear, despondency, envy, separation from what is desired, union with the undesired, hunger, thirst, old age, death, disease, sorrow, and the like, what is the good of the enjoyment of desires?" From this point of view salvation consists of rising above the world of illusion to the true spiritual reality where we experience the absolute divine oneness of all things, the union of Brahman and Atman (of Ultimate Reality and True Self). True spiritual consciousness erases all ignorant distinctions, desires, and any finite sense of self. This stands in stark contrast to the wishful thinking of those who see reincarnation as a wonderful way to keep on experiencing the world. *Samsara* literally means "to wander (across)" and the image is not that of a happy wanderer, but closer to that of a treadmill existence causing one to cry "stop the world, I want to get off!"

Nirvana

Nirvana is the Hindu answer to the question of our relationship to eternity. Nirvana is very different from the typical Western concept of heaven. It has been described in various ways as extinction, absorption, or ultimate God-consciousness. In general the belief is that the individual consciousness happily loses its individuality in an ultimate oneness with Reality, in the Seamless Whole. One popular image is of a flame joining the sun while a flame being blown out refers to extinction of the self (the Buddhist version which we will consider further in chapter 5 emphasizes extinction of the *ignorant craving* responsible for our misery and suffering). Another image for Nirvana is that of a drop going back into the ocean, or the more provocative and paradoxical notion that the drop absorbs the entire ocean of Divine Consciousness into itself. Walt Whitman celebrated this "Over-Soul" in his "Leaves of Grass" poetry, and along with New England transcendentalists like Ralph Waldo Emerson helped to bring this worldview to North America. Some think of Nirvana in a somewhat nihilistic way as a state of oblivion—in 1960s terminology "blissed out." As a generic term in popular idiom, nirvana has often been taken to mean a wished for but always unattainably sublime goal, something like a utopian version of Shangri La.

Jainism and Buddhism are two major reform movements that came out of Hinduism. Both rejected sacrifice, caste, and the absolute authority of the Vedic Scriptures. Buddhism is known for its theme of moderation. All desires are not bad. Only ignorant desires (cravings) for things we can't possibly have or can't possibly avoid are problematical. Jainism, from a word meaning conqueror (of desires), is known for its extremist notions of how to achieve victory over desires. Ironically, while Jains believe in extreme asceticism and self-denial as a spiritual path in this present world, their particular version of Nirvana—called Isatpragbhara—tends to be more affirming of the idea that separate individual souls have an eternal destiny. It is not surprising that within the Hindu worldview there would be many possible nuances regarding the ultimate eternal destiny, fulfillment, or transcendence of individual identity. To enter fully into God consciousness can be both to save and to lose one's life. When the famous mythology expert Joseph Campbell described the experience of heaven as "being so busy looking at God that you won't have time for your own experiences," it seemed to be more a description of Nirvana than of Heaven. But then, when the New Testament talks about one's life as being "hid with Christ in God," such language sounds more like Nirvana's Seamless Whole than Heaven's mansions and streets of gold. It is important to distinguish between concepts of Nirvana and Heaven in various ways, but also to recognize that the distinction is far from clear-cut or absolute.

The version of Nirvana that I find most compelling is that it is not a place or a destination of any kind. It is a present state of mind or consciousness, above all an awareness of the Seamless Whole (Shunyata)—an awareness that I am one with everything, that "I am the universe happening." It is very much like *realized eschatology* and *the eternal now*. Nirvana is the process of ending suffering by extinguishing wrongful and ignorant desires through insight into the nature of Reality. Among the most ignorant desires of all are the desire to survive death (the temptation to create what Ken Wilber calls "immortality symbols") and the related desire for absolute fairness and justice that we have been considering in this chapter. Dr. Hinkle tells of a therapy client who blurted out "It isn't fair!" Hinkle responded: "You're fifty years old and you're just figuring out that life is not fair! No wonder you're miserable. You are trying to have a kind of fairness you can't possibly have. You are trying to draw a square circle. It can't be done."

Facing reality involves becoming clear about what we cannot have just by wishing, about what we can and cannot control or change. This is another aspect of what it means to live in the moment. We do have many more options and choices for improving our lives than we might think we do, but there are also some things that we just can't do or have. This is the wisdom behind the serenity prayer which could also be stated as "Have the serenity to accept some things as impossible, the courage to do the possible, and the wisdom to know the difference."

The paradox of finding our ultimate, eternal, personal fulfillment by losing ourselves in what has been called "the beatific vision" (Campbell's "so busy looking at God") is another notion we find in biblical theology and mystical tradition that is similar to the concept of Nirvana. We might compare it to the experience of simultaneous orgasm with one's lover where the phrase "the two become one flesh" takes on real meaning. People tend to feel most fulfilled when they are making someone else happy. Think of how clearly we see the truth of the saying "better to give than to receive" when we look into the face of a child who has just given a homemade gift to a parent. Many long-married couples attribute their success to always trying to put the welfare of the other person first. In chapter 5 we will focus almost exclusively on this positive aspect of "losing self."

Paradox and Nihilism

There are great paradoxes in the philosophies of India. One of them has to do with the aforementioned notion that there is a strain of nihilism in these worldviews. A famous cave sculpture in Benares depicts a Divinity with three faces, one looking straight ahead and two on the sides looking in opposite directions. The sculpture is called the Mask of Eternity. Joseph Campbell explains that the two opposite facing heads represent the fact that everything in life comes in pairs of opposites—this and that, life and death, good and evil, being and non-being, past and future, thesis and antithesis, etc. The face in the middle looking straight ahead represents that we are to avoid being trapped or deluded by these opposites represented by the two faces on the sides. Instead of preferring one or the other, we are to accept that in some sense these are false dichotomies (something like the way in which eternity is not a dichotomy of "long time versus short time" but is about moving beyond the very concept of time). But in another sense we accept that life inevitably is made up of these opposites, and realizing this, we simply get on with it.

This way of looking at life is also typical of Taoism in China, and Elaine Pagels points out that much of the apocalyptic literature which did not get into the New Testament includes a similar affirmation of opposites—including feminine along with masculine religious imagery where both genders have positive and negative connotations. The usual objection to this affirmation of opposites asks how we can affirm evil, brutality, and suffering as equal to goodness, kindness and joy. The answer is "Reality!" Life is made up of these opposites, and although we may not value them equally, the sooner we get used to and accept them for what they are the better off we will be. Such awareness may not make us "happier," but facing the inescapable realities of life does have the potential to produce a profound sense of true well-being and serenity.

Those who accuse this approach to reality of being nihilistic typically argue that someone who just accepts everything would never try to change the world for the better—would not bother to resist brutality or an evil dictator, etc. If nothing we do will make any real difference in the long run, why bother? Part of the answer to these kinds of accusations is just to admit that there are indeed a lot of reasons to be nihilistic. We sometimes lament that "the more things change the more they stay the same." Politically, you throw out one set of rascals and another set comes in to take their place. Taoism teaches that it is folly to think that we have much ability to control or organize life. Taoists encouraged spontaneity and loved to make fun of the stuffy Confucian establishment. The book of Ecclesiastes in the Hebrew Bible proclaims "Vanity of vanities; all is vanity and a striving after wind." It is to the great credit of those who compiled the Hebrew Scriptures that they included this book of skeptical and cynical wisdom. Nihilism, skepticism and even occasional cynicism have their place. Ecclesiastes is very much in sync with the Buddhist realization that much of our suffering results from ignorant craving for things we either can't have (like a perfect world) or can't avoid (like death). We can't control everything to suit ourselves. We will never achieve absolute justice. We need to find pleasure in simple things.

But the three-faced Mask of Eternity reminds us that *everything* has its opposite, and the opposite of a nihilistic, fatalistic, or cynical approach to life is the activist mindset that gets involved in trying to change our lives and the world for the better! As with the struggle and relax (sense of moral urgency/sense of humor) paradox described in the previous chapter, this Indian approach to the "eternal round" encourages us to negotiate the back and forth between passivity and activism without losing our equilibrium. There can be times when we are very busy and excited trying to make a difference and times when we relax in serenity. There can be times when we think we have answers, and times when we think we have nothing but questions. We can move back and forth along the continuums of life not so much as a balancing act, but as actors on the world stage whose sense of equilibrium keeps them from going off the deep end in any direction, whatever those various deep ends might be, such as the opposite extremes of fanaticism and dilettantism.

The serenity-prayer tension we are considering can also be described as between the "is" and the "ought." When do we accept the way life in this world is, and when should we struggle to make things the way we think they ought to be? Disastrous personal and social consequences can come from beliefs and ethical systems that try to force the world to be the way we wish it to be when these wishes are out of touch with reality. Such wishful thinking can cause parents, for example, to reject their gay children—with multiple dire ramifications. Such parents wish life to be simple rather than complex and full of variety, not realizing that the real world of complexity and variety is much more interesting and fun than the boring world of predictability and simplicity that they think they want.

Another paradox found in various forms of Hinduism and Buddhism is also similar to the active/passive paradox of grace or faith described in chapter 2. In Zen Buddhism, for example, a person might put great effort into becoming enlightened only to discover that when enlightenment arrives it is experienced not as something earned or learned but as an "aha moment" that has "happened to" the person. Active seeking has led to passive receiving. Instead of earning a prize, the seeker receives a gift. Instead of grasping, we feel that we have been grasped.

It should be evident by now that the "letting go" aspect of all these paradoxes has a great deal of relevance to the subject of the individual's relationship to eternity. The theme is that we will be most in touch with eternity if we stop trying to grasp or hold onto eternity. This is the insight behind such phrases as "Let go and let God," "Religionless Christianity,"

"The Beatific Vision," or theologian Paul Tillich's famous interpretation of eternal salvation as based on "Accepting your Acceptance." Whether looked at in a religious way or not, death is the ultimate form of giving up all our attempts at control—above all, the control of our relationship to eternity. Whether we think of "Goin' to live with God" in terms of Heaven, Nirvana, Eternal Life or Eternal Peace, I think we need to see the "goin'" as metaphorical. Joseph Campbell liked to say that if you don't know how to experience eternity in this present moment, you never will. In other words, you *can* and *should* experience the eternal, timeless Seamless Whole right here and now. According to Time magazine, the last words Steve Jobs spoke before he died were "Wow! Wow! Wow!" I'm sure some would like to think that he was having the beatific vision of heaven, but "eternity" is most generally understood as "beyond time and space"—a concept that does not necessarily allow us to jump to supernatural conclusions. Perhaps we should rephrase the expression as "goin' to *be* with God"—a less "grasping" image of our relationship to eternity—and similar to the Spanish *adios* (go with God).

In his televised "Power of Myth" interviews with Joseph Campbell, Bill Moyers asked him what his understanding of heaven might be. Seeming to accept that heaven could be a meaningful concept, Campbell replied, as we noted earlier: "I think that in heaven you will be so busy looking at God that you won't have time for your own experiences." Considering his original Roman Catholic background, it is not surprising that Campbell would come up with this version of a "beatific vision"—which also, not surprisingly, makes heaven sound more like nirvana. I see Campbell as suggesting that we *imagine* death as an eternal beatific vision. This nirvana-like imagery is found especially in Colossians 3:3 where the author, who is "Pauline" if not actually St. Paul, suggests that Christians should think of themselves as already dead ("you have died") and of their life as "hid with Christ in God." This image of eliminating the distinction between life and death and of one's life as being hid with Christ in God sounds much more like nirvana than heaven! It clearly is in sync with the idea that we should live each moment in timeless awareness (realization) of the eternal now.

Imagining a journey to one or many next lives is not the only way to transcend death. Simply to live and die with spiritual serenity may well be the ultimate art of living and dying well, the best way to sing a song of life that transcends death.

CHAPTER 4

Evidence and Life after Death

WE HAVE SEEN SOME of the ways in which morality and mortality are related factors in religion. By contrast we should note that the ancient Egyptians certainly weren't overwhelmed with moral concern when they buried their royalty surrounded with vast treasures for the afterlife while large portions of the population barely managed to stay alive in this world. (Is there a modern parallel in the ability of immensely wealthy families to bequeath enormous fortunes to sometimes apparently undeserving or irresponsible descendants, while a vast number of everyday working people barely manage to survive?) Polls consistently show that a significant number of people who say they believe in God also say that they do *not* believe in life after death. Many even say that they definitely *want* death to be the absolute end of their lives. We will now consider as a distinct matter the underlying question of whether life after death is even a possibility. It is one thing to discuss various versions of belief in life after death. It is another thing to consider the very possibility or impossibility of life after death.

Evidence

The question of whether there is or can be anything even close to solid evidence for life after death is not easily answered. The quip about absence of evidence not being evidence of absence is clever, but it too easily gives people *carte blanche* to believe anything. Let us consider now some scientific, philosophical, and theological aspects of evidence and proof. Since it seems clear that Christianity has put more emphasis on "Resurrection of the dead "than have other religious traditions, keeping in mind what we learned in chapter 2 about the nature of the New Testament, we will first explore whether biblical writers and editors provide us with any real evidence for life after death. Was their central resurrection story fact, myth, or something else?

Christianity has typically presented itself as a religion whose very existence is based on a supposed proof of life after death. Many Christians believe that unless the resurrection of Jesus is a literal fact of history, Christianity is bogus. The (Lutheran) novelist John Updike published a poem "Seven Stanzas at Easter" in the Christian Century magazine in 1961 which included these lines:

> "Make no mistake: if He rose at all
> It was as His body;
> If the cells' dissolution did not reverse, the molecules reknit,
> The amino acids rekindle,
> The church will fall . . .
> Let us not mock God with metaphor, analogy, side-stepping
> Transcendence; making of the event a parable, a sign
> Painted in the faded credulity of earlier ages . . . "

I find it troubling that a literary artist would be so critical of metaphor and parable. But Updike certainly does capture the mentality of what I call naive romantic literalism. In fairness it must be noted that he wrote the poem at a time when the insights of the historical-critical method of biblical studies were not as widely known and discussed as they have been since then, and as they will be considered in what follows here. (I am writing this just after Updike's death and I am not privy to what his later views might have been on this subject; I am aware that his pastor in 1961 was famously conservative theologically.) My frequent criticism of the notion that the resurrection of Jesus is a "uniquely unique" historical event now has to be coupled with another potent critique. Updike's poem raises the even more pertinent and, I think in this case, devastating issue of science. His image of cells, molecules and amino acids doing a sudden about face, flies in the face of any credible science. The "uniquely unique" argument is weak enough, but when religious believers arrive at conclusions which contradict everything basic science clearly shows us, it seems crystal clear that wishful thinking has taken over.

Early in her career, Elizabeth Kübler-Ross, author of *On Death and Dying*, generally avoided discussing life after death. But eventually she came out with the surprising statement that, beyond belief in life after death, she was now convinced by evidence, beyond a shadow of a doubt, that there was life after death. What was this evidence? She felt that the remarkable similarity of all the supposedly independent anecdotal stories about near-death-type experiences constituted proof of life after death. (The 2010 movie "Hereafter" refers to similar "evidence.") Contrary to what many folks might expect, a number of Christian theologians rushed to criticize her statement. Their point of view tended to be that if you make life after death a matter of scientific proof, then it is also open to being disproven. Removed from the realm of faith, they felt the reality of life after death would become less rather than more certain. But this reliance on faith as certainty is painfully and embarrassingly close to "blind faith" and, again, wishful thinking. We may like feeling free to believe whatever we want, but I doubt that such freedom in any way bolsters actual certainty—unless you are willing to equate head-strong stubbornness with certainty.

Some will probably conclude that I am encouraging believers to lose their faith. But it would be more accurate to understand that I am suggesting only that they *change* their faith! I am suggesting that they *believe in* messages, themes and values—perhaps above all in the value of solid, empirical evidence for ascertaining truth. Similarly, as human beings we are unlikely ever to lose our aggressive "fighting spirit." But we can *change* how we fight and what we fight for. We can replace violent fighting with an earnest fight and mutual struggle (the basic meaning of *jihad*) for peace, wholeness (shalom), fulfillment, and justice—for "life abundant" here and now. We can struggle to create a "kingdom" that is "not of this world" only in the sense that it is not like the empires based on oppression, domination and violence—not like the Roman empire whose violent nature was exposed in its crucifixion of people such as Jesus of Nazareth who clearly sided with the victims of wealth and power. Even a Superpower can be a benevolent power as long as it has the drive, determination and insight to use its resources in ways that benefit humankind and the planet.

The often quoted King James translation of Hebrews 11:1 describes faith as "the substance of things hoped for, the evidence of things not seen." But the more recent and arguably more accurate translation in the Revised Standard Version puts it this way: "Now faith is the assurance of things hoped for, the conviction of things not seen." This translation forces us to recognize that conviction and assurance is not the same thing as evidence. To rely on mere faith or arbitrary belief as the basis for accepting an astonishing assertion as true is dangerously close to the attitude of "My mind is made up; don't confuse me with facts." We are going to take a look at some facts that relate to the supposed biblical "evidence" for resurrection of the dead. This kind of analysis is indebted to the historical-critical method of biblical studies, a method I prefer to describe as "radical literalism" because it analyzes the Bible word for word and letter for letter, using all the scientific techniques of historical and literary detective work to understand the human side of how the Bible came to be the kind of theological literature that it is. This approach traces the development of our human ideas about God and religion. (Karen Armstrong's early bestseller *A History of God*" would be more accurately titled "The History and Development of *Ideas about* God." Robert Wright's 2009 book *The Evolution of God* covers similar territory, blending in some Daniel Dennett-style scientific aspects of evolution.) As noted earlier, I recognize that this type of critical analysis does not necessarily prevent folks from interpreting the Bible as in some sense a "divinely inspired" Sacred Scripture. While I question the supernatural authority and special revelation of objective truth that is typically attributed to *holy books*, my appreciation of the spiritual value of such literature nevertheless remains high.

Most if not all early forms of religion wondered and speculated about what might happen to dead people. I think it is also safe to say that the limited "science" of earlier times made it easier to take the idea of life after death for granted. When Islam eventually followed in the footsteps of Judaism and Christianity, an afterlife of reward and punishment seems to have been accepted as a given. Considering this pre-scientific tendency to take some form of afterlife for granted, it is striking that the early Hebrew biblical tradition has not usually been thought of as emphasizing such belief. Jon D. Levenson, Professor of Jewish Studies at Harvard has written a number of books on the subject. Particularly helpful is his 2006 award winner *Resurrection and the Restoration of Israel—The Ultimate Victory of the God of Life*. This book argues that the roots of the developing Jewish belief in resurrection go back further and deeper than has usually been understood.

Levenson finds these roots in the psalms, in the Genesis theme of God as the ultimate source of all life, and in the theme of Sheol as a neutral "place of the dead" that significantly is never understood to be totally cut off from God. He finds more of these roots in the imagery of Ezekiel's valley of dry bones coming back to life as a symbol of the reconstitution of a defunct Jewish nation, and in the individual stories of Enoch and Elijah who are pictured as leaving the earth without dying. Despite seeing more roots than others have unearthed, Levenson nevertheless supports the common understanding that the idea of resurrection of individuals from the dead only becomes explicit in the book of Daniel at the time of the Maccabees around 164 BCE. He shows how these themes, variously developed in many rabbinic traditions, dovetail into the Christian belief in Jesus as the first fruits of a general resurrection of the dead.

While some within Judaism such as Levenson have emphasized the theme of resurrection, and others such as the author of Ecclesiastes in the Hebrew Bible and Rabbi Harold Kushner have not, the issue clearly is front and center in the Christian New Testament. In discussing this it is important to begin with the earliest Christian writings about resurrection. It will surprise many to learn that the earliest New Testament writing about resurrection are the letters (epistles) of the apostle Paul (originally named Saul of Tarsus) not the four Gospels titled Mark, Matthew, Luke, and John. I have named the Gospels in this order because there is broad consensus 1) that Mark is the earliest Gospel; 2) that Matthew and Luke largely copied from Mark; and 3) that John is a later work with striking differences from the other three Gospels. The fact that Matthew and Luke copied extensively from Mark explains the similarities between these three Gospels—usually called the "synoptics" because they present a "similar view" of Jesus. The fact that the differences between them often appear to be deliberate, suggests that these differences are not only a matter of witnesses and story-tellers having imperfect memories. These differences reflect variations in theology—different emphases and themes, as well as a variety of intended audiences in different locations.

Since the Gospels are not the earliest Christian writings about resurrection we will come back to them later. In 2012 Marcus Borg published *Evolution of the Word*, in my opinion a long-overdue New Testament and marvelous commentary with the "books" placed in the order in which they were likely written! Borg's commentary describes how both the New Testament and "Jesus as the Christ" *evolved* (see again my section on Midrash in chapter 2). Borg also makes it clear that the names of these gospels were attached later, after the early Jesus movement became aware of the existence of different gospels which they needed to distinguish from each other. The likelihood that the title does not indicate actual authorship is the reason why I consistently write, for example, "the Mark Gospel" rather than "The Gospel of Mark."

The secretive and still mysterious "mystery religions" such as those associated with the Persian cult of Mithra, show us that the theme of dying and rising Gods was nothing new in the larger world of Greek and Roman culture. It is also significant that the idea of holy warriors being rewarded in some version of paradise or afterlife was used by Homer in Greece before it was used either by the Maccabees around 164 BCE or by

Mohammed and his followers in the seventh century CE. In his 1958 Ingersoll lecture, Werner Jaeger suggests that "Poetry is man's immortality . . . it will make him survive in song so as to be known to future generations." Jaeger recognizes an irony in giving life heroically in order to achieve immortality. (You value life so much that you throw it away?) We might well wonder to what degree the New Testament gospels are picking up on this same theme when they picture Jesus as saying that those who lose their lives for his sake or for the sake of the gospel will actually find or save their lives. By contrast, in chapter 5 we will be considering the possibility that this interplay of saving and losing life is similar to the Buddhist understanding of emptiness or "no-self."

St. Paul and John Dominic Crossan

Before the gospel stories of Jesus were ever written, St Paul's letters to the churches in Thessalonica and Corinth expounded on the theme of resurrection. The letter of the apostle Paul titled First Thessalonians (about 50 AD) is most likely the earliest of all the New Testament writings—in a virtual tie with First Corinthians and possibly Galatians. A key word throughout Paul's epistles and some others is the Greek word "*parousia.*" A two-part word perhaps best rendered as "being again," *parousia* usually meant arrival, or return, or some kind of special visitation. New Testament scholar John Dominic Crossan argues that Paul uses the word as a metaphor based on the arrival of an emperor or other visiting dignitary at a city. All indications are that Paul probably never heard stories of Jesus coming out of a tomb or ascending to heaven on a cloud. Paul's experience of the risen Jesus, whom he had never met "in the flesh," is a vision of Jesus in heaven. Paul expects Jesus to return to this world. In his letter to the Thessalonians he writes that at this return "the dead in Christ will rise first. Then we who are alive . . . will be caught up in the clouds together with them to meet the Lord in the air; and so we will be with the Lord forever" (1 Thess 4:17).

This passage is the one most frequently quoted by the followers of nineteenth century British preacher John Darby who have cobbled together a bizarre "Rapture" theology, combining images such as this one about meeting the Lord in the air with convoluted readings of other symbolic or obscure biblical references, taken out of context. In order to make this "dispensationalist" system of a distinct series of "ages" hang together, dubious gaps, sometimes of thousands of years, are read into an artificial biblical chronology (see *The Rapture Exposed: The Message of Hope in the Book of Revelation*, by Barbara R. Rossing, 2004). Similar to rapture theology is "Christian Zionism" which supports modern Israel, not because it empathizes with the plight of Jews throughout history, but because it believes that the nation of Israel must be re-established before God's kingdom can come and destroy all nonbelievers—including all Jews who do not convert to Christianity!

Crossan suggests that the "return" in First Thessalonians 4:17 is a metaphor based on the fact that a visiting emperor would first encounter places of burial when approaching a city. This meeting of the dead would be followed by greeting the living inhabitants. Crossan contends that the image of being caught up in the clouds and meeting the Lord in the air should not be literalized. (Even "resurrection literalist" N. T. Wright agrees that this image is metaphorical.) As a visiting dignitary would enter a city, says Crossan, so Paul visualizes Christ as "being again" in a transformed world. The central point is that those who follow "The Way" of Jesus are already participating in a transforming world, being born again or raised as "a new creation" (2 Cor 5:16–18). Paul's main theme, for Crossan, is that Jesus' Way is primarily about transforming this world by resisting the Roman model of achieving peace through violent conquest and oppressive power, replacing it with the Christ-centered model of achieving peace by promoting justice and love!

Metaphorically based or not, the stark and unmistakable fact is that this first-to-be-written book of the eventual New Testament canon forces us to admit that Paul was mistaken in his expectation of an imminent, literal return of Jesus to this world! Two thousand years later and counting, talk of "any day now" has become little short of ridiculous. Paul's agreement with the notion in 1 Cor 7:1–31 (written around the same time as 1 Thess) that followers of Jesus should not bother to get married because the end is near, makes it crystal clear how wrong he was about this. The latter books of the New Testament canon demonstrate the ongoing attempt to hedge on the idea of "soon" or "near," as we saw in chapter 2. That Paul's literalism was mistaken, however, does not mean that the more than literal meaning of what he envisioned was wrong or useless!

To affirm Jesus as Lord (*Kyrios*—Master, Leader) challenged the Roman emperors who were *Sons of God* borne by human (virgin) mothers. Paul proclaimed "Lord Jesus" as an alternative Son of God. It was years later that the Luke and Matthew Gospels used the "virgin birth" idea to bolster the Lordship of Jesus (the Matthew version less effectively because it confusingly traces the genealogy of Jesus through a human father named Joseph, and mistakenly uses the translation of Isaiah's word "young woman" as "virgin"). The "John" who authored the eventually canonized book of Revelation (there are many other apocalyptic books) agreed completely with St. Paul's opposition to the brutal Roman empire, but somewhat like the Matthew Gospel, he apparently saw Paul's religious and cultural accommodation with Gentiles as compromising the integrity of the Jesus-as-Jewish-Messiah movement rather than as an effort to win non-Jews over to a different vision for humanity. Elaine Pagels thinks this "John of Patmos" did not yet identify with the new term "Christian" and still supported Torah "purity laws." The tension between Jewish and Gentile followers of Jesus ("Christian" might have originally been a nickname) was a huge issue in the early movement before it had become an institutional church with bishops, elders, and deacons. In his epistle to the Romans, Paul repeatedly insists that Jewish and Gentile converts must never feel superior to one another.

Crossan views spirituality as an ongoing process of both social and personal transformation. Life is not about reaching static goals, so it need not bother us that supernatural notions of the future possibly entertained by Paul or Jesus about miraculous interventions, or about living forever in a next life after death, might never materialize. Crossan suggests we should be satisfied with Paul's poetic metaphor of death as being at home "with the Lord forever," and content to live a future-oriented, compassionate life in the eternal now of realized eschatology. (I had originally intended to do my graduate work with the noted process theologian Daniel Day Williams at Union Seminary in New York City because this kind of process approach has always made good sense to me.)

It is indeed a hugely important question about the historical Jesus whether he has to be seen mainly as an eschatological, apocalyptic (revealing/uncovering) prophet who expected an imminent "end of the age," a divine, supernatural intervention in the trajectory of the world. Even though Jesus is pictured as saying that nobody, not even he, knows the exact day or hour of "the restoration of the Kingdom" (Acts 1:7), it could be that the historical Jesus did expect it fairly soon. The Jesus of Mark and Matthew categorically insists that "this generation will not pass away till all these things take place" (Mark 13:30; Matthew 24:34).

Underestimating the variety of beliefs held by Pharisees, Essenes and other groups such as the insurrectionist Zealots, as well as the difficulty if not impossibility of creating a consistent portrait of the historical Jesus based on such complex, convoluted, inconsistent, revised and redacted oral and written traditions—some of which he has described as *forged*—Bart Ehrman insists that Jesus and Paul were indeed part of a literal eschatological, apocalyptic movement. He says we must admit that they were just plain wrong—that, to be painfully blunt, their vision of a soon-to-come "new age" was delusional. (Considering their status under the heel of Rome, their apocalyptic beliefs might more fairly be seen as something akin to what we today would call a "Hail Mary pass.") I see a parallel in this kind of audacious hope with followers of Tolstoy, or with Marxists who for over a hundred years have been predicting the advent of a revolution toward true justice "just around the corner," and working to bring it about. When folks say "as slow as the second coming of Christ" instead of "as slow as molasses in January" they are expressing cynicism about supernatural apocalyptic mythology. I think we clearly need to outgrow this kind of supernatural apocalyptic (wishful thinking) scenario which is now as outmoded as the image of the sun standing still. We must focus instead on the kind of down-to-earth realized eschatology of process and transformation (or perhaps even some form of revolution) that Crossan describes.

Crossan and Borg echo what I see as a majority opinion that the very earliest layers of gospel traditions and stories about Jesus do not picture him as expecting a supernatural apocalypse—that it was the "post-Easter Movement" (in the context of the Jewish wars with Rome) which developed some of these images of Jesus. In his book *Forged*, Ehrman joins the chorus of those questioning whether letters such as Second Thessalonians were actually written by Paul, partly because they reflect confusion as to whether the transformations associated with resurrection are to come soon or at a later time, and Ehrman thinks Paul always thought it would happen very soon.

The bottom line here is that the New Testament and other early Christian writings present conflicting views on eschatological expectations and understandings of "the Kingdom of God"—which makes it both possible and necessary for us to choose the understanding that makes the most sense in our modern/postmodern world! Crossan's view is based to a significant degree on the sections of the Matthew and Luke Gospels that almost certainly were copied from an unknown earlier written source, dubbed "Q" for the German word *Quelle* (Source). This material, that likely is some of the earliest in the canonical gospels, has lent support to Crossan's thesis that the historical Jesus was essentially an itinerant, charismatic sage and healer who preached a not always well-received inclusive and egalitarian message of love and compassion. His life has most meaning for us because it was basically about countering the crucifying violence of the Roman Way with his Way of promoting distributive justice, peace, and the full humanization, healing, and salvation of humankind through reconciling, compassionate love for others—even for enemies, for other forms of life, and for ourselves ("love your neighbor *as you love yourself*"). Elaine Pagels explains that the author of the New Testament book of Revelation was a similarly passionate Jewish Christian, writing in wartime (around 90 AD) using a panoply of traditional symbolism, who is basically very angry at Rome for killing peace-loving and compassionate activists such as Jesus, Peter, James, and many other Jewish followers of Jesus.

In his book *God, Mystery, Diversity* (1996) Gordon Kaufman broadens the Christian message about a divine messiah: "Though centering on the man Jesus, the Christ-symbol is regarded as referring not only to this solitary figure but to the larger community of reconciliation that grew up in response to his work—and in principle, thus, it can be extended to all similar communities of genuine healing, love, and justice." Kaufman helps us see clearly the kind of inclusive vision that has the power to inspire a dynamic postmodern spirituality!

Literal messianic and apocalyptic ideas in our global, nuclear age are irrational and dangerous. That both Jesus and St. Paul may have had false apocalyptic expectations or may have believed in afterlife must not obscure the more basic and salient theme of realized eschatology. Looking forward to a coming new age encourages us to challenge any dysfunctional *systems* like that of Rome rather than merely to tweak the status quo with well-intended relief work. Realized eschatology is *a process version of apocalypticism,* the process of participating fully in the eternal now. The biblical motif of recurring advent puts the focus on process. The image of darkness being deepest just before the dawn can also be a helpful apocalyptic metaphor. Realized, participatory eschatology means we actually can celebrate the complex process which produced the often difficult and confusing jumble of mythic storytelling in the New Testament and other early Christian literature—storytelling that has challenged, enlightened, and guided much of the world for over two thousand years.

Reframing Themes and Spinning Stories

Rather than dismissing Jesus and Paul wholesale as delusional, we need to reframe themes, for example, the "Superman to the rescue" image of Jesus. "Jesus Christ Superstar" is artistic exaggeration, not fact. The image of Jesus as savior or rescuer can give the false impression that we are poor, helpless, and hopeless human beings, incapable of doing anything worthwhile. But this is not the condition from which we need to be saved. When Luther wrote about the "bondage of the will," or Schleiermacher wrote about our absolute dependency, they were saying in effect that we need to be saved from thinking we can go it alone—saved from denial about our nature as contingent beings dependent upon relationships. Ethically, we need to be saved from the Lone Ranger mentality which tells us that it is totally up to us as individuals to make ourselves and the world perfect. We need to be saved from ethical fanaticism, from religious zealotry, from fear-driven demagoguery, from magical and superstitious thinking.

Healthy spirituality does not encourage a "poor me" victim mentality, but it does encourage our dependence on relationships—what Buddhists call contingency. Jesus saves by connecting "God" with "compassionate love for your neighbor as for yourself" (a version of the Golden Rule). Self-esteem is, more accurately, about *valuing* yourself, and valuing yourself is about valuing your relationships with others and your contingent relationship with nature, the universe—your "ecological home." It is about having confidence in what you are capable of accomplishing, about having the courage to "take up the symbol of the cross" and follow Jesus in the humble way of compassion, justice, and peace. Being saved is about encouragement. We are saved not just *from* what is bad and destructive, but also saved *for* constructive engagement in all the facets and relationships of life. This way of thinking about salvation provides us with a more humanistic understanding of infant baptism as a symbol of our contingent, dependent relationships with other people, with the universe, and with the sacred.

On the subject of manipulating Scripture to create outlandish scenarios that sometimes have significant political implications I think we should take note of Jeff Sharlet's 2008 book *The Family: The Secret Fundamentalism at the heart of American Power*. Sharlet describes The Family as promoting an Ayn Rand or Machiavellian type of elitism that is the polar opposite of "victim mentality." This elitism suggests that Jesus slyly said different things to different audiences. According to the politicians who espouse this brand of religious fundamentalism, Jesus may at times have expressed an ethic of empathy for the poor and oppressed, but Jesus also promoted elite political and economic power in the service of free enterprise, success, wealth—and clout! (This attitude is similar to Rev. Moon's theology of communism as the devil's way and free enterprise capitalism as God's way—and also similar to preachers who sometimes promise cash-money blessings to believers "because God wants you to be successful.") It was folks coming from this particular fundamentalist perspective who first created the presidential prayer breakfasts during the Eisenhower administration. They like to point to a figure such as King David who had committed murder and other grievous sins and yet was used by God to accomplish great things. They like to talk about what God wants but, honestly, their transparent goal clearly is to bolster their own power trips.

We should do our best to understand what was really going on when Christian theology and traditions were being created, but we should not overestimate our ability to sort out every fact and metaphor. We need to debate the merits of various notions about the historical Jesus and Paul, but we must focus mainly on what to do now with such ancient religious traditions. We need artful yet honest interpretations that effectively address the spiritual situation of contemporary people.

Leaving aside, and to some degree counteracting, apocalyptic interpretations of Jesus and Paul, we now turn to Paul's first letter addressing the church he helped to establish in Corinth. *First Corinthians* contains the earliest lengthy discussion of the "resurrection" of Jesus that we have. Contained primarily in what was eventually numbered Chapter 15, there are four major points that must be underscored. *First*—what is the nature of the *resurrection appearances* that Paul describes? He uses the term eyewitnesses, but eventually puts himself "as one untimely born" in the same category with all these eyewitnesses, including "the twelve" (the story of Judas as betrayer likely was created later by followers of Jesus who were being kicked out of synagogues). The problem is that by all accounts Paul's experience was a *vision* of Jesus in heaven. By equating his visionary experience with that of the eyewitnesses, Paul in effect calls into question the nature of these appearances. Furthermore, the word translated as "appearance" is more accurately rendered as "made manifest," which has a less literal and more visionary connotation. Among other reasons Paul gives us to doubt that his understanding of resurrection has to do with the appearance of a revivified corpse is his use of metaphor and simile, especially when he writes about baptism as being crucified with Christ, daily death and resurrection so "we too might walk in newness of life (Romans 6:3–4), and "spiritual bodies." It is vital to remember that Paul likely never heard stories about an empty tomb or a bodily ascension of Jesus into heaven.

Second—in presenting the resurrection of Jesus as the first fruits of a general resurrection to come, Paul uses what seems like a backwards argument. Two quasi-religious/political groups, the Pharisees and the Sadducees, had long argued about whether there is any such thing as resurrection of the dead. (Many stories in the Gospels picture Jesus as being involved in these debates.) As someone who says he was associated with the Pharisaic movement, we would expect Paul to claim that the argument has now been settled because we have a case study, an actual example of a resurrection in the case of Jesus. But instead of arguing primarily from the specific instance of Jesus being raised from the dead to the general belief in resurrection, Paul's argument is that one first has to believe in general that resurrection is possible before one can believe that Jesus has been raised! This reversal or absence of the "case study" line of argument that one would expect is a dramatically revealing admission that resurrection for Paul is not a mere historical fact that somehow proves his assertions about "the risen Christ"!

Third—when Paul takes up the issue of what a resurrected person is, he struggles to come up with metaphors. His most physical one is that of a seed "dying" as it sprouts and becomes something greater. The Greek word often translated as risen or resurrected is more precisely the image of awakening—Jesus is pictured as waking from the sleep of death and being elevated to a new life in heaven. Paul's ultimate image is that "resurrection" is about becoming a "spiritual body." Such a notion is clearly paradoxical— a "non-bodily body." In Greek there are two words that can be translated as "body." One is *sarx* which is more accurately translated as "flesh." The other is *soma* which tends to refer to "body" in a more abstract or holistic sense. The paradox of a spiritual body is the best Paul can come up with to avoid both the over-spiritualized notion of the "immortality of the soul," and the overly physical notion of resurrected flesh. The eventual Christian doctrine of "the resurrection of the body" tries to avoid the Manichaean dualism which sees only spiritual reality as good and all physical reality as evil or unreal. (Paul does use the word immortality, but not immortality "of the soul.") Christian doctrine tried to express that there is something of eternal value or significance in that category which we describe with words such as form, shape, body, physical, material, substance, identity— although, as we will soon see, attempts to specify the nature of a "spiritual body" can lead us into ridiculous absurdities. Many contemporary

Christian theologians typically say simply that resurrection involves "the real you." When Bart Ehrman discusses this in *Jesus Interrupted* he seems surprisingly unaware of the distinction between *sarx* and *soma*. His discussion of "bodily" resurrection in an apocalyptic context seems to ignore both Paul's use of the paradoxical term "spiritual body" and Paul's insistence that resurrection is not about a reanimation of mere "flesh and blood." Some see resurrection as being about a shift in consciousness that transforms our perception of reality. Paul seems to envision a fluid relationship between matter, life, and consciousness in a way that only the most far-out theoretical physicists might find even vaguely credible.

Fourth—when Paul makes the bold and unequivocal statement that "flesh and blood cannot inherit the Kingdom of God" he seems to me (pardon the pun) to put the nail in the coffin of any notion that resurrection is about corpses coming back to life, flying through the air, or making literal journeys to heaven. In short, "Jesus is not Dracula!" For Crossan and Borg, Jesus "raised" essentially means Jesus *vindicated* as Lord rather than Caesar! For Professor Thomas Sheehan, what survives death is not Jesus but his Word, his message about "thy Kingdom (empowerment) come on earth." Neither physical nor spiritual "supernatural kingdoms" have much credibility in our postmodern world. The concept and reality of living in the eternal now of realized eschatology, however, can remain as a legacy of these artistic theological imaginings.

Turning now to the gospel stories, we must first remember how much later they were written than the letters of Paul, and how long after the presumed lifetime of Jesus, in a world without printing presses or other media technology. Next, for our purposes here I will be content to mention only that the discrepancies between the various accounts of the resurrection of Jesus strongly suggest that those who wrote and edited these stories and who canonized them as Scripture did not necessarily expect us to take it all as literal fact. Recall also what was said in chapter 2 about these gospels as theological portraits rather than biographies, and about the probability that Jesus is to some degree a semi-fictional character artistically created out of scenes, themes, and metaphors from the Hebrew Bible. One of the most startling yet often under-appreciated things in the parable about the rich man and poor Lazarus (Luke 16:19–31) is that Jesus ends the parable with these words: "If they do not listen to Moses and the prophets, neither will they be convinced *even if someone rises from the dead*" (italics added). This purports to be Jesus himself suggesting in effect that a resurrection from the dead would prove nothing!

One of the most significant things we must notice is the tendency of all these Gospel accounts to waver back and forth between presenting the resurrected Jesus as both physical and not physical. He is pictured as eating a fish or asking Thomas to touch his scars, but then he walks through walls or disappears suddenly. He seems willing to convince Thomas with evidence, but then praises those who have not seen any solid evidence and yet believe. This ambiguity is enhanced by the clearly theological and liturgical nature of some stories. Perhaps the best example of this ambiguity is the story in the Luke Gospel (24:13–35) where the risen Jesus is (strangely!) unrecognized as he compellingly describes a new interpretation of Messiah to a pair of grieving disciples walking on the road to Emmaus. But then when he enters their home and blesses the meal he is finally recognized only to vanish suddenly. This is clearly symbolic of Jesus as the unseen guest at the Eucharistic (Communion) Meal which, by the time this Gospel was written, likely had already become a defining ritual of the early Jesus movement. N. T. Wright turns all this ambiguity and inconsistency on its head, bizarrely insisting that the sheer ridiculously consistent oddity of these stories is what suggests that they really happened. I can only respond: "Nice try."

Bishop Spong has perhaps been the most direct in suggesting what really may have happened historically with Jesus and his followers. Spong theorizes that after Jesus was crucified, his followers, probably led by Peter, eventually realized how their experience with Jesus was so divinely inspiring that they could not let this "transforming peace movement" die. So they came out of hiding in the north and returned to Jerusalem, probably in autumn during the festival of Tabernacles (also known as Sukkoth or Feast of Booths), to proclaim that both Jesus and his movement were still alive. To put it in the words of a modern day folksong they were saying in effect "You can't kill me, I've already died!" Any reader who wants to follow up on Spong's evidence and arguments for his scenario should read his book *Resurrection: Myth or Reality?* In it he outlines his reasons for suggesting that the Palm Sunday story is actually about this brave return of the disciples from Galilee to Jerusalem in the fall, six months or so after the crucifixion. His evidence includes, but is certainly not limited to, an analysis of how the story of Jesus cursing a fig tree for not having fruit would make sense in autumn but not in the spring, the dubious use of "three days and nights" or "*after* three days" symbolism in the Gospel stories, how details of the fall Tabernacles festival fit with the Palm Sunday narratives, and how so many of the Easter narratives are connected with

Galilee rather than with Jerusalem. Spong's 2009 book *Eternal life: A New Vision,* updates his earlier insights.

So, what we do have evidence for is the changed behavior of those who became part of the Jesus Movement. *It was this movement that was resurrected! Movements take a licking and keep on ticking. Easter (creating the post-Easter Jesus) was more a process than an event.* Even many quite traditional Christian theologians have said that the best evidence for the resurrection of Jesus is not empty tomb stories but the emboldened lives of his followers in the face of violent forces and oppressive systems.

Immortality versus Resurrection

Another book we must consider at this point is the classic *Immortality and Resurrection,* an edited collection of four Ingersoll Lectures from the late 1950s subtitled "Death in the Western World: Two Conflicting Currents of Thought." This lectureship series at Harvard on "The Immortality of Man" began in 1864. The opening lecture/essay by German theologian Oscar Cullmann is titled "Immortality of the Soul or Resurrection of the Dead?" Cullmann illustrates his first point by focusing on the different ways in which the deaths of Socrates and Jesus are pictured. Socrates is calm because he believes that his soul will never die and is being released from the prison-house of the body. Jesus on the other hand is distraught, not just because of the manner of his death, but because he sees death as absolute and as total separation from God. Cullmann goes on to describe the New Testament notion of Resurrection as a miracle in which God raises a person back to an exalted form of life after that person has been one hundred percent dead. Both soul and body are dead. There is not an immortal part of the person that survives. Immortality of the soul is based on the type of Manichaean ethical dualism (evident in some forms of Christian Gnosticism and in the recently discovered Gospel of Judas) that sees the entire material world as basically evil, corrupt, and worthless. By contrast, Cullmann insists that God's material creation including the human body, while corrupted by sin, is essentially good and can be redeemed by God. Jesus is the very first resurrected "spiritual body" so resurrection is already here, but it is also "not yet" because we still die and all of our personal resurrections, and the resurrection of a new world, must wait until the end time of final judgment.

This idea of both personal and creation-wide resurrection is sometimes described by picturing death as a defeated enemy. Other provocative images picture death itself as being cast into a lake of fire or as being *eaten* (swallowed up) by God! Death is not a friend, and for this reason we are right to "rage against the dying of the light." But the view of folks such as Cullmann is that death is indeed defeated by God, who is able to raise the essential person (a "spiritual body"), a person in continuity with the former self. What is resurrected is "the real you," and ultimately the universe as a whole is restored. But while this "immortality project"—as Ken Wilber would describe it—is clearly different from the Greek notion of the immortality of the soul, it is important to remember that the New Testament was originally written in Greek, so that when Christian theology talks about the resurrection of the body it is using the Greek notion of *soma* (body) as opposed to *sarx* (flesh). This use of the more general or metaphorical Greek word for "body" suggests that resurrection is not to be understood merely as the resuscitation of a corpse.

However, we are left wondering what fleshless bodies, or what Cullmann calls "incorruptible matter," might be—as well as wondering whether this isn't all just clever wordplay. If we use the phrase resurrection "of the dead" rather than "of the body," I suppose the idea of resurrection as "miraculous re-creation" could be imagined as something like a new Big Bang in which our former consciousness is given new life. But while this might seem like a logical possibility in terms of rather dubious theoretical physics, I venture to say that it is almost certainly impossible. How would the new consciousness have continuity with the old? I have seen studies where interviewees ascribed more consciousness to corpses than to brain-dead people who were technically still alive in a vegetative state. The likely explanation for this is that once the person is completely dead, we can more easily allow our imagination to take flight. The Ingersoll lecture of 1956 by Harry Wolfson follows up on Cullmann's lecture by taking us through the philosophical machinations of the early Church Fathers over the notion of "spiritual body," machinations which to my mind become about as ridiculous as arguing about how many angels can dance on the head of a pin. The bottom line to me is that while imaginative metaphors are fine, imagining a literal reality that goes way beyond even the most bizarre science fiction is hard to take seriously.

We must note again that parts of the New Testament reflect a desire of some early Christians to emphasize the actual physical resurrection of the flesh. Elaine Pagels has pointed out that the fleshly suffering of Jesus and of so many martyrs provoked a desire also to be rewarded with a resurrection in the flesh. By contrast she observes that some Gnostic and related "heresies" tended to stress a more symbolic, metaphorical, or "transformation" understanding of resurrection, an understanding also supported by many things we have noted in the New Testament such as St. Paul's clear assertion that "flesh and blood cannot inherit the kingdom of God" (1 Cor:15:50). My perspective is that typical versions or understandings of being resurrected into some "other" supernatural world or dimension are untenable and out of date in our postmodern world. I think the way forward is shown by those such as Crossan and Borg who understand resurrection theology as the vindication and validation not only of Jesus, but of all who endeavor to make this a better world here and now—thereby revealing also a more realistic and honest way of dealing with mortality. The cross and crucifix make for strange jewelry because they are like a hangman's noose or an electric chair. But while the cross does remind us of violent systems of oppression and domination, its enduring celebration as a reminder also of resurrection (renewal, transformation, vindication) makes it a dramatic symbol of hope that love and compassion can ultimately prevail!

Cullmann's own approach to the "spiritual body" issue involves an arguably valid attack on the ethical and philosophical dualism which sees all aspects of the material world as essentially evil. He tries to explain how the good aspect of the physical body (*soma*) can be resurrected as the sin-infected flesh (*sarx*) rots, because he wants to affirm the significant tradition that God's original material creation is blessed with eternal value and significance. But he clearly gives the troubling impression that if mankind had not sinned, death would never have become a reality. His interpretation of the so-called fall into sin seems to be that before the fall it was intended that all persons born on this earth would stay alive in their original bodies forever—a "logical" notion if one reads Genesis literally, yet ultimately absurd! Other interpreters suggest that the story is ambiguous, and that as childbirth and labor were only to become more painful and difficult than they were before the fall, so death would only become more fearsome than it would have been before the fall. Since the tree of life associated with immortality is never mentioned until after the fall, some feel it is unclear whether the presence of this tree says anything about Adam and Eve being immortal before the fall. The question of whether death would have been possible in an original paradise raises a more basic problem with the (Persian, not Hebrew!) word "paradise" itself, because it suggests a state of primeval perfection totally incompatible with the evolutionary model of development from simple to ever more complex manifestations and adaptations.

The (scientifically discredited) idea of a perfect, original, literal, historical paradise would seem to raise the question of whether a God who couldn't get it right the first time around would be able to do so with a second try! This "second try" includes for Cullmann all the traditional and fairly literal doctrines of sin, atonement, and so forth, and culminates in the idea that only at the very end of actual history, the "end of the world—or ages," at the last judgment, will all saved souls and bodies reunite in relationship to both a new heaven and a new earth—a second chance creation or paradise that presumably this time will not be able or allowed to go wrong. He recognizes that many prominent theologians object to his suggestion that "souls sleep" while waiting for this reunion of body and soul at the end time. He tries to soften this interim period of those who "die in Christ before the end" by describing it vaguely as a time of "special nearness to God." He rejects Karl Barth's solution to the problem which claims that the dead are no longer in the realm of time, a solution which actually does recommend itself because the concept of eternity means "beyond time," as opposed to "forever" which refers to time that never ends. The notion of soul sleep could be seen as resurrecting the image of "eternal rest," which as noted earlier may be a more honest way of depicting our relationship to eternity.

Of the many questions that are begged by Cullmann's analysis, one that stands out is why Jesus doesn't have to wait to receive his spiritual body when everyone else has to wait? His answer to this and many other questions is typically: The Holy Spirit! Jesus as Christ is "with" and "in" God but is also near to all the living and to the sleeping dead in the form of the Holy Spirit. How convenient. Once you have a spiritual entity on board you are freed from the bonds of your otherwise concrete historical, metaphysical, and biological presuppositions. It is true that the New Testament does describe resurrection in terms of "life in the Spirit," but when the Spirit is concretized as the third person in a Trinitarian concept of God, even more vexing questions are raised. The bottom line for me is that none of the theologizing that Cullmann does about resurrection is anything other than speculation based on unproven assertions made by the New Testament writers. We are going to see in the rest of this chapter other "spiritual vagaries" that give far too much leeway for turning our wishes into realities.

In my view, Cullmann's scheme is both a masterful summary of classical biblical thinking about resurrection, and an illustration of why such resurrection theology must be seen as closer to the realm of art than of fact. He reads the Bible too much as pure history, taking it all too literally as if the Bible contained some higher form of science (knowledge). Santayana wrote: "Poetry raised to its highest power is then identical with religion grasped in its inmost truth." Krister Stendahl liked to quote the Swedish proverb: "Theology is poetry plus, not science minus"—meaning that religion must not denigrate science and its empirical methods, and that religion is basically an intense form of poetic art which tries to express truths greater than mere words can convey. Such poetic truth can be likened to scientific truth not in the sense that it is a higher form of scientific truth, but rather in its ability to help us live well in the real world and to influence our practical, ethical behavior in the eternal now. I very much appreciate Cullmann's validation of the material, physical world (the Creation) as good. But I would rather he had seen this in terms of validating the scientific, empirical, materialist understanding of reality!

Cullmann's "neo-orthodoxy" is science minus. Despite its detailed attempt to pin down the logic of New Testament resurrection theology, it provides no real evidence for life after death and actually appears to deny everything that true science tells us about the realities of life and death, change and evolution. He theologizes as if he is dealing with concrete facts that other approaches get wrong, but then he says we can "admire" other views and admits that the New Testament writers (as we've noted) are not always consistent in presenting the view he espouses.

Cullmann is particularly critical of Rudolf Bultmann's existential (art-like) approach to New Testament theology. He may be more or less on the mark in his distillation of New Testament resurrection theology, but when he presents his analysis as an attempt to discern the definitive *facts* about life after death he *mistakenly equates evidence about textual matters of New Testament interpretation with empirical evidence about Reality.* He also suffers from what Stendahl, editor of this Ingersoll collection and former dean of Harvard Divinity School, called theological hardening of the arteries—and what Joseph Campbell called "getting stuck in our metaphors." Yet I spy a potential for his rehabilitation when he says that perhaps the best portrayal of the resurrected Jesus is to be found in a famous painting by Grunewald. Cullmann ends his response to critics (who seem mainly upset with the notion of "soul sleep") by calling attention to Bach's *Mass in B Minor* and Handel's *Messiah*, and concludes that "the artists have proved the best expositors of the Bible."

So Open-Minded That Your Brains Fall Out

We need to turn back from these ideas about the nature of life after death to the prior question of whether there can actually be any such thing as real proof for the reality of post-mortem life, whether we are talking about the soul, resurrection, or immortality. In his book *Life After Death: The Burden of Proof,* Deepak Chopra uses a dubious version of quantum physics along with rather vague notions of consciousness and dimensions of reality to argue that the burden of proof falls on those who would deny the reality of life after death. There are a number of problems with his approach. First, it asks for proof of a negative, for proof that life after death does not exist, and it is a universally accepted maxim that you cannot prove a negative. Second, it ignores the trump-card axiom that "extraordinary claims require extraordinary proofs." The basic flaw in Chopra's argument is that he reduces all reality to "chemicals sending messages," and then posits that these messages—this intelligence—is the true reality. But how could this intelligence or consciousness exist without the chemicals?

Once you allow an overly ephemeral, non-material, and quasi-supernatural notion of intelligence or consciousness, anything becomes possible. The same thing happens when Cullmann brings The Holy Spirit into play. What is really at work here is unchecked imagination, and as with the notion of God being Almighty, anything can seem possible when you allow your imagination to run rampant—or as Bill Maher jokes, "when you are selling an invisible product." A similar jibe at those who believe things for which there is no concrete evidence or, worse yet, who insist that something is real or true in spite of a preponderance of contrary evidence, ridicules such folks for being so open-minded that their brains fall out.

When we say that religion is an artistic, creative product of our imagination, the underlying point is that Ultimate Reality is profoundly mysterious. We are saying that the word "God" is best understood as referring to this Ultimate Mystery. We are saying that all religions can be seen as attempting to express this Mystery with their own symbols and metaphors—but also that Ultimate Reality is beyond even our best metaphors and imaginings. We are *not* saying that any particular religious system or set of beliefs is *The Truth*! We are *not* validating a version of the famous philosophical "ontological argument" which would claim that simply because you can imagine some specific thing or article of faith it is therefore real and *must* be true. What we *are* validating, again, is the general notion, often championed by Albert Einstein, that Reality is ultimately mysterious.

Misusing Einstein

There have always been "scientists" who try to find a place for God in their equations. The book *Show Me God*, put together mainly by Fred Heeren, claims that "Hebrew revelation is the only religious source coming to us from ancient times that fits the modern cosmological picture." (page xv) But the parallel that Heeren draws between the progression of the six days of creation in Genesis and the progression of evolution is disingenuous. Heeren doesn't address the issues raised by the separate creation story in Genesis 2. The language about firmaments, the sun standing still, and the existence of days and nights (and light!) three days before the sun and moon are created, does not speak well for the compatibility of the Bible's worldview with the modern scientific worldview. On the other hand, the Hebrew Bible does contain beautiful, artistic poetry that invites us to "consider the heavens." Heeren's book jacket has a photo of Albert Einstein on the front cover standing before an astronomical chart. Einstein has been quoted as saying "Religion without science is blind; but science without religion is deaf." But Richard Dawkins has provided us with important clarifying quotes from Einstein: "The idea of a personal God is quite alien to me and seems even naïve." "If something is in me which can be called religious then it is the unbounded admiration for the structure of the world so far as our science can reveal it." " . . . Nature is a magnificent structure that we can comprehend only very imperfectly, and that must fill a thinking person with a feeling of humility." "*I am a deeply religious nonbeliever.*"

Any instance in which Einstein uses God language has to be seen in the context of this self-description and of these qualifications. When he said "Coincidence is God's way of remaining anonymous," he was talking about Reality remaining *mysterious*! Coincidences remind us of many things, including the synchronicity and interconnectedness of everything, and the amazing combination of random chance and order or structure in the universe—especially in the evolution of life. (Many coincidences are simply about paying attention to things we had not noticed before.) Einstein did not intend his clever image of God remaining anonymous to be understood as endorsing any anthropomorphic notions of God. He was just making use of colorful, artistic, poetic and metaphorical language. He prefaced his famous remark about imagination being more important than knowledge with "I am enough of an artist to draw freely upon my imagination."

Einstein's unbounded admiration for the magnificent structure of nature is also a theme found in Islam. Islamic art values intricately refined patterns—precise and elegantly crafted calligraphy, for example. Islamic theology identifies Allah with a structured, controlled, pre-determined sense of Reality. The requirement to pray five times a day gives a structure to the day that can provide a sense of serenity—as does the "plain and sober" design of most Mosques. These tendencies do also have their down-sides. Islamic art does not particularly value innovation, and when generalized, this lack of appreciation for innovation can impede progressive changes. Too much emphasis on control and order can result in overly rigid morality, authoritarian and even dictatorial governments, and a general hostility to features of modernity. The widely held belief that the Qur'an is but an earthly copy of a divine book that has existed in heaven for all eternity, can foster a general attitude that things are set in stone. On the other hand, Islamic appreciation for structure and pattern has sometimes led to fairly friendly accommodation with scientific discoveries and theories such as evolution. In the early days of Islam, the Arab world in which it originated was moving far ahead of Europe in its understanding of medicine, anatomy, and physics—not to mention business and trade. Arabic numerals were a godsend to mathematicians (imagine trying to do algebra with Roman numerals). This focus on structure and order also reminds me of a non-religious psychiatrist friend of mine who has no problem with his clients being religious because he realizes how important it is for people to have some order and structure in their lives. (He is like many who would say that religion, whether you believe in it or not, gives us structure, and we need structure.) One of the standard aspects of any good definition of religion will include the element of structure, pervasiveness, worldview, and a system for setting priorities.

Einstein's description of himself as a deeply religious nonbeliever seems close to my notion of "high church atheist," and also seems to me to be exactly the kind of profound paradoxical affirmation to which any thinking person can relate. His observation that "Imagination is more important than knowledge" (in *On Science*) holds true for both science and religion, but we must also remember that science is a translation of the Latin word for *knowledge* and it includes the empirical scientific method as the best means for ascertaining knowledge of factual truth! It is bad enough that folks like Heeren misuse Einstein to promote their narrow religious beliefs. Worse, Heeren's claim that the Bible is the one and only factual and scientific divine revelation is precisely the kind of arrogant overstatement that perpetuates religion as a source of bitter conflict. Imagination is important in both religion and science, but in religion its relationship to knowledge is more "tricky" because religion traditionally tends to be much more about interpretation than about facts. Science is virtually *synonymous* with a method for determining what is factual, whereas religion too often depends not on any particular method but simply on "special pleading" for authoritative "revelation."

Another book that attempts a scientific proof for God and life after death is Frank J. Tipler's *Physics of Immortality*. Tipler presents himself as a mathematician atheist turned believer. Claiming to have arrived at his Omega Point Theory proofs of God and immortality "in exactly the same way physicists calculate the properties of an electron," he at least admits that most scientists don't agree with him. We have noted previously that discussions of advanced mathematics and abstract physics can easily begin to sound like religious or theological discourse, but this is quite different from jumping to the conclusion that mathematicians and physicists can prove the existence or truth of any particular version of God, resurrection, or immortality.

Popularity Is Not Proof

Physics of Immortality is a thick book. Deepak Chopra has written many books and appeared on many television programs. But there are also a lot of television programs that feature supernatural story lines about everything from space aliens to clairvoyant spiritualism. We easily confuse quantity with quality. The quantity of anecdotal evidence, the sheer thickness and quantity of books, or the popularity of supernatural themes in television or movie entertainment does not constitute proof of anything! There is nothing intrinsically wrong with imaginary entertainments. But the fact that we find things appealing or even meaningful on some level is not the same as proof that they are factually true. Wilhelm Reich's book about the World War II era, *The Mass Psychology of Fascism*, demonstrated that the popularity of an idea can sometimes turn into mass hallucination, hysteria, or something even worse. Our imaginative use of God language can be poetically and symbolically full of significance, but if we start taking it too literally we risk making every day of our life into April Fools' Day.

In 2005 Mary Roach authored *Spook: Science Tackles the Afterlife*, in which she writes with engaging humor about scientists, engineers, schemers, and mediums who are all trying to prove (or disprove) that there is an afterlife. She submits herself to a few dubious and sometimes bizarre experiments or experiences, and presents typical psychic, near-death or other research studies. But I think one reviewer was right on the money by noting that she does all this "with a degree of skepticism and whimsical humor that leaves the reader unconvinced that anything of substance has been demonstrated."

Scientific Illiteracy, Anti-intellectualism, and Intelligent Design

I am bothered by the degree of both religious and scientific illiteracy that I detect in contemporary culture. I am even more bothered by the widespread anti-intellectualism that often accompanies scientific illiteracy. In his 2009 book *Unscientific America* Chris Mooney recognizes that much religious fundamentalism displays this kind of prejudice and illiteracy, but he also describes how liberals too sometimes stand in the way of science because of ideological agendas regarding such things as research using animals, or because of failure to appreciate the subtleties of statistics regarding, for example, vaccination. Scientific illiteracy and anti-intellectualism appear also in other subtle and insidious forms. In movies and television shows all too frequently the person who believes in supernatural realities is shown to have been correct and the scientifically oriented skeptical person is portrayed as mistaken, stupid or narrow-minded. In reality it is usually the case that those who believe in supernatural, psychic or other bizarre notions are the small-minded and deluded ones.

Dr. Bonnie Strickland, past president of the American Psychological Association, has done research suggesting that those who too enthusiastically embrace psychic and other supernatural notions tend to be helpless victim types, praying instead of acting, believing that things more often happen *to* them than happen because of their own efforts. Nobody ever won the hundred thousand dollars that magician James Randi offered to any Edger Cayce type who could pass his scientific tests for their supposed psychic or other abilities. Wishing doth not make it so, but the deliberate doubt which is at the core of the scientific method has produced true wonders such as space exploration or "miracles" in technology and medicine of which the ancients could only dream.

In a 2001 article "Looking for God at Berkeley" Mark Athitakis describes pro-God scientists as "exploiting scientific loopholes by appealing to the general public instead of submitting their research for peer review, or by pointing to areas of science where the research is incomplete or contradictory as proof of Darwin's imminent collapse." These scientists might point out, for example, that Harvard scientist Stephen Jay Gould questioned the notion that evolution always follows a path of steady progress. But a closer look at Gould's criticism would reveal that his concern was to refine the theory of evolution, not to discard it. He suggested that evolution took place in fits and starts and that although it always moved in the direction of greater complexity, this did not in every instance necessarily lead to progress or improvement. Ken Wilber refines the theory of evolution by describing how it can be a slow process, but can also speed up as whole patterns (he calls them "holons") combine in ways that rapidly repeat the phenomenon whereby the whole becomes greater than the sum of its parts (he describes this aspect of evolution with the phrase "transcends and includes").

One of the favorite arguments of so-called intelligent design theory is that while evolution may explain some things, other things are "irreducibly complex" at the molecular level. This notion that some parts of reality have always been extremely complex and could not have slowly evolved leads researcher Jed Macosko among others to assert that "natural phenomena can be caused by things that are not natural" (in other words, "supernatural"). But this kind of statement is tantamount to rejecting the very ideas of empirical reality and scientific evidence! Once you do that you are no longer a real scientist. In other words, intelligent design theory is not a *scientific* theory. Remember that in science when we call something a *theory* we mean that it is *the best explanation we can give so far based on all the available evidence!* A theory is not just a guess or a hunch. In science, an educated guess requiring considerably more evidence is called a hypothesis. A theory is much closer to being a law than to being a hypothesis. Would we say that gravity is "just a theory"? It is because evolution is a uniquely complex and multi-dimensional phenomenon that we tend to call it a theory rather than a law, but at this point in time for all practical purposes I think we can speak of both the law of gravity and the law of evolution.

Richard Dawkins makes it abundantly clear that life can only be understood as evolving from simple to complex. If one postulates the complexity of an intelligent designer at the beginning of the process, the question would immediately demand an answer as to who designed the designer. Trying to answer this question would lead to an infinite regression which is logically far more ridiculous than simply admitting that the very existence of anything at all is an ultimate mystery. Hasn't everyone heard the example of the child who, after an exasperated mother says that God just exists without being caused (or "just because!"), wonders why the universe itself couldn't just exist without a cause? The Jain Scriptures actually use this very argument to criticize belief in a creator God.

Dawkins also makes it clear how we must not think in terms of a choice between design and random chance. The gradual process and accumulated result of "natural selection" ("survival of the fittest" is a less precise phrase, more about the result than the process) is an elegant combination of randomness and "logic." Natural selection could also be described as a "natural *intention*" or tendency constantly to adapt, to "die and rise." The problem with the word design is that it implies the unjustified and inadmissible assumption that there is a designer, some "mind of the universe" or "*deus ex machina*" (a God external to the world) that pre-exists all developed complexity. The idea that complexity precedes development is the ultimate ridiculous example of putting the cart before the horse. The gradual evolution of a complex organ like the eye is not improbable when one understands the simple fact that the partial vision of an evolving eye is better (more useful) than no vision at all.

Rather than seeking to stifle debate on or to ignore these questions about scientific truth, we need rather to clarify where the discussion belongs. In science classes this discussion belongs under the heading of the philosophy and methods of science. In social studies the discussion might be largely in terms of church and state issues. In philosophy or humanities the relationship between religion and science would be the subject.

The implications of relativity theory, quantum physics and string theory—including multiple dimensions and parallel universes—are mindboggling. (Google "The Elegant Universe" or read *The Grand Design* by Hawking and Mlodinow or *The Tao of Physics* by Fritjof Capra.) But to jump from the baffling issues of relativity theory and quantum mechanics (particles versus waves, etc.) to the conclusion that science can validate supernatural realities is highly problematical, as I think Robert Wright at least somewhat concedes in *The Evolution of God*. Those who claim to have psychic powers usually resist the idea that any scientific tests can be devised to verify their abilities. A person such as Uri Geller, for example, consistently tells people to drop their doubts and focus on making something happen. This approach encourages deliberate belief and wishful thinking. It basically rejects empirical evidence (science) as the most reliable standard for finding out what is true or real. It operates in the realm of "my mind is made up; don't confuse me with the facts."

The scientific method by contrast is based on deliberate doubt. Reality is discovered by repeated attempts to demonstrate that a hypothesis does not hold up with further testing. Only when a thesis withstands this kind of rigorous empirical, results-based testing does it begin to move toward being an accepted theory, an accepted truth. I contend that this kind of scientific methodology has produced the real miracles. It has put human beings on the moon where astronauts were able to look back 240,000 miles and see the earth with its 6 billion people appearing to be the size of a quarter! It has saved my life (not to mention the lives of President Bill Clinton, David Letterman and many others) with heart bypass surgery. (And I should mention that in contrast to anecdotal accounts such as the hype about "90 Minutes in Heaven," I had absolutely no consciousness of anything from the time they put me under until the time I came out of the anesthesia.) What science has accomplished by banishing supernatural, superstitious wishful thinking or fear-mongering ("junk science" and a lot of science fiction included) should be adequate compensation for the loss or change of some popular beliefs.

Belief and Faith

Of course, there are many emotional beliefs that can't be proven. A belief, in this sense, is better understood as a value commitment. A typical dictionary definition of faith is "a belief in the truth, value or trustworthiness of a person, idea, or thing." We have emotional commitments to (we believe "*in*") the meaning and value of love, trust, courage, freedom, risk taking, etc. Frequently when we use the word faith, we are thinking in terms of dreams, wishes, hopes or general optimism. But when this understanding of faith veers off into the notion of accepting something as factually true without logical proof or material evidence, it becomes more a matter of merely "believing *that*" something is true. Believing *in* or having faith *in* something or someone is based on a kind of "emotional evidence" or subjective valuation.

In the famous story of doubting Thomas from the John Gospel, Jesus shows Thomas evidence that he has risen from the dead but then says "blessed are those who have not seen and yet believe." Does this mean that the gospel writer is promoting the idea of believing something without any evidence? Like other New Testament writers, this storyteller presents the resurrection with great ambiguity, sometimes as a physical and sometimes as a spiritual phenomenon. We have considered this earlier, but here the point is that the doubting Thomas story depicts both the notion of belief based on evidence and the notion of faith as pure trust in a person, idea or message. In other gospel stories Jesus upbraids his followers for their "little faith"—their fear and lack of courage. It takes courage and trust to live life *confidently*—"with faith." "Be Not Afraid!" is a biblical mantra!

The bottom line is that we often use the words faith or belief to mean different things in different contexts. In *The Future of Faith*, Harvey Cox says that belief is more like opinion and Christians should return to calling themselves not "believers" but followers of *The Way* of life that Jesus represents. Faith can be simply a deep personal confidence and trust that life is worth living. The word "confidence" comes directly from Latin meaning "with faith," and other derivatives such as "confidant" clearly reveal the intensely personal, subjective and emotional aspect of trusting faith. Both faith and belief can involve a combination of evidence, experience, and subjective feeling, and both can also be thought of as policies. Policies are neither true nor false but are just useful or not useful. Optimism as a policy tends to be more useful than pessimism.

Faith can also be an expression of what you inwardly most prefer in spite of reality. You may have a clear faith in goodness, love, truth, and beauty, because they are what you prefer. Sometimes described as having "faith without hope," the idea is that you affirm what you prefer as an "article of faith" regardless of outcome. Robert Fulghum, who likes to praise childlike wisdom, puts it this way: "I believe that imagination is stronger than knowledge—myth is more potent than history—dreams are more powerful than facts—hope always triumphs over experience—laughter is the cure for grief—love is stronger than death."

The cliché "hope springs eternal" speaks to the resilience of our ideals. This kind of faith or belief may explain why regular churchgoers tend to outlive non-churchgoers. The habits, stability, optimism, contemplation, and commitment associated with spiritual/religious faith seem to have intrinsic survival value. The philosopher Santayana wrote that while prayer "accomplishes nothing material [it] constitutes something spiritual." He describes how faith "ceases to be a foolish expectation of improbable things and rises on stepping-stones of its material disappointments into a spiritual peace." The kind of Pollyanna optimism offered by many self-help books and positive thinking preachers too often leaves us in the lurch when the going gets tough and outcomes are not what we had hoped. Optimism that does not take into account the uncertainty and inevitable failures in our lives is shallow and naïve. Like an Olympic athlete in training, a spiritual person embraces the paradox of preparing both to win and to lose, realizing it is the effort that matters.

I think the best hope for the future of biblical religion is to lose its supernatural baggage, and to recover its heart and soul by reclaiming "God" as Ultimate Divine Mystery, by reclaiming and re-imagining early Christian opposition to personal, political, economic and social systems of exploitation and domination, and by opposing ethical/religious fanaticism. I would also suggest that we pay more attention to "the *art* of worship," and that we consider using descriptions such as shalom service, celebration of liberation, transcendence exercises, or centering meditation, as more appealing and meaningful alternatives to the term "worship."

When belief is seen as a matter of affirming the reality of specific *supernatural* phenomena, it is by definition not subject to empirical (natural, sense-based) testing or proof. A supernatural belief can only be asserted, not proven or known. If we can prove something with solid evidence, then by definition it is no longer super—above or beyond—natural. It is not a mere belief. It is solid knowledge. (My no-nonsense college professor who taught Greek and ancient history, Alfred E. Haefner, liked to say, "People believe a great many things. They actually know very little.") So we return to the point that religious language, symbols, and metaphors are best seen as artistic expressions rather than as either strictly factual knowledge or as supernatural beliefs. They are expressions of faith, trust, and commitment to values such as compassion, freedom, justice, creativity. These imaginative, poetic, sometimes playful allusions and creative stories are not one-dimensionally scientific or historical. They have to do with realities such as interpretation, meaning, purpose, motivation, inspiration, education, economics, and culture—with all aspects of everyday life and especially with the values that we hold sacred.

I value and have faith in creativity as sacred. I resonate with Gordon Kaufman's understanding of "God" as a metaphor and symbol for the naturally occurring, evolutionary phenomenon of "serendipitous creativity." I value grace and compassion as sacred. I have faith in religion as a deeply spiritual, multi-dimensional, and highly valuable art form that sings the song of life in a way that brings us as close as we can come to transcending death.

CHAPTER 5

Psych Yourself Out With Buddhism

To UNDERSTAND RELIGION AS a creative art form is to understand that the supernatural stories and many if not most of the specific beliefs of particular religions are not real or true in the sense of being strictly factual. Our consideration of the general Swedish and Danish indifference to religion and related tendency to discount belief in life after death, suggests that a growing number of twenty-first century people no longer believe in any supernatural notions of life after death. The HBO television series "Big Love," which I mentioned in chapter 3, featured a "renegade" polygamous Mormon family that based much of its behavior on beliefs about the afterlife. Many who viewed this show probably saw these sincere people as foolish to be counting so heavily on the next life to provide the basis for their values and decisions in the here and now. As I've suggested before, we might prepare ourselves to be surprised regarding the very unlikely possibility of life after death, but I do not recommend putting any, let alone all, of our eggs in that basket.

That artistic religious ideas or supernatural images are seldom if ever literally *factual* does not prevent them from being *meaningful*. As has been illustrated in the previous chapters, religious metaphors and constructs can legitimately serve to encourage compassion, empathy, non-fanatical morality, hope and optimism. Creative imagination is never wasted when it produces these fruits. The problem is that not all religious belief and imagination can or does produce such fruits.

Buddhism without Superstition

We turn now to a growing movement in Buddhism that emphasizes its compatibility with science in general and with psychology in particular. This approach views Buddhism not as a set of religious beliefs and practices but as a way of psyching ourselves out, a method for coming to terms with Reality, a method that doesn't involve wishful or magical thinking. Buddhism has always been about the relationship between mind and matter, but in two different senses. One is the supernatural or magical sense where a person expects reincarnation, miracles of healing, or other special effects through the power of "mind over matter." The other kind of Buddhism, that I am promoting here, is about the power, not of an entity called the mind, but about the power of our *thinking*! This kind of Buddhism puts the emphasis on how we see and construct our reality by the way we think. It stresses the element of truth in the notion that we *are* what we think. Like the little engine that could, if we think we can do something we just might be able to do it; and if we think we can't do it or lack the imagination to even conceive of doing it, we probably can't and won't do it.

To give another example, the current body of evidence demonstrates the ineffectiveness of the "scared straight" approach to reforming juvenile offenders by taking them to prisons where hardened criminals make intimidating presentations about how terrible it is to be in prison. What has been shown to be the truly effective way of reforming criminal behavior (and of reducing recidivism) is to change the way offenders think! When they stop thinking that criminal behavior is a way to solve problems or to achieve their goals, and begin thinking instead of more effective ways to achieve desirable outcomes, their behavior improves. (This is another instance of the way in which "personal construct psychology" works.)

Central to this focus on *the power of our thinking* is discernment of our personal reality as a mind/body continuum. Mind and body, mind and brain, "body and soul"—these only refer to different (not separate) aspects of the same reality. Instead of viewing mind and body as two separate and different "things," or viewing my "self" as a thing, I *think* of my *"self"* as an ongoing, integrating (contingent), thinking, and interpreting *process*! (This focus on the process of thinking is also central to some of the most prominent currents in contemporary schools of philosophy.) Education about the brain is becoming available to ever-larger portions of the population, teaching everyday folks how they can use their minds to understand their brains. When we pay attention to and integrate the instinctual (reptilian), emotional, and intellectual aspects of our thinking process, *our minds will understand how to make better use of our brains* in a way that will enhance our lives! This is a scientific version of what Buddhism calls mindfulness.

Also central to this "thinking" version of Buddhism are the notions of emptiness, no-self, the seamless whole, and nirvana. Two authors who have focused on this non-supernatural version of Buddhism are Stephen Batchelor and Steve Hagen. Oprah Winfrey's "guru" Eckhart Tolle also is in this mode. We have previously noted Batchelor's book *Buddhism Without Beliefs*. Hagen has written *Buddhism Plain and Simple*, and another book intended for a general audience titled *Buddhism Is Not What You Think*. Hagen means "not what you think" in two senses. On the one hand his point is that Buddhism is not so much religion as it is psychology. On the other hand, he means that Buddhism is about living in the moment without getting stuck in beliefs, ideas, and thoughts. Both of these insights have always been features of, or possibilities inherent in, a Buddhist mentality.

To focus on the psychological aspect of Buddhism is neither to deny its spiritual dimension nor to contradict the notion of religion as an art form. An artistic approach to religion both underlies and validates the creative development of a scientific, psychological approach to spirituality. Both art and science are about being open to multiple perspectives. Art, spirituality, and psychology focus on seeing and relating to reality by thinking creatively and imaginatively.

On the subject of life after death, this psychological approach encourages us to embrace every moment of the life we have here and now because "this is it!" You can only experience eternity beyond all sense of time in present moments, and if you don't experience it *now*, you almost certainly never will. Buddhism has often been understood as a form of atheism similar to its rather austere "cousin"—Jainism. When the de-emphasis on gods is combined with the "thinking" psychology of Buddhism, the focus is no longer on reincarnation, but on the realization that not believing in any form of life after death makes this life all the more meaningful and important. This awareness also makes tragedy all the more profound— whether it occurs through war, disease or other calamities. The beauty of something is enhanced by recognizing its end. The death of a beautiful young soldier, or of young children murdered by a deranged lunatic, is all the more tragic when we realize that we should not talk about them as being "in a better place." Not believing in afterlife intensifies the gift of compassion! A beautiful young person is dead and gone forever. Don't lie to cover up the tragedy. The recognition of the *impermanence of everything* increases our gratitude for the gift of this moment, for conscious awareness of the eternal now. Intense sensitivity and compassion in the face of tragedy and suffering makes true moral discernment and gratitude for the gift of this life here and now all the more important and necessary—and makes any decision to engage in war all the more horrendous.

In a famous story of the Buddha, he holds up a flower as if to ask what the meaning of the flower might be. One disciple indicates with his knowing look that he understands. The meaning of the flower is simply that it is real there in the moment. Moments, and flowers, and we ourselves all pass away, so we need to be fully awake to the intrinsic value of our moments. When the prophet Isaiah writes that all flesh is like grass or flowers, and that only the Word of God endures forever, we get a Hebrew version of this kind of realism. What does it mean to say that only the divine word is forever? Like the images of "living with God," "dwelling in the house of the Lord forever" (Psalm 23), or the John Gospel's poetic picture of Jesus as the incarnation of divine eternal *logos* (Word or Wisdom), the "eternal word" is an image that raises the issue of our relationship to eternity without necessarily suggesting either a continuation of our separate identities after death or a literal pre-existence of Jesus. (In the opening of the John Gospel, the use of the pronouns "he" and "him" in some English translations indicate that the Greek word *logos* is a masculine noun, not necessarily that Jesus as a person has literally existed from all eternity or is himself the actual creator of the world!)

I have emphasized that the Christian notion of realized eschatology is very close to the Buddhist stress on living in the moment. Whichever of these traditions we affirm, it is important to be clear that living in the moment does not mean that we shouldn't make plans or work toward longer-term goals. Living in this eternal now means appreciating both the immediately present moment and also the larger "here and now" of this world in every way possible. Such appreciation is part of the gratitude that has been encouraged throughout this book. Even when we are in pain we will sometimes say that at least the pain reminds us that we are still alive.

Those who invest so heavily in preparing for a next life might well ask themselves how they are going to appreciate a next life if they fail to fully appreciate every moment of this life. Furthermore, the lengths to which even very devout Christians will go to stay alive for one more day, week, month or year, suggests that they are hedging their bets on the afterlife. It also seems oddly inconsistent that those who supposedly value life after death so highly are so often opposed to most of the options available to folks in agony who wish to die. The catchy phrase "everybody wants to go to heaven but nobody wants to die" also captures this sense of hedging one's bets on life after death.

As I am writing, health care is front and center in United States politics. On November 22, 2009 an excellent segment of CBS TV's "60 Minutes" illustrated the need for Americans to become better at facing their mortality. They need to consider whether their insurance system can afford to spend skyrocketing sums of money on people who clearly are in the last stages of life. Americans are sometimes told to fear rationed care ("death panels"), but if they fail to set reasonable (power of attorney) limits on end-of-life procedures, they could destroy their entire economy. The wealthy will always be able to afford big end-of-life heroics. But I wouldn't consider spending a few extra weeks or months to die, hooked up to machines or undergoing endless tests, as one of the perks of being rich. There is also a moral issue that the amount of money involved in keeping only one terminal patient alive for a short time could be spent keeping a much larger number of people alive for many years. (These mortality issues raise even larger ones about global politics, economics, weapons trading, and the like.) Time magazine devoted virtually the entire March 4, 2013 issue to a nuanced explanation of "Why Medical Bills Are Killing Us" even though medical care itself in the United States is first rate.

Contingent Emptiness and "No-self"

The Buddhist notion of emptiness or no-self is the most basic aspect of the psychological approach to Buddhism. While it can seem difficult to understand, at the risk of appearing cavalier or simplistic I will try to make it as clear as possible: *What we think of as our "self" is constantly changing. "Self" is not a static thing but part of the process of contingency (interconnectedness) and change. Therefore, we need not fear losing in death a self we never had in the first place. My sense of self is not an independent, lasting, essence, substance, or thing, so my sense of self is ultimately "empty of self nature." This "contingent emptiness" is also called "no-self."* As mentioned in chapter 1, some will criticize this approach as nothing more than a fancy way of saying "when you're dead, you're dead—get used to it!" But this kind of Buddhist realism is not at all cynical, nihilistic, or negative. It is simply refreshing honesty.

There are, of course, many ways to describe what Emptiness means. Emptiness means contingency, that everything is interconnected with and dependent on everything else. Emptiness means that nothing is self-caused (everything is determined by a universe of interdependent factors) and, therefore, everything is empty of "self-nature." No-self is a form of emptiness. No-self means that our sense of self is a construct, a concept—not a thing, essence, or substance of permanent reality. No-self is one specific instance of contingency. *On the broadest possible level of awareness, emptiness means that our sense of separateness from other beings and from the universe is an illusion, because our interrelated contingency ultimately transcends our individuality.*

Change in and of itself is not the main meaning of emptiness, but change is an essential aspect of the contingency that makes "self" such an empty and ephemeral concept. Coming to terms with our mortality is about coming to terms with emptiness and no-self. The resulting awareness means that we no longer worry or wonder about life after death. We are wise to meditate on these realities at least once in a while because so many of our moments generally are (and have to be) spent living as separate selves in a world of specifics. Regularly grounding ourselves back into awareness of the Seamless Whole of contingent Emptiness is something like what others might call worship, but there is no reverence for an authority involved, only reverence and appreciation for Reality. Instead of praying for miracles, we are psyching ourselves out—we are working on our attitudes.

Psyching yourself out about your "self"—fully embracing the notion that you don't have a self to lose—is easier said than done. We do become attached to our memories, experiences, and relationships—to people, places, and things. In a sense we are the sum total of our memories. Letting go of these can indeed be sad. This is why in the next chapter we will consider the wisdom of having a paradoxical, dialectical, ambivalent attitude toward death.

To understand emptiness is to realize that *you are not just "part of" the universe,* looking at the universe, but that *you are the universe happening!* Others would describe this as being about understanding that your consciousness *is* the very consciousness of the universe. To put it still another way, don't think of "yourself" as in any way separate from ultimate Reality—from your *ecos* (ecology/home)! These are better ways of saying what can also be described by using the mind-stretching image I mentioned previously of the self as an individual drop of cosmic consciousness taking in the whole ocean of cosmic consciousness. The less striking version of this analogy is the image of the cosmic ocean absorbing a drop of individual consciousness. If this ocean is thought of as Nirvana, we get a misleading image of the self seeming to "go somewhere," which is a distraction from the point that enlightenment (being awake and aware) is about *now—the eternal now*. Enlightenment is about participating in present moments without losing an underlying sense of the Seamless Whole (Shunyata).

No Suffering, No Difference, and Paradox with No Contradiction

The change, contingency, and impermanence theme in Buddhism is often explained by using the image that you can't step into the same river twice. It is always flowing, ever changing. But it is also sometimes said that you can't even step into the same river *once!* This notion of life as empty, unconnected, "non-dual" moments is quite abstract and difficult to comprehend. Most of us are more aware of the apparent continuities of our lives. I think part of what is meant by empty, unconnected, non-dual moments is perhaps similar to the random movement of tiny particles in quantum physics that Albert Einstein once mocked as "playing dice with the universe." The idea seems to be that individual moments of the eternal now are just that, individual moments, and any connection between them is so ephemeral as to be virtually non-existent. All matter, whether in the form of large objects or the smallest particles and cells, is in fact mainly empty space—emptiness. When we get to this level of theoretical physics, the entire concept of cause and effect begins to be called into question. One possible implication of all this is that "anything can happen" (theoretically!), but as I cautioned in chapter 4, we can't use this kind of possibility thinking as an excuse to be so open-minded that our brains fall out. The point ultimately is the mysterious nature of Reality.

Another Buddhist concept is called "no difference." There is no difference, for example, between Nirvana and Now. The Buddhas and the saintly bodhisattvas are not other-worldly celestial (supernatural) beings or entities who literally return to this world out of altruistic compassion to help those still in the here-and-now. There is no difference between then-and-now, as there is none between Nirvana and Now. At this level of Buddhist thought, Nirvana is not a place or a state of mind that you enter only when you die. Nirvana, awareness, awakened consciousness and enlightenment are about *ending suffering* here and now. This "Buddha Nature" is a state of mind one can enter here and now—in fact, *only* here and now!

To a significant degree, all Buddhist teaching comes down to the idea of ending suffering by getting rid of *ignorant craving* for that which we can't have (total perfection, for example) or can't avoid (physical aches and pains, for example). Dr. Hinkle illustrates this kind of ignorance by describing the misery and frustration of a person who is constantly trying to draw square circles. It can't be done! I find most instructive the example of those who go through life always dissatisfied and unhappy because they demand that life be "fair." We can try to increase justice and fairness in the world but, as we've noted before, absolute and total fairness will never be in the cards. Getting rid of ignorant craving also involves a basic awareness that we can't have anything without also having its opposite. We can't have life without death; we might even say that the major cause of death is—birth! We can't have creation and growth without destruction and decay. (The God Shiva is a great Asian symbol for these opposites.) We can't have pleasure and avoid all pain. We cannot always and only have an optimum rate of change in our lives. I remember how former U. S. Vice President Hubert Humphrey described his chemotherapy as "bottled death"—it tries to kill both you and the cancer, and the hope is that the cancer will die first. This is an intriguing dialectical twist on the expression "a matter of life and death"—cheering one form of death onward to triumph over another form of death.

Bart Ehrman titled his book on suffering and evil "God's Problem." I think he should have called it "The Problem *is* God," that is, certain concepts of God. When you postulate the concept of an almighty and benevolent Sky Daddy God, you have set yourself up for inevitable disillusionment. *For every claim that God intervened to help someone in dire straits, there are infinite examples of worse tragedies in which it is painfully obvious that no divine aid was forthcoming!*

No wonder there are so many jokes about God being incompetent, an under-achiever, or asleep at the switch. Ehrman sides with Ecclesiastes in concluding that suffering and evil is inexplicable, and that the best we can do is try to minimize it. But Buddhism and Taoism, partly by avoiding the concept of either an almighty God or a malevolent devil, do not understand suffering as inexplicable. It is just simple Reality that everything has its opposite. The basic concept behind any notion such as Satan or Devil is *opposition.* You can't have joy without sorrow, pleasure without pain, love without indifference, beginnings without endings, or beautiful weather without natural disasters such as tornadoes. We can do things to minimize evil and suffering, but we can't eliminate this aspect of experience. Inventions, medicines, therapies, laws, and a host of other things can reduce some forms of suffering and evil, but the ultimate relief has to be found in the way each of us thinks. Our greatest ignorant craving is for a world that can never be!

Buddhism does not teach that desire itself is a bad thing. It is *ignorant* desire and uncontrolled craving that cause unnecessary suffering and lead to the greatest forms of misery. Even the enlightened still suffer, but it is not the kind of suffering that poisons the consciousness. One may still experience the sadness that inevitably accompanies empathy for self or active compassion for others, the pain of illness or accident, even the numbing grief that comes with death and other forms of loss. But none of this need be the kind of soul sickness that kills the spirit. The corollary teaching about moderate non-attachment does not mean that we always live a bland middle of the road life, devoid of any intense moments or feelings. Non-attachment means rather that we avoid unnecessary suffering by not craving permanence. Nirvana and rebirth are about resilience, renewal, and reinvigorating change. The Hebrews wrote, "As long as I have breath I will praise the Lord." The Buddhist says "As long as I have breath I will celebrate and embrace the moments of life."

As long as I have breath! Psychologist Dennis Hinkle says:

> "Consciousness is an activity of a functioning brain. I will treasure this very moment of consciousness when I accept that my consciousness will end forever when my brain dies. Attempts to see mind or consciousness apart from the interaction of brain, body, society and world are delusional. Mind and body are not separate entities. My fear of death vanishes when I realize that I cannot be conscious of my own death, only of the process of dying. The ending of this fear is a great liberation."

These observations about consciousness from Dr. Hinkle remind me of Woody Allen's famous quip: "I don't mind dying; I just don't want to be there when it happens." Hinkle's comments also can encourage us to meditate on the fact that we don't feel great trepidation about the millions of years of our non-existence before we were born. Many Buddhists meditate on the breath because it is so intrinsically linked to the moment-by-moment gift of life. Here we have reached perhaps the true bottom line on the question of life after death, and the answer is: When you stop breathing and your brain dies your opportunity to appreciate moments has come to an end! This prospect of personal oblivion should make every moment all the more precious to us. So *carpe diem*! Seize the day! A popular Christian hymn that I particularly appreciate because it is one of the few that explicitly celebrates the human intellect, also says: "Take my moments and my days; let them flow in ceaseless praise." While I no longer understand the "praise God" imagery of this hymn literally, I think I have long appreciated and celebrated the value of moments and days. Perhaps I have long been a budding Buddhist.

The concept of non-duality or no-difference reminds us that the word paradox means *apparent* contradiction. We can and do make all kinds of dualistic distinctions in our thought processes, but in some sense Ultimate Reality has to be understood as unified, with duality, difference, or contradiction only *apparent*! It is our subjective perspective—our view of reality—that can appear contradictory. To say that Reality Itself is self-contradictory makes no sense.

It is my impression that Buddhist teachers typically hesitate to make their paradoxes explicit. They beat around the bush using all kinds of stories and examples, often baffling ones, that lead the struggling students or disciples to come to an awareness of the paradoxes slowly and on their own—sometimes the goal is to teach the student to bypass the rational intellect and become more intuitive. I often find myself wishing that Buddhist dharma (teaching about Reality) would spell out its paradoxes sooner and more explicitly. (I also have this feeling about any theologians who are struggling with a paradox but don't get around to addressing it explicitly.) On the other hand, all this hemming and hawing so typical of Buddhism can also be seen as reflecting appropriate open-mindedness and an awareness of complexity and Mystery. Being content with metaphors, symbolism and stories is an important way of avoiding strident absolutism.

The paradoxes of Buddhism echo the paradoxes I have encountered in Christian theology—and both traditions understand that paradoxes are only *apparent* contradictions. To repeat an example: When saying that we should live each day as if it is our last, and at the same time as if it is the first day of the rest of our life, we are talking about experiencing two frames of mind *as if* they are one. Simultaneously holding in mind two contradictory thoughts such as these can be the secret to healthy equilibrium and attitudes about life, as we saw in chapter 2. To use the typical Buddhist expression, these apparently contradictory thoughts are two but not two—they are "non-dual." Some might describe it as simultaneous awareness of the opposite sides of the same coin—or simply as *facing Reality.*

In Christian theology the doctrine of Sanctification ("the work of the Holy Spirit") can be stated in paradoxical terms by saying that because of

God's grace you *are* a saint, now *become* the saint you already are. This "become what you already are" is connected to the concept of realized (proleptic or anticipatory) eschatology—the notion that the future is always already here in the eternal now. Similarly, but with less focus on the issue of a person's ethical status, the idea of non-duality means that we can understand ourselves as already Buddhas, already in Nirvana. The Buddhist version of what I call the "paradox of grace or faith" in chapter 2 is that we struggle to achieve salvation while at the same time realizing that there is no salvation to be achieved, because we already have it as a gift. This line of thinking about every moment of life as a gift to be savored for all it is worth, reminds me of a great adage that is called into service particularly when a young life it cut short: "Youth is not preparation for life; youth is life itself." This sense of life as a gift also reminds me of the way many Muslims think of their religion itself as a gift. Schleiermacher's emphasis on religion as a feeling of absolute dependency, Luther's sense of our dependence on grace alone, as well as McGill's "gospel of neediness" all resonate with this theme of life as a gift. None of this is about a helpless victim mentality. It is about contingency, interconnectedness, interdependence, and valuing every moment of life and consciousness here and now.

A lot of paradoxical understanding ends up being about humor. Chinese Taoism in particular has always emphasized the unpredictable, uncontrollable, paradoxical, humorous nature of life. Malcolm David Eckel, associate professor of religion at Boston University, describes how the Dalai Lama gave a presentation at Harvard where "his holiness" first gave a long technical explanation of Buddhist teachings, but then with a sly smile asked the audience "who is it that is telling you all this?" His answer: "Mere I." The Dalai Lama exudes an aura of lightness, buoyancy, and the humility of one who does not take himself (his ego) too seriously. This should remind the reader of my earlier point about the importance of combining our sense of moral urgency with a sense of humor. Theologians of more than one tradition have sometimes imagined life in this world, with its unbelievable mixtures of grandeur and horror, pathos and heroic idealism, the sublime and the ridiculous, as a grand cosmic joke that is being played on us—and have then suggested that faith is about getting the joke. A profound sense of humor is a divine gift of grace, just as trusting faith and optimism is a gift—gifts that are an antidote to cynicism. Everything in life can be either tragic or funny depending on our circumstances or our frame of mind. The impulse to laugh or to cry is the same; we laugh, for example, at cemetery jokes at times when we feel safe from the threat of death, but we can't help crying when death is close on our doorstep. Comedy is tragedy plus time or distance. Many of my motifs in this book are presented with great humor in *Heidegger and a Hippo Walk through Those Pearly Gates* by Thomas Cathcart and Daniel Klein, a book I heartily recommend.

Buddhism has been accused of being nihilistic or fatalistic, of not taking anything seriously enough, because of the dharmas about emptiness, no-self, non-attachment and moderation, or because beliefs about reincarnation and karma tempt one to put things off to a future lifetime. There is an element of truth in the Buddhist and Taoist notions that it is folly to think we can control life. Shakespeare reminds us of the slings and arrows of outrageous fortune. I love the clever aphorism that says "if you want to make God laugh, tell her your plans." It can at times be very wise to recognize that "whatever will be, will be." But since in these religions everything has its opposite, we also know there are times to shun fatalistic nihilism and act on the awareness that change and emptiness open up infinite possibilities.

I have heard Professor Eckel describe a scene he witnessed involving intense worship of a glorious statue of the Buddha. Then he described how the same worshippers were asked to meditate on their entire ritual and worship experience as being an illusion, creatively imagined. This sounds a lot like the kind of creative, artistic spirituality that I have called high church atheism, the kind of worship that understands virtually all of our religious language, personifications, and images as metaphorical, symbolic, and imagined. Traditional worship services are in many ways like putting on a play—a kind of dramatic spiritual make-believe. If the worship of a statue of the Buddha is an exercise in creative imagination, what does that suggest about the person the statue represents? Many scholars say that it is difficult to detect an actual life behind the highly stylized literary portraits of Siddhartha Gautama who becomes Buddha (Awakened). But, as with Jesus, the religion based on stories about Siddhartha can be true and valuable, even if they are primarily artistic creations. Furthermore, obsessing about whether they are real historical people can become for us a wasteful and futile distraction from living in the present moment.

For many who understand Buddhism as basically a way to psych oneself out about the nature of life, the most helpful image is perhaps that of *"The Seamless Whole" (Shunyata)*. A way of visualizing nirvana consciousness, this image is about contemplating our participation in all eternity, all reality, beyond yet including time and space. The Seamless Whole is partly a version of the Hindu teaching of the unity of Ultimate Reality (Brahman) and the self (Atman). The Buddhist attitude toward self is surely somewhat similar to the New Testament Gospel image of finding your life by losing it, or losing it by seeking to save it. But in Buddhism, finding your life by losing it is ultimately a matter of no longer worrying about the self at all, in any way! Those who meditate on the Seamless Whole consider themselves extraordinarily blessed when an awareness of this Reality sweeps over them. It may not happen often, but even just an occasional intense experience of the Seamless Whole can suffice to make us feel that we have truly experienced "the peace that passes all understanding."

A paradox here is that one makes an effort to achieve this awareness, and yet when it comes, it is experienced not as something achieved, but as something that comes over us. We are the passive recipients of a sacred gift—a gift spoofed with delicious humor in the "Serenity Now!" episode of the Seinfeld TV show in which the George character's curmudgeonly father, who is anything but serene, periodically screams "Serenity Now!" in a failing effort to reform his persona. The perhaps most famous "Seamless Whole" joke is: What did the Buddhist order at the hamburger stand? Answer: "Make me one with everything."

We've noted the charge commonly leveled against people who call themselves atheists, namely that they are just as much doctrinaire, absolutist "true believers" as are those who promote religious faith. Sam Harris himself acknowledges that his last chapter of *The End of Faith* has been criticized by some as capitulating to or promoting the type of psychological Buddhism I have been describing here. It is a fair point. Is this approach to Buddhism just another form of the absolutist missionary mentality? Is this a claim to have the last word on the only proper religious worldview? Are these ideas of change as the only reality, of emptiness, no-self, The Seamless Whole and Nirvana just another, albeit perhaps more subtle, form of arrogant absolutism? Does Buddhism really have the one and only complete explanation for why people suffer and what to do about it?

Dennis Hinkle may well be correct when he says that Buddhism is the least dogmatic of any religion and that it emphasizes conceptual freedom. But "least dogmatic" could imply "best," and one has to be careful about saying things which appear to suggest that a given religion has a monopoly on truth, freedom, or highest consciousness. I am particularly concerned with the kind of Christianity that arrogantly devalues any religion that isn't mainly about "salvation" defined as getting to an afterlife, especially when it is the kind of "Christianism" that claims to have the only ticket to that afterlife. Instead of focusing on afterlife, I think the issue should be framed in terms of our need to have an emotionally *and intellectually* satisfying spirituality which helps us deal with our mortality while also enhancing our meaningful participation in the eternal now. I hope to bring this kind of spirituality into sharp focus in the next chapter.

It has to be kept in mind that there are many different versions of most religious traditions, and that virtually all of these traditions have their mystics. Part of my goal here has been to provide at least an inkling of how these various traditions can be presented in their best light. Often they have the same priorities and concerns, but simply come at them in different ways. It is not fair to present one tradition in its best light against another in its worst. My main problem with Christopher Hitchins is that although he did a great job of skewering the dark side of religion, he seemed determined to present every religion only in the worst possible light. Thich Nhat Hanh and Matthew Fox, on the other hand, are among those who have provided us with examples of how to bring out the best and most helpful aspects of various religious traditions.

Any religious worldview inevitably is liable to appear on some level as mutually exclusive of other views. How could it be otherwise? Religion by definition tackles the big questions that are sometimes called the "boundary questions," the persistent or perennial questions such as: What is the meaning of life? Why does anything exist at all? What is my purpose in life? Just as physicists struggle to come up with a "theory of everything"— as string theory and M-theory now aspire to be—theologians struggle to comprehend the whole enchilada. All that is required is a proper dose of humility in this quest. Buddhism demonstrates this modesty partly by its use of so many metaphors, stories, riddles, and the like that we can become frustrated when Buddhist teachers don't more quickly get to the point. All the artistic hemming and hawing and seemingly endless explaining, however, is not unique to Buddhism, and it can be a part of the process that actually helps all of us to avoid cavalier absolutism and missionary arrogance.

Much of traditional Buddhist piety and practice is quite clearly the expression of creative artistry. But evidence-based-Buddhism, with its long history of observations that focus on *seeing* Reality rather than speculating about the nature of Reality, is more akin to science, psychology in particular, than to religion. Buddha supposedly said, "Of things I do not know I will not speak." To maintain that this version of Buddhist enlightenment is compatible with a scientific worldview is to praise its method, not to claim that Buddhism as religion trumps all other religions. This type of Buddhism is not based on the authority of a teacher or a book, but on the authority of direct observation. Take for example something mentioned earlier. *No matter how many divine miracles have been attested by various claimants, the vast infinity of unmitigated tragedies throughout history provide evidence that the notion of a benevolent intervening deity is untenable and even ridiculous!* This is facing Reality with no sugar-coating (too much sugar is never good for us). This is the comfort of Truth as opposed to the feel-good security of wishful thinking and speculation. In the words of Carl Sagan "It is far better to grasp the universe as it really is than to persist in delusion, however satisfying and reassuring."

Integral Spirituality and A Brief History of Everything

Many people are not clear about the fact that Buddhism developed in India as a reform version of Hinduism. Within India, Buddhists tended to assimilate back into the Hindu culture. But as Buddhism spread into China, the rest of Asia and beyond, it was better able to maintain its distinctive identity. The influence of the Buddhist/Hindu worldview begins to appear in the United States most notably with the so-called transcendentalists such as Ralph Waldo Emerson and Walt Whitman. One could make a long list of those twentieth-century thinkers in the cultural West who have promoted a type of Buddhism similar to what I am describing in this chapter, but a short list would include Alan Watts, Joseph Campbell, Matthew Fox, Sam Harris, and Ken Wilber. Alan Watts came to the United States from England with a background as an Anglican clergyman and his book titles *This Is It* and *Beyond Theology* clearly indicate his Buddhist leanings. Campbell became a more or less self-educated expert on mythology who particularly favored Gnostic/Buddhist style interpretations of Christianity. Matthew Fox, who began as a priest and Dominican monk, founded The Institute for Culture and Creation Spirituality, and the title of his book *The Coming of the Cosmic Christ* reflects his unique blend of Buddhism and a scientific worldview with biblical theology. Sam Harris is a current atheist writer who nevertheless, as mentioned above, concludes his book *The End of Faith* by recommending what he grants is a Buddhist-style consciousness and worldview.

Ken Wilber is the contemporary writer who arguably has developed the most comprehensive version of an essentially Buddhist perspective on life and the cosmos as a whole. We have met him already at various points, and I have both recognized his contributions and criticized some of his use of jargon. The titles of his later books, *A Brief History of Everything* and *Integral Spirituality* (both 2007), together with his founding of an Integral Institute, give a good indication of his desire to comprehend, integrate, and promote his understanding of Reality as a whole. He has developed a system that depicts Reality consisting of three dimensions described variously as *self, culture, and nature*; or as *Beauty, Goodness, and Truth*; or as *art, morals and science*. (Each of these three ways of describing the three dimensions also corresponds with the basic linguistic structure of I *(self-beauty-art)*, We *(culture-goodness-morals)*, and It *(nature-truth-science)*. The first two dimensions—described either as *self and culture*, or as *Beauty and Goodness*, or as *art and morals*—are by definition singular/individual *(self, Beauty, art)* and plural/social *(culture, Goodness, morals)*. The three dimensions become four dimensions (or "quadrants") if you also divide the third dimension of objective empirical Reality (nature/Truth/science) into singular and plural—that is, single (individual) truths or organisms on the one hand, and complex "organic" systems on the other hand. I realize that it is difficult to understand Wilber's notion of "everything" without seeing his charts and graphs, but for our purposes it will suffice to summarize his most salient points here (in addition to those I have mentioned elsewhere). (Don't let it bother you if you had trouble following the above paragraph.)

One of Wilber's central contentions is that *the modern, enlightened "age of reason" with its focus on materialism and empirical science has tended to ignore the understanding of Reality that can be described as spiritual, holistic, visionary, symbolic, metaphorical, pluralistic, and above all, integrated or integral!* But, and this is a huge but, we cannot and will not recover the various aspects of this spiritual worldview by downplaying or ignoring the dimension of reality that the scientific worldview reveals to us. A Wilber's mantra is that evolution "transcends and includes" what has come before. *The empirical worldview is not wrong. It is just too narrow and limited.* It must be both included and transcended. In *A Brief History of Everything* Wilber writes:

> "... the rational-industrial worldview, and roughly, the Enlighten-
> ment in general served many useful and extraordinary purposes.
> We might mention: the rise of democracy; the banishing of slav-
> ery; the emergence of liberal feminism; the widespread emergence
> of empirical sciences; an increase in average life span of almost
> three decades; the introduction of relativity and perspectivism in
> art and morals and science; the move from ethnocentric to world-
> centric morality; and in general the undoing of dominator social
> hierarchies in numerous significant ways."

While the empirical worldview in many ways has made and is making the modern world a better place, Wilber continues, "the idea that there is simply a single empirical world or empirical nature, and that knowledge consists solely in mirroring or mapping this one true world . . . fails to take into account the self that is making the maps in the first place." There is a subjective, personal and arbitrary element in the creation of any worldview. The history of the evolution of worldviews is indeed restrained by some realities such as basic chemistry or laws of physics that prevent these worldviews "from being merely collective hallucinations" (which religions sometimes seem to be when they fly off into a more or less bizarre fantasy land that followers are expected to take literally). It is subjective human beings who artistically map out worldviews—and theologies! Marcus Borg also stresses the subjective aspect of spirituality in *Meeting Jesus AGAIN for the First Time* where he describes his experiences of "nature mysticism," of "radical amazement" (a term coined by Jewish theologian Abraham Heschel), and of overwhelming, tremendous mystery at the center of existence—"the holy mystery that is all around us and within us." Like Wilber, Borg fully affirms both the empirical worldview and *the subjective experience of sacredness*.

Rudolf Bultmann has been one of the most famous Christian theologians also to embrace the scientific worldview (*Weltanschauung*) and question supernaturalism. His anthropological, psychological, subjective and existentialist understanding of the truth(s) behind biblical mythology marked a major development in the history of theology. In the 1950s he wrote: ". . . the very fact that it is possible to produce a secularized version of the New Testament conception of faith proves that there is nothing mysterious or supernatural about the Christian life." (I'm quite sure he meant that "Christian life" was "not mysterious" in the sense that Christians are not enamored with the bizarre, the spooky or the supernatural.) Reflecting Luther's emphasis on grace, he demythologized authentic "life in the Spirit" as the abandonment of all self-contrived security or certainty—any attempt to "save ourselves." Life in faith, or trust in God, he said, is about opening up here and now, not clinging selfishly or desperately to "life in the flesh," and committing oneself unreservedly to the future. When he writes about "crucifying" our attachment to security and certainty in this world, the metaphorical use of "crucifying" illustrates his subjective and existential understanding of theological language. In my view, Bultmann unfortunately did not sufficiently demythologize Christ, God, or "cross and resurrection." He continued to proclaim Christian faith as based on "uniquely unique" (sic—code for "miraculous" perhaps) historical and "revelatory events *par excellence*" in a way that still carries a hint of the supernatural. He used male pronouns in reference to "God." He used the language of being "in but not of the world" in a way that seemed to down-play the cause of justice and peace here and now. He was quite aware of the history of philosophy, but not so aware, it seems to me, of the issues raised by the existence and contributions of other major religious traditions such as Buddhism.

For Wilber, an empirical worldview is great and important as far as it goes, but it is not the whole story. When it becomes "Scientism," it ignores *the spiritual dimension of self, culture, morals, beauty, art.* Bultmann simi-larly offered much of value by combining a postmodern empirical, down-to-earth outlook with a subjective, existential, psychological, and artistic approach to the spiritual dimension. Unfortunately, he did nevertheless remain perhaps unconsciously accustomed to the use of some traditional mid-twentieth century Christian terminology.

To illustrate what he means by Spirit or Soul, Wilber says, "You can look at a brain, but you must talk to a mind." When he says "Interpretive knowledge is just as important as empirical knowledge," I think he has corrected Einstein's (perhaps deliberate) overstatement about imagination being *more important* than knowledge. Improving on the notion that a personal God can tell us something about our worth that the neutral sun as a part of nature cannot tell us, Wilber maintains that it is our *higher, in-ner, spiritual consciousness* that interprets the meaning of either a beautiful sunset or of a burning desert sun. "Nature," he writes, "is a self-organizing dynamic system" that is "the objective manifestation of Spirit . . .definitely not a static or deterministic machine . . . The very processes of nature are spiritual processes . . ." Evolution moves, albeit in fits and starts, in a di-rection of increasing complexity, differentiation/integration, organization, relative autonomy, and progress—progress, that is, within the limits of in-evitable decline in any complex system (entropy). Based on this evolution-ary direction, Wilber sees the universe as having consciousness, meaning, intrinsic value, pattern, and grace woven into its very fabric.

Instead of a purely mechanistic universe, Wilber sees the spiritual dimension that he describes as Self, Soul, Beauty, or Art, as the highest source of an evolutionary process in which "Spirit empties itself into man-ifestation." Another way to express Wilber's point that *the very processes of nature are spiritual processes* is to repeat what I said earlier about the natu-ral evolutionary world as a dynamic blending of random adaptation with *an inherent, intrinsic sense of logic and order.* (It is both scientifically and spiritually delusional to argue that evolution is a *purely* accidental process.) Harvard theologian Gordon Kaufman described this "spiritual process" as a manifestation of sacred or "divine" creativity. His book titled *In the beginning . . . Creativity* (2004) develops the understanding that "God" is basically a metaphor for the ultimate mystery of creativity. Kaufman clearly does not envision the existence of a supernatural creative agent. He coined the term "serendipitous creativity" to express the meaning of the "God symbol," and he understands this sacred, serendipitous creativity as a *natural phenomenon.* (This reminds me of Daniel Dennett's book on *Religion as a Natural Phenomenon.)* Joseph Campbell traces the origin of the word "serendipitous" to its Sanskrit root in stories about wanderers having adventures. The image is not so much of "accidental" occurrences but of marvelous, open-ended journeys. Kaufman's *serendipitous creativity* imagines the universe as on a journey of this nature—a Macro-Journey in the context of which our individual lives are micro-journeys.

The Buddhist aspect of Wilber's thought is clear in his phrases about highest Consciousness. He describes highest Consciousness as "radiant Abyss and ultimate Ground . . . Your very Self intersects the Self of the Kosmos (sic) at large—a supreme identity . . . that undoes the knot of the separate self and buries it in splendor . . . The stages of transpersonal growth [take the] observing Self to its ultimate abode, which is pure Spirit or pure Emptiness . . ." For Wilber, Emptiness has two meanings. One meaning is a particular "discrete, identifiable state of awareness . . . classical nirvana." But the second and most profound meaning of Emptiness is not that of one state among others, but a *totally non-dual mysticism*—often described as *"Suchness" (Tathata)—an abiding sense of being one with absolute reality, one with the true nature of things beyond all concepts and distinctions, one with The Seamless Whole (Shunyata), one with the Mystery!* Wilber continues: "You don't look at the sky, you are the sky . . . awareness is no longer split into a seeing subject in here and a seen object out there. There is just pure seeing . . . you simply rest in pure observing awareness . . . relax into present experience . . . duality is not present in the immediateness of real experience . . . you do not *have* an experience, you *are* every experience . . . The sound of one hand clapping is the sound the Big Bang made . . . the sound of supernovas exploding in space . . . the sound of the robin singing . . . the sound of the entire manifest universe—and you are that sound." "The sound of one hand clapping" (technically called a *koan*) famously symbolizes an awareness or experience of timelessness in a moment of time, the awareness that "I am the universe happening"—the sound of *Reality* beyond logic and reason, beyond time, beyond words, beyond sound. (This paragraph should make you aware of what meditation is all about.)

The unity of Spirituality and Art is absolutely central in Wilber's analysis. The "upper left quadrant" or "dimension" in his chart of basic Reality is the "higher" dimension that is described as Spirit, spiritual, holistic, visionary, integral and artistic! But art also relates to all the other quadrants and dimensions as well. Art transcends, includes and integrates consciousness, empirical science and culture. Art is about holistic world-centric perspectives. (I like to use the spelling *wholistic* to emphasize the connotation of wholeness or all-encompassing completeness which is also associated with the Hebrew word *Shalom*.) Wilber argues that we needed the postmodern movement to counteract the ways in which enlightenment science "had begun to crowd out consciousness, aesthetics [art], and morals." Higher and deeper spiritual consciousness necessarily includes a global and multicultural perspective.

This spiritual consciousness also encourages a *post-conventional imagination* that Wilber defines as "what if" and "as if" thinking. "What if" thinking puts me in mind of the phrase that the Kennedy brothers borrowed from fellow Irishman George Bernard Shaw: "Some see things as they are and ask why; I dream things that never were and ask why not." Dr. Hinkle says that this kind of "what if" thinking is the kind of "propositional thinking" that was a central part of his education with his mentor George Kelly, who linked it with "skill in considering alternatives." Hinkle describes how Kelly often said "Well, that's one way to look at it. What are others?" Hinkle describes his own clients as coming in as concrete thinkers, and leaving therapy as propositional thinkers. They had been in the world of certainty with its locked-in attitudes, but in therapy they entered the world of creative possibilities. They had been in the world of hidebound religion, but in therapy they entered the world of spiritual, scientific, artistic openness and freedom. Once again it is appropriate to remind ourselves here that many of the most creative, productive, and influential people in the history of the world have led very unconventional lives!

We have already encountered Wilber's objections to "immortality symbols." Any such immortality projects are for him a matter of lying about our mortality by pretending that we are above or separate from nature. Living in the present moment essentially rules out any notion of surviving death or living another life on the beautiful isle of somewhere.

Living in the eternal now is about psyching ourselves out regarding our mortality—not about goin' somewhere, not about a personified God watching over us. Waxing poetic Wilber writes:

> "(The *Spirituality* which is) present throughout the entire evolutionary process becomes increasingly conscious of its own condition . . . There is no end limit, no foundation, no final resting place, only Emptiness and endless Grace. So the luminous Play carries on with insanely joyous regard, timeless gesture to timeless gesture, radiant in its wild release, ecstatic in its perfect abandon, endless fullness beyond endless fullness, this miraculously self-liberating Dance, and there is no one anywhere to watch it, or even to sing its praises."

To go back to a great line about mythology and spirituality quoted in the introduction to this book: "[Spirituality] is the song of the universe, music so deeply embedded in our collective unconscious that we dance to it, even when we can't name the tune.

CHAPTER 6

Humans as Mystics

IT IS PROBABLY SAFE to say that the people who really and truly believe in heaven as an actual place where Jesus and their loved ones are waiting to receive them with open arms, who believe that they will be reincarnated back into this world, or who believe that there is some other way in which we survive death, are becoming a smaller proportion of the population— especially in the developed world where the results of science have often been little short of miraculous. Life after death is no longer routinely taken for granted as it apparently tended to be in earlier phases of human history. Some of the earliest archeological evidence we have for human religiosity is found in the European Paleolithic cave paintings, and in the ritual burial of skulls which suggests a formal procedure for coming to terms with death, while the massive pyramid tombs of Egypt are an ultimately bizarre reminder of early human preoccupation with life after death. Educated younger people in particular, despite their immersion in the special-effects fantasy worlds of modern movies, are increasingly skeptical about supernatural theological doctrines and beliefs. I think they understand that the word dead means exactly what it means! In spite of hype about near-death, out-of-body or other such experiences, people are beginning to understand that *by definition* death means the end. By definition, death means not surviving—not coming back. By definition, death means that there is no supernatural "after."

Don Cupitt's book, *After God: The Future of Religion,* challenges us to accept the fact that "supernatural belief is out of date and intellectually in poor shape." He argues that even those who "hold their supernatural beliefs in a literal or realistic sense do not in practice behave as if they take their own beliefs seriously." They expect more from science and technology (modern medicine, for example) than they expect from their supernatural beliefs. "Supernatural belief lingers," Cupitt writes, "because it has social prestige for historical reasons, but it is now 'fringe' as far as the serious business of life is concerned." Conservative and mega-churches may seem successful, but in the larger society they are nevertheless a fringe phenomenon with a questionable future. The traditional religious language which embodies a sense of objective and absolute truth still has its appeal, but it is more nostalgia than reality. In the postmodern scientific age, Cupitt insists, we need spirituality that is comfortable with "some form of pragmatism that has given up on the idea of objective truth, and is content in every department of life with ways of speaking that work well enough to get by with—for the present." In other words, we need to embrace realized, participatory eschatology and live in the eternal now. President Obama affirmed this kind of pragmatism in his second inaugural speech when he cautioned against confusing rigid absolutism with standing on principle.

In Stephen Greenblatt's view, "The Swerve" was a new opening for critical thinking, the beginning of the end of supernatural superstition, and the advent of a more humanistic way of dealing with death—by focusing on the *fear* of death! He writes that the Renaissance was the beginning of a swerve (turn) away from an authoritarian system that exercised control by promoting guilt (especially about sexual pleasure) and "the fear of some horrendous punishment waiting for one in the realm beyond the grave"—an eternal torment in hell, sometimes lambasted by critics of such torment as an egregiously unjust "infinite punishment for finite sins." Focusing on *the nature of things* as the ancient philosophers Lucretius and Epicurus understood the world to be, Greenblatt celebrates their foresight, their prescient understanding of life and the world that pre-figures the modern scientific, empirical worldview. As we saw in chapter 2, the Epicurean focus on pleasure and happiness is similar to the focus on human and planetary *well-being* that Sam Harris holds up as the central ethical precept in his book *The Moral Landscape*. The idea that the ultimate criterion of moral goodness is whatever contributes to this well-being is very much in sync with the classic ethics of utilitarianism—the affirmation of whatever is useful for creating "the greatest happiness and good for the greatest number." This ethic is a more positive version of the Hippocratic Oath which reminds doctors to "do no harm."

Although Woody Allen has sometimes portrayed a character who trembles at the prospect of going out of existence, his own view seems to be expressed in his previously mentioned joke: "I'm not afraid of death; I just don't want to be there when it happens." The joke suggests that the only legitimate fear of death is not the prospect of oblivion but of a painful and unpleasant dying process. Robin Williams often wrestled with issues of death and mortality in his stream of consciousness comedic way. The mixture of humor and seriousness in his movie roles also embodies this dialectic. In her humorous but also very serious one-woman show about becoming an ex-Roman Catholic atheist, Julia Sweeny compares her brother's long and torturous death from cancer with "the bad weekend" that Jesus suffered for our sins. Her rant on this subject reminds me of a bumper sticker I saw which said, "If Christ died for my sins, he over-reacted"—which in turn reminds me of Ibsen's Peer Gynt character who can be seen as a vacuous non-entity unworthy of either heaven or hell. The point is not to compare levels of suffering or evildoing—I suspect that for most of us the sins of omission far exceed the sins of commission. The overall point here is that the fear of death, if we embrace an enlightened scientific world view, will be transformed into concern for issues such as palliative hospice care and the right to die in a manner of more or less one's own choosing. Existential angst about death is best countered by resting in the serenity which comes from having lived life to the fullest and, as death approaches, recalling with gratitude, as we are able, all the joys of life that we have experienced.

Both *The Swerve* and *After God* focus on overcoming negative feelings about oblivion, nihilism, nothingness. What Wilber calls "luminous Play" Cupitt calls "the Blissful Void." Affirming "the fleeting insubstantial emptiness of all existence," Cupitt writes: "You must learn to experience nihilism as levity, lightness. The strange unexpected happiness this brings is a wonderful deliverance from the fear of death, loss, and suffering . . . casting oneself unreservedly into the flux of existence, spending oneself, living as hard as one can, burning without being afraid of burnout." Rather than being a bleak absence of meaning and value, Stephen Batchelor says that emptiness is "an absence of what limits and confines one's capacity to realize what a human life can potentially become." Greenblatt puts the emphasis more simply on the joy of being free from the "terrible affliction" of dread about what might happen after death. His straightforward advice is to not waste this life worrying about a next life that doesn't exist. For those who would ask why we cannot enjoy pleasant fictions and must instead "rub our noses" in the reality of death, I repeat the poetic observation made by Keats: "Beauty is truth, truth beauty—that is all." Pleasant fictions about going to heaven may be poetically justified, but only if we face the *truth* that they are essentially metaphorical and imaginative images.

Hedging Your Bets on the Afterlife

We observed earlier that even many traditionally devout Christians, when face to face with the Grim Reaper, will go to extraordinary lengths to stave off death and live just one more hour, day, week, month or year. I suggested they were hedging their bets on the afterlife. I chuckle to recall that at the church camp where I spent a lot of time in my early years we could sing "You are lost and gone forever, dreadful sorry Clementine" with more gusto than we sang hymns about Easter and heaven. When addressing the possibility of life after death in *When Bad Things Happen to Good People*, Rabbi Kushner writes that "since we cannot know for sure we would be well advised to take this world as seriously as we can, in case it turns out to be the only one we will ever have, and to look for meaning and justice here." In the same way that Richard Dawkins says only that there "almost certainly" is no God, I am saying that there almost certainly is no life after death in any of the ways it is typically envisioned.

Once again we need to return to the kind of paradoxical "as if" thinking in which we hold two opposite notions in our minds at the same time as if both are true. We live in the moment *as if* there is no life after death, while at the same time we live in the face of death *as if (imagining!)* our life is eternal. (If it comforts someone to imagine walking and talking "in the garden" eternally with God, far be it from me to deny anyone such an image.) As noted before, it is not unreasonable to consider the unlikely possibility of being graciously surprised after death. Such openness is openness to the Ultimate Mystery for which the word God is shorthand. Science by definition is always open in this way also. But over-confident promotion of the notion of surviving death can become the kind of arrogant absolutism that is inappropriate for mere mortals. A major purpose of any meaningful concept of God must be to keep us from absolutizing our ideas and beliefs—especially beliefs about "God!" More than anything else it is precisely such arrogant theological certainty that keeps us from fully engaging the Ultimate Mystery in which we live and move and have our being.

That we must resist our desire to have more certainty or security than we can possibly have is an important message in the story about Adam and Eve tragically eating from the tree of knowledge because they wanted to be like God. The story suggests that they were already "in God's image" as relational and creative beings with amazing potential, but that this wasn't enough for them. The emphasis in this story is on avoiding the self-centered temptation to think of ourselves more highly than we ought. This emphasis has often mistakenly been seen as a demand for blind obedience, and has typically kept interpreters from dealing with the fact that our innate curiosity and moral sense of right and wrong are actually essential features of our humanity! The so-called "fall into sin" has to be seen in some ways as a good thing, as a fall *up* into our humanity where animal instinct is not our only guide. Our curiosity and desire to expand our knowledge has great survival value. We need to take stories like Adam and Eve ("adam" is basically just the Hebrew word for "human being" by the way!) for what they are fundamentally about, and not make the mistake of thinking that every single element in the story conveys an equally great truth.

Those who say that God made Adam and Eve, not Adam and Steve, are too enamored of structure and order. They fail to notice that because of the anti-fertility-religion theme the two distinct creation stories in Genesis actually play down sexuality by focusing in the first story on humans as "in God's image," and in the second story on man and woman as equal companions more than as sexual partners. If the emphasis were on sex and we—foolishly—took the second story in Genesis 2 literally, it would seem as though in this story God originally had bestiality in mind for Adam, who does not find any of the animals to be a fitting mate. The main message in Genesis about the "structure of creation and reality" is not about the certainty of static heterosexual order. It is about our dynamic relationships—to divinity (the sacred), to each other (same-sex couples certainly can be loving companions), and to our environment. The message is conveyed above all by the garden imagery that symbolizes the incredible diversity of nature, *including the diversity of sexualities!* (Consider the androgynous sea horse!)

Another significant example of the problematic nexus between rigid patriarchy and biblical literalism regarding sexuality and gender is the vehemence with which some insist that God must be a "He." If someone were to ask if God has a penis, many who insist on using male pronouns for God would likely be shocked and offended. God must be male; society must have a clear and certain patriarchal structure, but please, no talk about a penis! My point here is that those who make such a big deal out of taking the Bible literally can end up feeling embarrassed when forced to consider the unsettling implications of their literalism. (Outspoken biblical literalists also embarrass themselves whenever they put a star and wise men in a Christmas manger tableau because neither of these appears in the manger story.) When the youth department folks of The American

Lutheran Church (TALC) published *Called to be Human* in the early 1960s, in order to spark conversation about humanism, the humanity of Jesus, and perhaps also to counteract sex-negative tendencies in Christian theology, one of the authors sometimes brought up the question of whether Jesus had a penis under his robe—typically revealing the emotionally charged relationship between sex, gender, and religion. Sadly, when the National Council of Churches in the USA began publishing gender inclusive language materials it actually received death threats!

Commenting on Christian fundamentalism in her book *The Battle for God*, Karen Armstrong emphasizes the notion I mentioned in the Preface to this book that in a strange way the current brand of fundamentalism is "scientific." Instead of recognizing the artistic, mythological, metaphorical, and symbolic element in religion, contemporary fundamentalism insists on reading the Bible as scientific fact, so creationism becomes Intelligent Design, which is claimed to be scientific. Virtually all the stories in the Bible are claimed to be historical facts. I once heard a biology professor from prestigious Pepperdine University in Malibu, California insist that the biblical story of Noah's Ark is scientifically plausible—in spite of the indisputable fact that there are two contradictory versions of the story regarding the animals on the ark. An elderly Lutheran Bishop in Iowa told me that he believed heaven was on another planet somewhere. I have also heard it seriously suggested that heaven will be right here on earth where all the oceans would be dried up, creating much more land for habitation by the saved.

In other words, these kinds of fundamentalists are claiming in effect that there is no such thing as the supernatural—that everything they believe is "factually natural." There is little or no need for symbolism and metaphor because their religious beliefs are plain scientific facts that, as the word "science" suggests, can be known rather than merely believed. This attempt to obscure or destroy the distinction between natural and supernatural (as I noted in the Preface) makes a mockery of what we mean by science. Science is about a method for determining what is real and true based on evidence. Real evidence is not based on arbitrary "authorities" such as holy books or anecdotal storytellers. Real evidence is empirical and it shows concrete results. The kind of "science" promoted by religious fundamentalism would never have figured out how to do open-heart surgery or how to go to the moon. We have here another example of "by their fruits (or lack thereof!) ye shall know them."

It is much more honest for fundamentalist believers just to admit that they believe in the supernatural. It is not surprising that some of these believers condemn Harry Potter and other magical storytelling. The ancient laws of the Hebrew Torah condemned witches and sorcerers to death. Magical, supernatural storytelling is an expression of creative imagination similar to religious storytelling, which is correct to see itself as in competition with non-religious magical miracle stories. As art forms, both kinds of stories are capable of opening us up to and expressing a sense of Mystery. After all, as movie special effects wizards and great composers know, or as magicians (even amateurs such as I) like to point out, the emotion and sense of wonder engendered by an illusion can be authentic even though that sense of wonder and awe is produced by a form of trickery.

The biggest problem I have with Harry Potter or the "Twilight" vampire type of storytelling is that in worlds where anything seems possible, life can begin to seem repetitive and pointless—or we can become desensitized. Characters can be terribly injured or killed, and yet they are right back up again, enlivened by one special effect after another. Movies that rely too much on special effects typically leave me emotionally cold or even put me to sleep. They don't engage me with the kind of meaning that comes from an awareness of limits and consequences. The joke about two old golfers in heaven getting holes-in-one every time and then complaining "what's the point?" very effectively illustrates the desirability of boundaries and fixed limits.

In his 1985 novel *The Catholic*, David Plante observes that for believers "divine grace was so powerful it could transform a dead human body into a resurrected and glorified body that would exist forever in a world more real than this," and then adds his own more sober sentiment, "but I wanted my life to be free of images that were fantasy." Oakley Hall paints a very bleak picture of life and the history of the world in his novel "Warlock." Sleepless in the early morning (an occupational hazard for writers it seems) he muses "the only justification is in the attempt, not the achievement, for there is no achievement." He asks "Is not the history of the world no more than a record of violence and death, cut in stone?" He describes "those brave ones who will fall in hopeless effort for us all, whose only gift to us will be that we will grieve for them a little while . . . " Bringing religious imagery to bear he wonders: "Can I look out at these cold stars in this black sky and believe in my heart of hearts that it was this sky that hung over Bethlehem, and that a star such as these stars glittered there to raise men's hearts to false hopes forever? This is the sky of Gethsemane, and that of Bethlehem has vanished with its star."

Hall's attitude suggests to me that we should focus on Ultimate Mystery more than on ultimate meaning or a quest for certainty and immortality. Our sapient ability to ponder abstract, theoretical meaning or to seek changeless stability can prevent us from having a life that is worth living. Our relationship to eternity should be about feeling comfortable and at home with the mysterious nature of Reality, adopting a compassionate, global perspective, and focusing on the joy of being alive in the moment. *Meaning and purpose is something we create as we participate in all the relationships that make up life's dynamic interplay of stability and change.* The value, worth, meaning, and purpose of life is *intrinsic—inherent.* Human life in particular has all these qualities by its very nature and essence. The search for some extraneous purpose beyond our amazing lives here and now is a fool's errand.

Why focus on misery when even for those who face formidable challenges or limitations, who barely eke out a meager living or toil in jobs with few rewards, the good moments can outnumber, and meaningful relationships far outweigh, moments of dissatisfaction and discomfort. Down moments can help us appreciate up moments. This was a theme of the famous "last lecture" by Carnegie Mellon professor of human-computer interaction Randy Pausch, who shared with the world his thoughts about dying of cancer at age 47, leaving his wife and three young children.

The surprising thing is not that there is evil and suffering in the world, but how much goodness there is. Living in the moment with a sense of wonder, awe, and mystery, is possible for anyone. As the musical *Spamalot* recommends, "Always look on the bright side of life!" Retain your childlike imagination. "Twinkle, twinkle little star; how I wonder what you are." Even though, unlike the Hebrew Psalmist, we know that the starlight we see now has come to us through countless light years from a star or from an entire galaxy that may have died long ago, it is still awe inspiring to "consider the heavens." There is a sense in which we are all made of stardust, and when we do anything that enhances life on this planet, we can be like stars whose light shines on long after they have died.

Christmas—More Popular than Easter

Christmas, with its star in Matthew's story and its angels in Luke's, has always been more popular than Easter with its empty tomb, it seems to me. We have seen how the Hebrews rightly condemned various aspects of fertility religion, particularly child sacrifice. But despite the specter of such misguided and abhorrent rituals, both the real and the symbolic connection between sex, life, fertility and birth, remain an important and positive motif in all great spiritual traditions. Birth imagery is the more usual way in which most early religions picture the creation of the world. Scientists frequently talk about the *birth* of the universe. Easter and reincarnation are often associated with themes of renewal, hope, and transformation, but also with the image of rebirth. Easter eggs and fertile rabbits are secular symbols of birth and rebirth. The words "Easter" and "Lent" are both related to "spring," the season when life (and hope!) is reborn. So Easter could conceivably be understood as virtually another version of Christmas in which birth is the primary motif. When St. Paul compares resurrection to a seed dying and then springing back to life, he is making a flawed analogy at best. A seed is more like an egg. Neither "die," but both contain all the potential for life and transformation.

When Easter is visualized in terms of birth, rebirth, and renewal, I think we wisely move away from associating it with life after death. We move back toward an earlier, more honest Judaism, for example, where the notion of a future life is associated with future generations, with our children and descendents both individually and as the human race. Judaism was not the only tradition to connect the erotic drive to reproduce with some sort of immortality. The desire for immortality is not necessarily a problem unless it is directed exclusively and foolishly toward pie in the sky when you die. (Besides, having too much pie in heaven would kill you again—unless you subscribe to the notion of comedian Father Guido Sarducci that since you're already dead when you arrive in heaven you might as well throw caution to the wind and live it up!) The erotic drive of our "selfish genes" to stave off mortality by reproducing can actually become a problem if it results in over-population, genocidal wars, disastrous climate change—or when it spawns hysterical promotion of heterosexuality and fertility at the expense of sexual minority groups. (Is the Vatican listening?) When we consider how unimaginably crowded the earth would be if every woman had as many babies as possible, or every person ever born were still alive on the planet, we begin to get a whole different perspective on our fear of death and our desire for immortality.

In the Doge's palace in Venice, now an art museum, hangs what is said to be the world's largest framed painting. It takes up an entire wall of what used to be a huge ballroom. It depicts paradise—heaven. Various figures float around the heavenly throne. It is crowded, and it would not be my idea of paradise—I wouldn't want to spend ten minutes there. Among other things, seeing this painting made me think about a calculation I once saw of how deeply stacked with bodies heaven would be if it were a very large planet containing even a small percentage of the humans who ever lived. Many depictions of heaven remind me of the aphorism "Those whom the gods would punish, they grant their desires"—or of film critic Mick LaSalle's suggestion that serious movie presentations of heaven and afterlife would be better left to the imagination.

We can't focus on Christmas without returning to the relationship between art, music and religion. Christmas is surely one of the main reasons for anyone with a Christian background to reclaim their religion. The music alone is of inestimable value, in spite of its exploitation and over-exposure during the holiday shopping season. While angels are one of the most prominent themes in Christmas carols (helping to explain why so many people have told poll-takers that they believe in angels), my own personal favorite angel music is the eight-part double chorus in Mendelssohn's oratorio "Elijah" with its text: "For He shall give His angels charge over thee, that they may protect thee in all the ways thou goest." I absolutely adore this music and its text—and it was probably one of the choruses to be immediately encored about four times at the oratorio's premier performance in Birmingham, England. But I do not believe that angels actually exist. What I find so wonderful in the text of this chorus is the sense of encouragement, support, future orientation, feeling at home in the universe, and optimistic hope that it expresses. It reminds me how to approach death without fear.

I am a tenor, and my favorite aria (that I have at times described as my theme-song) comes at the end of "Elijah" when Elijah has been carried to heaven in a fiery chariot. The text is "Then shall the righteous shine forth as the Sun in their heavenly father's realm." I like to describe this song as "expressing an upbeat attitude toward the mystery of existence." Let me make it perfectly clear one more time: A big part of the reason I emphasize reclaiming what is worthwhile in traditional religions is that great religious music inevitably will continue to be sung and played, in spite of the fact that much of the verbal imagery that may be involved is extremely fanciful, dated, or supernatural. Fewer and fewer people will be taking the supernatural images literally, but they will still find the music uplifting and meaningful. Heaven imagery with God and The Lamb on a glorious throne, as in the ending of Handel's "Messiah," will be in a similar league with the image of "going to dance in all the galaxies"—a "secular" poetic metaphor coming from a person whose identity (soon to be revealed) may come as a surprise. The music of Ravi Shankar seems to me a marvelous blending of secular and sacred sensibilities. Music is a major part of religion everywhere around the globe.

In his memoir *Nothing To Be Frightened Of,* self-described agnostic novelist Julian Barnes describes the Christian religion as "a beautiful lie . . . a tragedy with a happy ending." He also describes the soul as "a story that the lump of meat called the brain tells itself." He does not indulge in the arrogant self-centeredness of imagining that a cataclysmic destruction of the earth will happen in his own lifetime, but he does lament the fact that even the sun will eventually die and that all our science, art, and literature will be obliterated. Yet he embraces nostalgia about the meaning he finds in the Mozart Requiem, Italian painting, German music, French stained glass, and church architecture. He questions whether moments of meaning and relationships add up to happiness. But as Garrison Keillor highlights in his New York Times review of Barnes' "beautiful and funny" book, "In this meditation on death, he brings to life, in short sure strokes, his parents, Albert and Kathleen." A birthday cake becomes an important memento of his mother, and this focus on birth in the context of a return to his own parental origins is a telling comment on the way many of us bookend our lives with meaning.

The spiritual that imagines "Goin' to live with God" also proclaims "I want to meet my mother" (and other family members), but what if this is a pipe dream? What if it isn't actually going to happen? I contend that what such sentiments really mean is that our parents, family and in fact all the people who have ever lived, have gone before us into death, and that there is significant comfort in knowing that we all walk the same walk from womb to tomb, from cradle to grave. Our parents, particularly our mothers, brought us into this opportunity to experience the eternal now, the Seamless Whole, and like them, we will also come to the exit. I find it not the least bit surprising that when soldiers feel they are facing imminent death they often will instinctively call out for mommy. Many people in the later part of their lives return to the area where their lives began, where they were born.

I was some time ago friend and pastor to a spiritual nonbeliever who, because of her long-term health issues, had an intensely symbiotic relationship with his wife of more than fifty years. As she lay dying in the hospital she would occasionally call out to her long-deceased brother, and my friend would make the corkscrew circle around his ear and point toward the ceiling to indicate to me that she was trying to communicate with her brother. He clearly thought this was silly. But not long after her death, he would expect people who visited him at home to greet his wife as if she were still there. He would occasionally ask me if I thought he was crazy, and the best I could come up with was to tell him about serious studies showing that a large proportion of people feel that they are still in some sort of contact with deceased loved ones, especially spouses. What this tells us is that our emotional needs sometimes trump our rational nature, and that memories, images, or imagined experiences can seem very real on an emotional and non-rational level. Unfortunately, many people use this as an excuse to delude themselves about the true nature of Reality. There is nothing wrong in living with a certain amount of fantasy. But if it becomes "living a lie" our personal integrity and even sanity can be at stake.

One of our family friends with an acute sense of humor wrote her own obituary which became quite a cause celeb in St. Paul/Minneapolis, Minnesota—garnering special attention from both newspapers and television. Part of the humor was that in listing those who had preceded her in death she included "millions of people buried the world over." She also wrote "survived by you, the reader." Further, she cautioned whimsically against anyone planning to join her soon in heaven because she figured she would be "spending at least the next twenty years in purgatory playing bingo." (It's clear to me that these kinds of jokes betray how we don't really believe that the afterlife we imagine is a literal reality.) As is true in so many other ways, there is great comfort in knowing we are not the only one, that we are not alone. Death has been described as the great leveler, but I think it is more meaningful to characterize it as an ultimate experience and manifestation of our common humanity—and of Reality.

In valuing Christmas over Easter I am suggesting that some metaphors may be better than others—and that in order to keep Easter metaphors in particular from becoming dissembling lies we must demythologize many of these images. Again, the endless jokes involving "the pearly gates" and other images of what we might encounter in heaven, suggest that we really don't take that whole scenario seriously. Does anyone really believe literally in what they are saying when they talk about deceased loved ones as being with angels or turning into angels, flying around with cumbersome wings, spending all their time in heaven looking down on us, or forever enjoying a favorite earthly activity, etc.? (The 1984 ballad by Seals and Setser about Seven Spanish Angels who "take another angel home" expresses a lovely sentiment about devoted love and it appropriately pictures death as "going home," but it is clearly a poetic metaphor.) Would we really want heaven to be an endless family reunion? (Sadly, for many people a family reunion that lasted a mere month would seem more like hell than heaven.) When a Hollywood award recipient says something like "I know my mom is looking down proudly tonight on her daughter," I think it goes without saying that a more accurate and honest version would be "I like to imagine my mom smiling down from above . . . " What one is really doing is projecting how the deceased person might be feeling if they were still with us—and that we wish they still were here with us! We are utilizing culturally accepted ways of expressing our struggle to come to terms with the death and loss of someone we continue to love and cherish.

As the great leveler, death is indeed a type of reunion—with the whole human family! If we tell children that their grandma or their pet dog is "in heaven" we need to do it in a way which allows them to realize eventually that this is an imaginative and pleasant fiction intended to help us cope with a painful reality. We also must make it possible for children eventually to become aware that fairy tales such as Little Red Riding Hood, with its dark elements, as well as horror movies and "death defying" amusement rides, perform the necessary function of helping us prepare or "rehearse" for the bad things that will inevitably happen in life. We have to be very careful about lying to children. It can lead to a situation in which they hardly believe anything that adults tell them. It has been claimed that little or no harm is done when we employ pleasant, imaginative fictions. To some degree that may be true. But taken too literally, these fictions can do great damage to our *intellectual integrity* which is such an essential aspect of our humanity. Furthermore, it remains a sad fact that many of those who take such fictions and other beliefs literally often tend to promote bigoted or narrow-minded religious, moral, social and political views—thereby giving their entire religious tradition a negative reputation. At the time I am writing this, sad to say, instead of Christians being known "by their love," too many who claim the name are known by their judgmental and bigoted prejudices!

When I first began my teaching career in California I developed and taught well-attended college courses on death, loss and grief. Many of the students were only freshmen or sophomores, but they felt a real need to deal with their mortality. Famous death and dying expert Dr. Elizabeth Kübler-Ross, whose book on the subject was one of our standard texts, died when I was in the early stages of writing this book. (I once had an interesting conversation with her about facing one's own death as a supposed expert on death and dying.) In one of the published obituaries she is said to have visualized her own death and destiny as "going to dance in all the galaxies." (Minneapolis Star Tribune 8-26-04). It's a lovely sentiment that sounds much more poetic than factual, but it also does express a very real scientific fact about the universe which is worth repeating here—that from the point of view of physics and astronomy, we are all stardust.

As we saw in the previous chapter, the Buddhist version of this awareness about how matter "gets around" is that everything is contingent, a seamless whole, interbeing (Thich Nhat Hanh), interconnected (Matthew Fox). Emptiness is the realization that everything is empty of self-nature ("self" is only an idea or "construct"), and emptiness is another word for contingency. And *contingency means that everything is contingent on and interdependent with everything else.* Astronomer Carl Sagan's famous way of explaining it was to say that if you wanted to make an apple pie truly from scratch, you would have to reinvent the entire universe.

When we consider the imagery in Scriptures, or in poetry and hymns, we can try to see how the metaphors and symbols are functionally and artistically appropriate even though we don't find them to be literally factual. There may be nothing wrong with a comforting image as long as we recognize its metaphorical nature. Hymns such as "Children of the Heavenly Father," "This is My Father's World," "Mothering God, You Gave Me Birth," and "When I Come to Die, Give Me Jesus" can help Christians feel at home and at peace in the universe; they can evoke positive, childlike (not childish) qualities—a feeling of belonging and of being unconditionally accepted. I can still sing "by heart" a popular church camp song without feeling the need to change any of the wording: "Living for Jesus a life that is true; striving to please him in all that I do; giving allegiance glad-hearted and free, this is the pathway of blessing for me. Oh Jesus Lord and Savior, I give myself to Thee, for Thou in Thine atonement didst give Thyself for me. I own no other master. My heart shall be Thy throne. My life I give, henceforth to live, O Christ for Thee alone." Of course, it seems laughable now how controversial it was back in the day to consider replacing "Thee" and "Thine" with you and your. But dated as this language is now, it need not detract from the meaning of the song with its metaphor of one's heart as a throne for Jesus and for the values such as compassion and self-giving love that he represents.

Feeling at home in the universe can also be described as "resting" in the Universe, as a child rests in the loving embrace of a parent's arms.

Songs about being "Saved by Grace" can bolster ones sense of humor and tone down dangerous perfectionist tendencies. Grace theology, we must remind ourselves, is not about our helplessness. It is about not taking ourselves too seriously—and that also means not taking the *concept of self* too seriously! A Scripture passage such as "In my Father's house are many mansions" can easily translate into the image of feeling at home in eternity, as can the poetry of Michael Sherer (inspired by G.J. Neumann) which encourages us to "celebrate the time between . . . as from God to God we go." St. Francis pictured death as "kind and gentle" because it "leads home the child of God." We are not actually going anywhere, but the image of peacefully coming into and going out of existence, moving between time and non-time (eternity), can be a helpful and beautiful way of visualizing our participation in the Seamless Whole of Reality. I think the popular images of heaven as a huge banquet in "the church triumphant" or as a grand family reunion are overused but nevertheless meaningful. Notice all the related metaphors (italicized) in these classic hymn verses: "Yet *she* (the church) on earth hath *union with God* . . . and *mystic sweet communion* with those whose *rest is won*. O blessed *heavenly chorus*, Lord, give us grace that we, like all *the saints* before us, *on high* may *dwell with Thee*."

All words and languages are symbolic and metaphorical, even the chemical table of the elements and quarks. But there is at least a sense in which descriptions such as Ultimate Mystery, The Seamless Whole, or Reality are not metaphors. All the above italicized metaphors are symbolic expressions. But Mystery as discussed in the Introduction to this book is The Real Deal. Mystery, The Seamless Whole, and Reality are attempts to name the ultimate Referent of spirituality. "God" is a personified metaphor referring to something else, to Ultimate Mystery. But Mystery, Seamless Whole, Reality, or other similar expressions are not metaphorical of something else. These expressions, if they are symbols at all, are attempts to symbolize a point beyond which symbolism is redundant.

Kenneth Patton, Universalist minister in Boston, knew how to celebrate Mystery, mysticism, and the feeling of "at-home-ness" in Reality—in the universe/multiverse. His *Services and Songs for the Celebration of Life* (available online) gave him a reputation as one "who taught a monotone rationalism how to sing . . .a stumble-footed humanism how to dance."

Various images or versions of "Goin' to Live with God" can legitimately continue to help folks cope with mortality and become comfortable with their relationship to Ultimate Mystery. Hymns such as "For the Beauty of the Earth" and "Immortal, Invisible God Only Wise" with its mystical verse "in all life thou livest, the true life of all," or Haydn's great chorus "The Heaven's Are Telling the Glory of God" (which I have conducted and sung) can enhance our consciousness and sense of gratitude and wonder. The arrangement of "O Day Full of Grace" by F. Melius Christiansen with its powerful last line "And there we shall walk in endless light—in endless light!" is a marvelously uplifting metaphor. Images such as "Beautiful Isle of *Somewhere*" can signify appropriate metaphorical caution, but I think it is better to affirm and reclaim more specific and less sentimental images in a way that validates the artistic integrity of individual religious traditions—as long as we realize that this explicit imagery is metaphorical and symbolic. Recalling the image of the stone rolled away from Christ's empty tomb, for example, we might contemplate rolling away any obstacles that keep us from boldly stepping through doorways into new and abundant life, or as Dr. Hinkle would put it, that keep us locked in concrete certainty and prevent us from embracing creative possibilities.

The Genie (like God, Santa, and Satan) may be permanently out of the bottle—never to be understood literally—but such images nonetheless can remain meaningful and useful in our postmodern world. I suspect that many people have always related to religious images, themes, hymns and other poetic expressions in the way I am suggesting here. They don't need me to tell them how to appreciate the emotional and spiritual insights of these art forms apart from the literal sense of the images. The purpose of this book is to acknowledge the elephant in the room. I am simply challenging religious/spiritual people to more honestly, explicitly, and thoroughly acknowledge the symbolic and metaphorical nature of religious language.

One of the greatest mistakes too often made with religious language is to confuse words intended as comfort with words of explanation. "The Lord giveth and the Lord taketh away" must not be seen as an explanation of how everything that happens is God's will or is according to some divine plan. The valid meaning of such sentiments is that, eventually at least, it can be comforting to place everything we experience in the context of the endless change, the endless give and take, the endless yin and yang of life! It is in this sense that we can sing some favorite songs without needing to change the wording. For example, here is a very popular hymn that I can type out without looking it up: "What a friend we have in Jesus, all our sins and griefs to bear; what a privilege to carry everything to God in prayer. Oh, what peace we often forfeit; oh what needless pain we bear, all because we do not carry everything to God in prayer." Comedian Bill

Maher, who has both Roman Catholic and Jewish heritage, enjoys teasing believers about their imaginary friends. But as children know, sometimes the imaginary ones are the best. One can easily understand this hymn non-literally as encouragement to take a Gods-eye view of the troubles of the moment. Like most comforting sentiments, not even this lovely hymn can do much to help a person who is in the immediate throws of unbearable grief and loss. But on some level and at some point, this kind of meditation/prayer can help us come to terms with the yin and yang of life. A "secular" song by Billy Hill expresses a similar sentiment: "You've got to give a little, take a little, and let your poor heart break a little . . .win a little, lose a little, and always have the blues a little: That's the story of, That's the Glory of Love."

An exquisite example of comforting New Testament poetry, often used when the worst of tragedies has occurred, is Romans 8:38–39: "For I am convinced that neither death, nor life, nor angels, nor demonic forces, nor things present, nor things to come, nor powers, nor height, nor depth, nor anything else in all creation, will be able to separate us from the love of God in Christ Jesus our Lord." The point here is that spiritual seren-ity is the ultimate source of true comfort—not that God, Jesus, angels, or demonic beings are actual, supernatural entities floating somewhere in space or in another dimension of reality. God, Jesus, Heaven, and other such symbols should not be used to *explain* or to whitewash tragedy. They are Symbols with a capital S that we use to express our solidarity with and compassion for each other (and for ourselves) in good times and bad. Literalists certainly can be comforted by these images. But belief in the after-death survival of deceased loved ones is so questionable in our post-modern world that even for literalists the value of such belief as a uniquely effective source of comfort appears to be fading.

Religious symbols come into play when we are overwhelmed—when words fail but we can't stand the silence. Sometimes our silent, empathic presence is the best comfort we can offer to someone who is suffering. One of the ironic ways that some deal with such things—preferably only after significant time has passed—is by resorting to so-called "sick jokes" or gallows humor. An upbeat Pollyanna alternative, such as picturing school children killed by a crazed gunman as happily dancing into heaven, can have the unintended consequence of giving mourners the further agony of feeling that their pain is not being validated or taken seriously. One of my all-time favorite Peanuts cartoons has Lucy screaming at Charlie Brown "I don't wanna feel better!"—cutting off his attempts to cheer her up when what she wants and needs is a chance to "vent." Even relatively true assurances such as saying "You will feel better in time" or "I know just how you feel" can be counterproductive if and when it appears to invalidate the sufferer's feeling of uniquely intense grief and pain. What can be very helpful are the cultural and/or religious rituals that accompany the grieving process—rituals that typically unfold in stages, based on an awareness of the fact that grieving can be a very long and complex process.

While some classic hymns, prayers, liturgies and the like may be best left in their famous and classic forms, based on the assumption that users understand the traditional, metaphorical and symbolic nature of the language, I offer this example of an updated mealtime prayer: "We give thanks for the grace that nourishes us, for the compassion that makes us human—may we be always mindful of the needs of others . . . in the Spirit of Jesus (Mohammed, Elijah, the Buddha, etc), Amen." I have begun working on revised hymn stanzas and liturgies for use in a Christian context—since that is the particular tradition that I wish to reclaim—and I hope others will do the same for their traditions. A lot of work has been done in the Christian tradition to create more contemporary musical settings, but wonderful as these may be, as mentioned before, I feel that much of this effort is like rearranging deck chairs on the Titanic! Much more needs to be done to promote postmodern theological sensibilities, revising liturgical texts and creating new expressions of devotional and contemplative themes. I hope that others more artistically talented than I will take up this challenge and vocation.

I grew up with a 1930 copyrighted German/American Lutheran hymnal that included this then popular hymn:

> "Work for the night is coming, Work thro' the morning hours;
> Work while the dew is sparkling, Work 'mid springing flow'rs;
> Work when the day grows brighter, Work in the glowing sun;
> Work for the night is coming, When man's work is done.
> Give ev'ry flying minute Something to keep in store
> Work for the night is coming, When man works no more."

This is only half of the text, and after sixty years I can still recite most all of it from memory. Whenever I am teaching about the protestant work ethic I almost always reference this hymn. While the meter of the hymn is probably too repetitive to be redeemed, it would have some potential to express postmodern "eternal now" spirituality by changing just one word:

> "Live for the night is coming, Live thro' the morning hours;
> Live while the dew is sparkling, Live 'mid springing flow'rs;

Live when the day grows brighter, Live in the glowing sun;
Live for the night is coming, When man's work is done.
Give ev'ry flying minute Something to keep in store . . . "

But while some things can be revised or adapted to avoid supernatural and other outmoded features, there are also artistic images that we should drop altogether. The saintly (but very frugal and strict) woman who adopted my mother as a five-year old was the grandmother with whom I sat in church every Sunday for the first few years of my life, because my father was the pastor and my mother was a musician. Grandma Wetterling had had a rough life, so it was not hard to understand that her favorite hymn began with the words "I'm but a stranger here, heaven is my home. Earth is a desert drear, heaven is my home." While set to a very nice tune by Sir Arthur Sullivan of "Gilbert and Sullivan" fame (someone should write new lyrics for this tune!), I remember my first college religion professor questioning how anyone could sing about the world of mid-twentieth century America as a desert drear. I had to agree and still do. (The Eisenhower era did have its pluses, and my grandmother did enjoy her family, her friends—and growing beautiful plants and flowers.)

There are, of course, emotional reasons why a person might believe in life after death. Some, like my grandmother, are dealt a difficult hand in this life and hope for a better life to come. Disabled folks can feel alienated—even more so when subtly patronized with well-meaning euphemisms such as "differently abled"—and may look forward to being "normal" in a future life. I think they would do better to forget "normal" and take a cue from Stephen Hawking's 2011 declaration that "there is no heaven." I suspect that some folks secretly resent the strict moral restraints that have been placed on them by their religion and feel robbed if they cannot count on being rewarded in a next life for the sacrifices they made or the pleasures they felt forced to give up in this life. (I find it terribly ironic when puritanically indoctrinated suicide bombers are told they will be rewarded with 72 virgins and other perks in a next life.) Rabbi Kushner says that the many dying people with whom he has spent last moments have never been afraid of dying. They understand that death is now the only cure for their ailments. If they regret anything, it is that they have no more time to rectify misplaced priorities or to regain missed opportunities and experiences.

Since I have mentioned world-famous physicist Stephen Hawking's conclusion that there is no heaven, I feel obliged to comment here on the much publicized 2012 claims made about the existence of heaven by neurosurgeon Eben Alexander. Amazing experiences such as those he reports having had during a coma connected with a bad case of bacterial meningitis have been widely understood to be the same as those which can be produced with psychedelic and other drugs. His experience in no way proves that consciousness can take flight when the brain is completely dead! It has been proven that many of our dreams which seem to be incredibly complex, and to go on for a very long time, actually last for an incredibly short time. Much can indeed happen in the brain very quickly as one is drifting in and out of consciousness, whether this is related to sleep or to some type of coma. I trust the judgment of expert neuroscience scholars far more knowledgeable than I (or than Eban Alexander!) who are shocked at his naiveté and at the apparently scientifically illiterate editors of the newsweekly magazine who promoted Alexander's book with a big cover story in their final "swan song" print edition.

Another lyric set to music by Sir Arthur also needs to go—the famous "Onward Christian Soldiers, Marching as to War." In post World War II Minnesota it was one of our favorite hymns in Sunday School along with a stirring song that went like this: "We are soldiers in an army and we fight for Christ our king; Where he leads we gladly follow as our marching song we sing: March, march, march, march, march, march, forward, forward, ever forward we must go. God will make us brave and strong to conquer every foe!" We children would have sung this song every Sunday if they had allowed us to do so—which they almost did. This rhythmic march is one of the first church songs that I learned to play on the piano. Not long after September 11, 2001, I heard a woman call a radio talk show and complain about Muslim holy war saying that Christians have nothing like it. I was driving my car at the time and started singing this marching song. I also had to resist the urge to shout at the radio about the Crusades, the inquisition, colonial imperialism, and the many wars throughout history in which Christianity has been a major factor.

In fairness it must be noted that *jihad* basically means "effort," and its connotation has to do with the struggle to live a good life. Similarly, the war imagery in Christian hymns and Jewish Psalms is generally metaphorical of the same struggle, although, sadly, the religious connection to actual warfare is all too common. Not to belabor the point, but Reginald Heber's early nineteenth-century hymn still appears (unfortunately, I think) in many hymnals: "The Son of God goes forth to war A kingly crown to gain. His blood-red banner streams afar . . ." The hint of tribalism in "This is the feast of victory for *our God*" fatally detracts from its intended reference to "death swallowed up in victory." Happily for many years I have not been called upon to sing or to play either "Onward Christian Soldiers" or that other old chestnut "Stand up for Jesus, ye soldiers of the Cross!" It has to be one of the ongoing tasks of religious leaders and teachers to both clarify and sometimes discard the images and metaphors that we use. Clearly, it is not necessary or prudent to drop all traditional symbols and images, even those that are problematical, because they are often forms of artistic and musical expression that would be a great loss were we to banish them. (I can't imagine giving up some of the great religious music that I love, even though many of the words and images cannot and should not be taken literally!) This is why I emphasize reclaiming aspects of our old religious traditions by learning how to interpret and reinterpret their iconic images and symbols. That some folks will not develop this midrashic reinterpretation is no reason for the rest of us to throw the babies out with the bath water.

By what might be considered a serendipitous coincidence, the word "spiritual" includes within it the word "ritual." Reflecting the heart of a true pastor, Jim Burklo includes a wonderful discussion of the value of ritual in his book *Open Christianity: Home By Another Road* (2000). Giving examples of how rituals have been able "to heat up the coolest Mr. Cool," Burklo reminds us of how ritual can express "meaning at many levels—sensual, intellectual, poetic, emotional, spiritual." He writes: "A ritual is a consciously planned event that gives expression to a force that might otherwise express itself in unconscious and perhaps undesirable ways." He gives examples of how rituals can be reshaped to jibe with postmodern sensibilities; I have suggested similar alterations in relation to infant baptism. (I also appreciate Burklo's focus on the metaphor of "home" as a central component of spirituality!)

When Tillich famously insisted that a symbol was not just a symbol but that it "participated in the reality to which it points," he was referring to the multidimensional relationship of words to reality, of facts to meaning, of physical to spiritual. In his way he was expressing what Buddhists call the multidimensional Seamless Whole in which overwrought separations are overcome. Oftentimes, as with music, the language and images of ritual do not need to be discarded; they simply need to be understood as metaphors and symbols expressing varying facets of "the embodiment of the sacred" (sacraments).

Another thing I recall from my childhood in church is feeling very sad about the little plaques under stained-glass windows in memory of people who had died. I felt this same ennui when visiting Westminster

Abbey in London and realizing how little if anything was left of even the most famous people who ever lived—including the king of King James Bible fame. I have always sensed that pie in the sky is scant comfort to the dying, or to the grieving as they go on with their lives. Death is sad.

What about St. Paul's advice that Christians should not "grieve as those who have no hope"? The best response I have been able to come up with is the paradoxical theme that sadness validates joy. If we constantly take pills that numb us to pain, they can also make us immune to joy. Buddhist moderation or detachment may eliminate needless suffering, but it does not eliminate all sadness. As Joseph Campbell said to Bill Moyers during interviews at Skywalker Ranch, "Life is a wonderful opera—except that it hurts." The 2009 French movie "Paris" does a wonderful job of evoking the bittersweet reality of living always in the moment as opposed to relying on the bromide of immortality symbols. Spiritual nonbelievers do not give up hope. Rather, we change what we hope for and what we think hope is! Harvey Milk was famous for saying "You've got to give 'em hope." But he knew that you also must tell the truth. Hope is an aspect of the "life force" or "instinct," but hope is most importantly about acting for positive change while also accepting the universe, Reality, as it is!

When I was 17 years old I created a Christmas display that filled our entire front yard in St. Paul, Minnesota with a little village of houses surrounding a church and, mounted on the roof of our house, 143 blue bulbs spelling out "Silent Night." This colorful display, with its three-dimensional twinkle light stars, had lines of cars going by and it won many first place awards in the religious division of the city's outdoor lighting contest—and in later years it graced other towns as well. In St. Paul we played Christmas music on a record turntable with outside speakers. My mentally disabled sister, Margaret, enjoyed monitoring these records. At the time I thought the carol "Deck the Halls" was too secular, and so Margaret, who could focus like a laser on certain details, would remind me to skip it on any record we played. I've come a long way since then, and the display is now in storage (begging to be put up again). Since I have come to recognize the symbolic and metaphorical nature of Christmas, God, angels, heaven, mangers, and virgin births, I have also come to realize that the secular and sacred meanings of Christmas music are not about separate Realities. I have come to embrace the themes of secular humanism. I have come to realize that the problem is not that Christmas is too commercialized and materialistic, but that it is not materialistic enough! We typically give too many things to people who have more than enough stuff when we should be putting more effort into sharing good things with those who desperately need the products of our commercial economy.

Deeply spiritual nonbelievers are those who understand that many truths of religion can be re-stated, and often better stated, in humanistic terms, while at the same time the spiritual dimension of life and truth can be fully embraced.

An Appropriate Attitude Toward Death

I have long felt that the most appropriate attitude toward death is one of profound ambivalence. This is a corollary of my overall thesis that as a creative art form religion helps us to become comfortable with the truth of uncertainty, and with the need for multiple perspectives. On one hand we can accept death with equanimity, while on the other we resonate with the famous Dylan Thomas line, "Do not go gentle into that good night . . . Rage, rage against the dying of the light." Even though we may have come to terms with the reality, inevitability, finality, and even desirability of death, we may still be apprehensive and sad about the pain and grief that is likely to accompany this ending of every single one of our relationships.

The reality is that tears and pain accompany both birth and death. It's the circle of life. But even if we still see death as an enemy, it can be as a defeated enemy, in the spirit of the Brahms Requiem: "O Death—where is thy sting?" Because our uniquely human self-consciousness causes us to anticipate the moment or extended moments of our death, we have to find ways of transcending our fearful anticipation. One of the functions of religion as an art form is to help us transcend death without the pie in the sky of immortality symbols, to face the challenge of our mortality without anxiety. Religion as art form prevents our anticipation of potentially unpleasant future moments from destroying our appreciation and enjoyment of the eternal now—the present moment! We can do this partly by focusing on the positive quality of the vast majority of our moments. We can also do it by focusing on the unique advantages we enjoy during each stage of our lives, when we are young, middle aged, and old. To quote the Jesus we meet in the Matthew Gospel: "Do not worry about tomorrow. Tomorrow will take care of itself." Nikos Kazantzakis, the author of *Zorba the Greek* and of *The Last Temptation of Christ*, chose this insightful epitaph for his tombstone: "I hope for nothing. I fear nothing. I am free."

In a previous book, I called one section "Love over Logic," the point being that somewhere along the line in life there always come times when loving relationships supersede concerns about justice, consistency, explanations, or rationality. There always come times when emotion trumps intellect—a phenomenon somewhat similar to the placebo effect. While it may not be intellectually or literally factual to describe a deceased loved one as "with Jesus," it can be emotionally and symbolically real. Metaphors can be about something *real* without implying the existence of a supernatural reality separate from the empirical universe. To enter the non-rational mode is not to be irrational or anti-intellectual. It is about embracing a holistic mindset where reason is only one factor. In these moments we stop worrying about what is right or fair, literal or metaphorical, and like the dying Buddha with his disciples, focus simply on how we have been and are surrounded with care, love, and unconditional compassion. We support one another with the kind of love (agape) that St. Paul describes as greater than either faith or hope! If we are loving and compassionate persons ourselves, we are most likely to be surrounded by this same kind of love and compassion, not only at the time of our death, but throughout our lives. Thornton Wilder's most quoted sentence is said to be "There is a land of the living and a land of the dead and the bridge is love, the only survival, the only meaning."

A Rest Along The Way

When one reads the books of Daniel Dennett or other philosopher scientists, it becomes apparent that science is a wonderful but in some ways exhausting and never ending process. I have come to the conclusion that for people in this postmodern world, religion is not so much the result of the "failure of nerve" (the switch from demanding things from the gods to begging the gods on bended knee) described by Sir James Frasier in *The Golden Bough*. Religion today seems linked more to exhaustion and impatience. When we confront the seemingly endless scientific process where every good answer to every good question raises even more good questions than answers, religion and Mystery serve as a "rest along the way"—an image found in a popular Christian hymn. Religion is partly about not delaying our commitment to values, priorities, and a sense of the transcendent until all the facts are in, because science indicates that all the facts will never be in. I am not promoting a "God of the gaps" mentality in which religion and God become increasingly less viable explanations for the way things are. What I am suggesting is that religion and spirituality can be viewed as a legitimate shortcut to stasis, serenity, and wholeness as we continue our never-ending quest for knowledge and truth.

I very much appreciate the way deeply scientific and spiritual nonbeliever Albert Einstein expressed his feeling about religion when he wrote: "One cannot help but be in awe when one contemplates the mysteries of eternity, of life and the marvelous structures of the universe. It is enough if one tries merely to comprehend a little of this mystery every day." (I think Socrates would agree!) To stand in awe of mystery is to understand that *one of the major functions of reason is to deal with the limits of reason, with the role of non-rationality in our lives and in our spirituality.* Just because emotions, dreams, intuitions and impressions may be difficult to pin down, they are not meaningless or unreal. The spiritual nonbeliever is neither hyper-rational nor irrational but is simply in tune with what Judaism calls *Shalom* (wholeness), and with what my father meant when he closed every one of his sermons by invoking "the peace of God that passes all understanding."

We should not, however, use the Mystery of Reality—a Universe that seems incomprehensible no matter how we look at it—as an excuse for believing "too loudly" in our favorite impossible possibilities. Possibilities are not likelihoods. If we connect belief in God with the idea that anything is possible, it should mean only that we are keeping our options open and that we embrace the mystery of life. The intriguing notion of parallel universes, which regularly comes up in discussions of "string theory," does remind us that we must not be overly skeptical about mind-boggling possibilities. But we also cannot ignore the dangers of offering false hope and mere wishful thinking. We must further beware of asking nonbelievers to prove a negative. It bears frequent repeating that "extraordinary claims require extraordinary proofs"—extraordinary evidence. I suspect that we will never conclusively answer the question of *why* there is something rather than nothing. This question "exists" simply because we have evolved to be—as far as we can tell at this point—the only creatures capable of asking it. And there may be no answer to the question except the child's wisdom that says "just because!"

Art Reveals Questions Hidden By The Answers

The earliest image we have of Jesus dying (in the Mark Gospel) is an image of apparent despair focused on only one question—*why*? ("My God, why have you forsaken me?") What we mean when we say "God only knows" is that we must learn to live with the question! Awe and wonder are paradoxical (or dialectical, if you prefer) blends of fascination and dread, of both wanting and fearing to know why. Paradoxically also, very often the question is the answer. James Baldwin wrote: "The purpose of art is to lay bare the questions that have been hidden by the answers."

There is a great Jesus-story about his visit with sisters Mary and Martha found only in Luke 10:38–42 which ends with Jesus saying to a busy and distracted Martha: "Martha, Martha, you are anxious and troubled about many things; *one thing is needful*. Mary has chosen the good portion, which shall not be taken away from her." This echoes Psalm 27:4, "One thing have I asked of the Lord, that will I seek after; that I may dwell in the *house* of the Lord all the days of my life, to behold the beauty of the Lord, and to *inquire* in his temple" (italics added). What is this "one thing needful . . . the question I have asked . . . that shall not be taken away"—the quest that Mary in this story is sharing during her encounter with Jesus? I think it can only be the ultimate inquiry or question itself of meaning and purpose, related to a sense of awe, wonder, and mystery—the quest that will never be taken away from us! The one thing needful is like the pot of gold at the end of the rainbow that doesn't "exist" but that, like the rainbow itself, is exquisitely real as a process and as an experience—the eternal process and experience of change, development, and questioning.

No specific "imaginary friends" or "invisible products" (which Bill Maher rightfully skewers as overly literal subjects of devotion) are ultimately real. The Quest Itself for "the one thing needful" *is* the one thing needful! The Quest itself is ultimately real, vital, and inevitable! It is the one Quest/Question—the impossible dream—that every kind of God-talk is ultimately about—the one ultimate thing that cannot be taken away from us! This Quest/Question has always been an obvious bottom line of religion, spirituality—art. It is the basic meaning of devotion to Allah/God. It is the basic meaning of "Seek ye first the Kingdom of God . . ." It is the basic meaning of koans such as "the sound of one hand clapping." It is the Ultimate Reality about The Way Things Are that is beyond all categories of thought. It is Kaufman's elusive "God" symbolizing our attempt to imagine an ultimate point of reference for understanding everything. It is the scientist's quest for a theory of everything.

With its nod to mind-boggling science in its reference to the unreachable star, one of the best spiritual/artistic/musical expressions of this Mysterious and Glorious Quest is the universally familiar show-stopper from the musical *Man of La Mancha*:

"To dream the impossible dream,
to fight the unbeatable foe,
to bear with unbearable sorrow,
to run where the brave dare not go;

to right the unrightable wrong,
to love pure and chaste from afar,
to try when your arms are too weary
to reach the unreachable star.

This is my quest, to follow that star,
no matter how hopeless, no matter how far,
to fight for the right without question or pause,
to be willing to march into hell for a heavenly cause.

And I know if I only be true to this glorious quest
that my heart will lie peaceful and calm when I'm laid to my rest,

And the world will be better for this,
that one man scorned and covered with scars,
still strove with his last once of courage
to reach the unreachable star!"

Changing Relationships—The Ultimate Reality

A lot has been said in this book about change—our need for an optimum amount of change in our lives, the importance of understanding what we can and cannot change, change itself as the basic and only absolute fact of life, change as the process of questioning, of evolution, and of artistic creativity. Now we come to another great paradox: Imagining an *unchanging* God of Love is actually about affirming the inescapable reality of change, uncertainty, and Mystery! Christian theologians who acknowledge that "God" can be understood as a symbol representing the evolutionary process—as a symbol for the very process of creation itself (serendipitous creativity)—nevertheless often will say that the only thing which never changes is God's steadfast love, because what they mean is that *the reality and importance of contingent (interdependent, fluid, and changing!) relationships never changes!*

Since "God" (like a rainbow) is an image and not a thing, since (as Tillich says) God does not "exist" but is "Being Itself" (the Ground of Being), what these theologians are saying is that *transcendent reality is about relationships—especially those relationships that involve compassion and love! Contingency is about ever-changing relationships, whether quantum or personal. Our existence will always involve relationships. This relational quality of life never changes as long as there is life.* Change itself is the unchanging reality of life, and spirituality is largely about coming to terms with this Reality!

In addition to highlighting the ineffability of "God," the doctrine of the Trinity with its "God in three *personas*" underscores the relational nature of Ultimate Reality. The Trinity doctrine should be seen as expressing the various ways in which we experience our relationship to Sacred, Divine Mystery, not as a riddle about how three can physically (ontologically) be one. Martin Buber's famous *I and Thou* is likewise relational. All biblical theology is relational. Subatomic physics is a web of relationships.

Some Christians exaggerate and overly literalize the "imaginary friend" aspect of their "personal relationship with Jesus Christ," but the importance of the relationship theme itself is not off the mark. I appreciate Martin Luther's idea that we should all be "little Christs" to our neighbor. The famous New Testament summary of all ethical and theological teaching as being a matter of loving God above all, and your neighbor as yourself, can be seen as primarily about valuing the incredible chain of contingent relationships in our lives. Spiritual human beings understand these relationships to be most rewarding when they involve love, with all of love's many levels of meaning, including compassion, empathy, caring, sharing, and mutual regard. The 2010 George Clooney movie "Up in the Air" is like a classic sermon on the importance of relationships. (I highly recommend it!) Harking back to what I reported earlier about the Scandinavian countries, studies of why the Danish people have been judged the happiest on earth suggest that the most important reason for their happiness is that they value their individuality while at the same time seeing it as enhanced by their interpersonal and societal (democratic socialist "welfare state") relationships. By contrast, people who come to emergency room psychiatrists for help typically are very much alone in the world.

In writing about "meeting Jesus again for the first time," Marcus Borg describes his spiritual journey as moving "beyond belief to relationship." He sees himself not as a believer, but as an aspiring mystic or Spirit person—similar to what I have called a spiritual nonbeliever. He speaks of his experience of the *mysterium tremendum* as entering into a relationship with Mystery/Spirit/God, "a relationship that involves one in a journey of transformation." Much of the literature discovered at Nag

Hammadi, Egypt in 1945 is in the form of imagined dialogues between Jesus and a welcomed questioner who in the course of the conversation undergoes spiritual transformation resulting in serenity, courage, hope, and refreshment. This kind of transformation (change), says Borg, gives us the unconventional, compassionate wisdom to oppose harsh divisions of economic status, race, culture, gender and sexuality—divisions and boundaries which are a major part of the "purity/holiness systems" typical of ethnic/cultural groups such as the Israelites whose status in the world was particularly precarious.

Sacred transformation frees one from the kind of narrow-minded or pathological conventionality that tends to demonize anything or anyone perceived as different. On the other hand, this transformation also curbs the pathological individualism that cares little about "promoting the general welfare." For Christians in particular this transformation is about "believing in Jesus" in the sense of becoming "more and more compassionate beings" like the Spirit Person, Jesus. To quote one of my favorite texts of a Bach cantata: "If Jesu's spirit be not yours, ye are not his." (A childhood bedtime prayer of mine ended with "Help me every day to be good and gentle, more like thee.")

Some of my seminary professors insisted that while the New Testament says "God is love," we cannot reverse it and say Love is God. I think they were wrong. (This is partly just about semantics, of course.) What can it mean to say Love is God? I think it means that if we stay clear about what is most valuable in life, we will be surrounded by the Mystery of Compassionate Love, both individually and collectively, as long as humanity survives in the universe. If we understand how important (and effective!) it is to give love, it is much more likely that we will receive love. Compassion begets compassion.

The notion of Divinity as Love and Compassion provides an important contrast with the message of the stony-faced and impassive Mask of Eternity in the cave at Benares. The insight of this sculpture is that spirituality must take into account all of life, both its beauty and its harrowing sense of the sublime that transcends ethical categories of good and evil. This sculpture helps us come to terms with the powerful, horrific, and destructive aspects of nature without being judgmental about these aspects of reality (which have been cleverly described as the non-intentional "ignorant crimes of the universe"). A purely impassive and stone-cold sense of reality, however, is too sterile, static, and one-dimensional. We need images that help us touch the deeply personal and spiritual dimensions of life. To say both "God is Love" and "Love is God" is a step toward embracing all dimensions of the sacred, but especially the good, positive, ideal aspects of the universe that we "prefer" and deem "worthy of worship."

The bottom line here is that the *mysterium tremendum* is not just about intellectual insight into the nature of reality. Mystery is a warm, personal *experience*. Part of the resistance to the phrase "*Love* is God" has to do with the hard-to-break habit of thinking that we can only express this warm personal experience by personifying God, nature, or the universe with gendered (too often male) pronouns or with expressions such as "One who" is compassionate, etc. (Borg is typical of many who still slip into the use of this personifying language—although he also distances himself from this language by reading prayers, for example, as poetic, dated, yet lovely artifacts whose images we may no longer take literally.) "Love is God" or "Compassion is divine" may be more abstract and less personified images than "God is love." But such images or metaphors are still fully human because the very ability to create and imagine such images is precisely what being human is all about. Only humans create personifications, metaphors, and abstract language!

Even though Jesus has been portrayed as using the personification of calling God his Father with whom he was "one," our postmodern sensibility requires us to limit our view of Jesus Christ as divine to the understanding that Jesus exhibited divine qualities such as love and compassion. Jesus may personify these and related qualities for us, but we should not personify (literalize, reify, objectify) Jesus as God incarnate! The Christian doctrine of Incarnation needs to be modified so that it is seen as being about the ways in which Jesus and his followers *embody divine qualities,* rather than as about the notion hammered out at the Council of Nicea in 325AD but not clearly and consistently present in the New Testament— the notion of an ontological, supernatural entity becoming human. As an older Christmas carol and a popular mid-twentieth-century song in combination put it: "Love came down at Christmas" so "they'll know we are Christians by our love, by our love; yes they'll know we are Christians by our love."

It is commonly pointed out that the word love is quite vague, but I see it rather as multi-dimensional. This is the reason that Greek is said to have at least eight versions of the word and one version is *agape, the unconditional love* that St. Paul describes as "the greatest" in his famous first letter to the Corinthians (chapter 13). Paul is not writing there about a God "who" loves us. He is basically describing the compassion for one another that was expected to pervade Christian communities: "Love is patient and kind; love is not jealous or boastful; it is not arrogant or rude." When he writes about knowing in part but then knowing or understanding fully as we have been fully understood, he is remarkably close to overcoming the subject–object split in the same way that it is overcome when we say "I am the universe happening." He does not have to be viewed as personifying some Supreme Knower "out there." He is not far from compassionate contemplation of The Seamless Whole. It is important to note that God is never mentioned in this famous and perhaps most poetic of St. Paul's writings, and that he strongly criticizes "religiosity" as well: "If I have all faith so as to remove mountains, but have not love, I am nothing." Paul could be interpreted as saying that there is "no difference" between knowing and being known—that you don't "have" an experience of knowing or of being known. You simply are every experience. You are "Knowing Itself."

Resurrection as Transformation and Transcendence

Once more I must return to the music that for me trumps theology. My two favorite symphonies are "From New World" (number 9) by Dvorak and Gustav Mahler's second symphony in C minor, which is usually called "The Resurrection Symphony" mainly because of the words sung by the chorus in the dramatic and soaring finale. Mahler himself never gave it the title of "Resurrection." He was always dubious that any attempt to put the meaning of such music into words could ever be satisfactory. He described his music as "symphonic universes" and at most one can say only that in his second symphony he struggled with notions of immortality, resurrection and salvation.

Mahler admitted that he converted from Judaism to Roman Catholicism mainly to further his music career. He was a confirmed agnostic, clearly sympathetic with understanding language about God and heaven as basically a celebration of creativity and nature. One of his last great works was "Song of the Earth" based on ancient Buddhist and Chinese texts which suggest more a reconciliation with mortality than a triumph of immortality. He set to music Ruckert's "I live alone in my heaven, in my loving, in my song." His last fully completed symphony (number 9) evokes a sense of timelessness in which life is contemplated in all its paradoxes.

Conductor Michael Tilson Thomas says that Mahler struggled all his life with the tension between major and minor, joy and sorrow, heroic striving and tragic fate. He wrote some of his most blissful music during the darkest periods of his life. In his first symphony he put a happy French tune in a minor key that made it sound like a funeral march. He mused that ugliness could be beautiful in its truthfulness, and contemplated the idea that life might be a cosmic joke on us. He clearly enjoyed sexuality and was ambitious and hopeful, but he was also haunted by death—many of his siblings and later his own daughter died very young; he was ill during his last few years and, like Michael Jackson, died when he was only fifty. The Adagietto movement of his fifth symphony was used to great effect in the film version of "Death in Venice" in which the main character in the novella is changed from an author into a Mahler-like musician in decline. I find Mahler to be symbolic of Germany itself with its incredible highs and lows as a people and as a culture.

Mahler's music grew exponentially in influence and popularity during the twentieth century and continues to resonate in the twenty-first. He touches a chord within the contemporary milieu that equals for me a kind of religious transcendence. From the tragic hammer blows of the sixth symphony to the soaring hopefulness of the Resurrection Symphony, Mahler does for love and death what Woody Allen does in humorous movies and Ingmar Bergman does in serious movies. I want to leave you with this final image of the power of music in general and Mahler's in particular: I have sung in performances of Mahler's Resurrection Symphony, including with Eugene Ormandy and the Philadelphia Orchestra, but even my participation in these performances cannot match what I experienced at the end of a performance I attended in Davies Symphony Hall in San Francisco. For such a huge piece I like to sit in the very back of the top balcony because the sound seems best there. When the final tremendous chords and crescendos and the long standing ovation ended, I noticed a young man of about 19 or so turn to leave. Tears were streaming down his face and the memory of it makes my own tears begin to well up as I type this—tears from being overwhelmed by the sublime. I rest my case.

In chapter 1, I was rather critical of Richard R. Niebuhr's study of the relationship between history, reason, nature, theological method (hermeneutics), and resurrection. But he certainly deserves credit for recognizing and struggling with the problematic nature of resurrection which is arguably the central feature of Christian theology. I appreciate his critique of those who have tried to write off resurrection as a mere analogy to ideas or beliefs that are less problematic. He deserves credit for tackling head-on the basic problem of defining what we mean by nature, reason, and "historical event." I am not sure that he ever comes up with particularly satisfying definitions, but he has made some worthwhile contributions to our understanding of what he often describes almost too glibly as "the resurrection event." He provides an insightful summary of the earlier versions of the quest for the historical Jesus in relationship to the resurrection theme. What he says about David Strauss' psychological and philosophical "negation of negation" reminds me in some ways of Buddhist emptiness and Tillich's image of "the God beyond God." He describes Harnack and Renan as examples of those who avoid the issue of history by totally spiritualizing resurrection and finding its significance in a *supra*-natural or metaphysical world.

Niebuhr's bottom line seems to be that historical events are always independent and unpredictable, unique and spontaneous. Bart Ehrman makes this same point quite eloquently in *Jesus Interrupted*. Niebuhr speaks of "the mystery of historical causality itself." This leads me back to my original criticism of his assertion that the resurrection is only "similar to an historical event" or "an event unlike any other." This just says that anything might be possible. It makes any discussion of evidence moot. Ehrman clarifies the problem when he explains that, unlike scientific experimentation, historical events cannot be repeated and tested. *Hence, an historical event is actually incapable of proving anything!* (Even if Jesus appeared to be dead and then came back to life, what would that really prove? Many would no doubt just call it a fluke.) Historians can speak only of probabilities when recounting past events, and can say nothing certain about what might happen in the future. Of course, even scientists such as Richard Dawkins use the phrase "*almost* certainly" when discussing most topics. Scientific methods cannot prove a negative, and I would argue that scientific discoveries tend to make us more rather than less aware of Ultimate Mystery.

Niebuhr does leave us with valuable and helpful insights that are worth quoting. His observation that dying and death are intrinsically alien to us reflects the "death as enemy" theme, and his words about the disciples creating a Lord greater than death suggest the understanding of resurrection as a *process* which vindicated and transformed the Jesus movement rather than as a singular event:

> "The resurrection . . . does not provide the early church with the secrets of the future, but only gives the community an impetus toward the future and a confidence in it." "(Resurrection) runs directly counter to our contemporary understanding of history, because it represents the unfathomable and irrational power of history itself." ". . . the resurrection of Christ can never be made

> wholly reasonable . . . But, for that matter, neither can death be made wholly reasonable to us. The thirst for life is too strong, and despite the great familiarity of dying and death, together they are intrinsically alien to us." ". . . the subjectivity of the disciples must always be taken into account when we try to understand the historical figure of Jesus Christ . . . whom they had helped to create . . . a Lord greater than death . . ."

Harvey Cox likewise sees the core of Christianity as a transforming and transcending spiritual community. Islam at its best has similar aspirations. One of the reasons Dvorak's Symphony number 9 has long been a favorite of mine—beyond the fact that the music excites my Czech blood—is that it is titled "from the New World." My Jech family settled in the area of south-eastern Minnesota and north-eastern Iowa around the time that Dvorak visited there on his trip to "the New World." I like to think of this image in broader terms as the new world that the New Testament dreams of in contrast to "this world" of oppressive and violent domination systems. The future is synonymous with transformation. The future is synonymous with hope!

Niebuhr does not definitively demonstrate that a physical, historical event of the raising of the dead body of Jesus ever occurred, and I doubt that it was ever his intention to do so. He does, however, put us on the right track to confidence in and hope for the future. I find John Shelby Spong's approach to resurrection and transformation equally helpful and hopeful.

Sing and Be Merry for Today We Are Alive

In the last chapter of his impressive 1994 book *Resurrection: Myth or Reality?* (the gist of which I described in chapter 4), Bishop Spong describes the "massive research" he has done on life after death, on the last page writing:

> "Those books on life after death that I read in my earlier life will remain in a row on a shelf in my library. I will not open them again. I will treasure those persons with whom my life is emotionally bound today, and I will enjoy the expanding privileges of their friendship. When they die, I will grieve at the loss that my life will experience. I will not speculate on how, if, or in what form I might see them again. That is not my business. My business is to live now, to love now, and to be now . . . Let us eat, drink, and be merry, not because tomorrow we shall die but because today we are alive . . ."

It is striking how similar Spong's overall attitude is to the Buddhist perspective we considered in chapter 5. On the subject of life after death he continues "I possess no concepts. I am reduced to silence before this ultimate mystery . . . a profound, reverential silence." This sentiment reminds me of the aforementioned lectures on eternal life by Joseph Sittler. His bottom line was that we may believe in eternal life but we really have no idea what it means when we sing the spiritual about goin' to live with God for all eternity. I, of course, am not quite so silent on the question of life after death. In the light of a scientific, empirical, postmodern sensibility I see more problems with believing in it than with not believing in it. I question belief in anything for which there is no real evidence—in the spirit of "extraordinary claims requiring extraordinary proof" and "wishful thinking doth not make it so."

Spong sharply criticizes the use of life after death as a reward and punishment tool for behavior control. He confesses to being an agnostic on the amazing amount of speculation that parapsychology has produced on the subject. He describes how liberal or revolutionary politics may be somewhat naive in the attempt to provide a substitute this-worldly utopia or paradise. He does recognize, however, that belief in life after death can act as a "deterrent to any passion for building a just society"—which is the ultimate God-like passion as authors Borg and Crossan see it. Kaufman and many others likewise see resurrection theology as about hope for the resurrection here and now of a new human community of love, justice, freedom, equality, forgiveness, and compassion. Many Christian congregations, for example, are learning to refocus on involvement in their local communities as essential for the rejuvenation of their "faithful" efforts to promote these values. Naïve utopian dreaming needs to give way to a practical process of working toward a deeper and fuller realization of these values.

If resurrection were simply about the relationship that each of us individually has to eternity it would be a much too egotistical and short-sighted concern. Any resurrection theology worth its salt has to be multi-dimensional, especially the multiple dimensions of "today we are alive"! Another version of the saying could well be: "Eat, drink, be merry, and do what you can to make it possible for others to do the same!"—even if all you are able to do is to reduce your own consumption of the world's resources and your carbon footprint.

Bishop Spong is sure that there was some kind of inexpressible "core experience" that inspired the Easter legends about Jesus, an experience of a timelessness that is one expression of the ultimate mystery called God, an experience that is "beyond the capacity of our language to capture or of our minds to understand." He feels that creatures with self-consciousness can commune with the limitless, the eternal, the ultimately real, and that "If one does that completely enough it could well be said of that one that his life had been incorporated into God at the moment of his death." Spong describes this core experience:

> "For Jesus it seemed to mean something like communion with God. It meant being in touch with something that transcended all of one's human categories, including a transcendence of the self that one is. It meant having one's eyes opened to see dimensions of life not normally seen and to have one's ears open to hear melodies and harmonies not normally heard."

Spong goes on to describe finite moments slipping into or becoming infinite, timeless moments. This seems to be exactly the same thing as awareness of The Seamless Whole and Contingency that Buddhism ponders! Spong's notion of transcending the self also seems to be virtually the same thing as the Buddhist notions of emptiness or no-self. His attitude is very much in sync with the writings of Steve Hagen, Stephen Batchelor, and Ken Wilber. Batchelor's book *Buddhism Without Beliefs* is echoed in the subtitle of Bishop Spong's 2009 book *Beyond Religion, Beyond Theism, Beyond Heaven and Hell*. The common point is about getting beyond ideas and intellectual constructs to living in the moment, living in Tillich's "eternal now." We need not force ourselves to believe in some fanciful "next world" notion of life after death, to embrace some type of immortality project, in order to get beyond our fear and anxiety about death.

The language about God's unconditional love and grace is Christian symbolism for feeling at home in the universe, feeling totally "safe" in the universe, resting in the universe (resting in the questing), being at peace with Ultimate Reality. Such language is not and should not be about a reified ("thingified") God (Sky Daddy) who loves us. *A proper understanding of unconditional love/grace means that we are freed both from worrying about afterlife and from wrangling about questions such as which religion is the only true religion!* Equally important, we are freed *for* full engagement ("life abundant") in the eternal now, in the process of creating an environment, an ecology (home!) conducive to the flourishing and well-being of all its inhabitants.

A Buddhist might express what it means to feel at peace with reality by saying Reality wins! Truth wins! Truth and Reality trump feel-good bromides that deceptively promise to satisfy all our desires, needs, and preferences. The Taoist would say that life has to be the way it is, a marvelous and sometimes terrible combination of opposites, and the sooner we accept it for what it is the better off we will be. When we feel safe and at home in the universe as it really is, we experience the Seamless Whole and Contingency—which is what Bishop Spong has come to see as the real message in the John Gospel's language about Jesus being identified with God and with the Truth that sets us free. Jesus the Christ is *logos* in this gospel, a somewhat technical (and masculine) Greek term which can be translated as Word, Speech, Reason, but also as Reality or even as Wisdom (the latter reflecting both Jewish and Greek personifications that have feminine connotations).

Spong insists, however, that "God" is not a supernatural being who comes to rescue the world. His 2009 book, the main title of which is *Eternal Life: A New Vision*, identifies the John Gospel instead with the arrival of a new level of human consciousness about Reality. Luther and others have described John as the "most spiritual" gospel. (Spong is working on a book about the John Gospel as I am preparing this book for publication.) Eternal life is not about living "forever" or "again" (both "time" words!). It is about *living compassionately now in awareness of timeless eternity*. Eternal life and God, says Spong, are about a "universal consciousness that is shared"—corresponding to the interconnectedness of all matter and energy. This notion of shared consciousness is about the ultimate reality and value of contingent *relationships*. Spong concludes his Epilogue:

> "If in life we have touched the transcendent and the eternal, and have shared through self-consciousness in the life, love and being that flows through the universe, then I believe we can find the courage to lay this phase of that journey down . . . I would feel the same even if I were convinced that there was nothing more to come . . . I want to live well while I am living and to die well when I am dying, and both because I believe that life is holy."

Once you have been consciously alive, there is a sense in which your relationship with life has been eternal—timeless. Bishop Spong sees the Jesus of the John Gospel as saying that eternity is within us "as the Father is in me and I in Him." Celebratory spirituals about living eternally with God express joy at being able to experience life abundantly (John 10:10) in a way that encompasses past, present, and future. We can feel a relationship with the future just as we can feel a relationship with all the history that has happened before we were born. (I occasionally find myself wishing my college major had been history.) But we should not kid ourselves that we (or Jesus) literally existed before we were born, or that we will literally exist after we die. All the debates that have gone on in the history of Christianity about the nature of "afterlife" lead me to conclude that rather than focusing on living forever in some version of an afterlife, we should focus instead on transcending death by transcending the *fear* of death. The theme "Be Not Afraid!" is one of the most pervasive in the entire history of biblical religion in particular and of all religion in general. When Bishop Spong says "even if" he were convinced that there was nothing more to come, I think he is recognizing that there may well be nothing more to come for us personally beyond this life here and now. "Being raised into the eternity of God" means that we are beyond death's power.

Feeling safe and at home is what makes it possible for us to have the Shalom (wholeness, peace, serenity) that comes when we meditate on the Seamless Whole, realizing our total, mystical, interconnected oneness with all reality, with all life. The personification of a God who loves unconditionally is best understood as meaning that *if there were* such a thing as God, "He" would be like the one described frequently in the Hebrew psalms as "gracious and merciful," "abounding in steadfast love," "good to all," with "compassion over all that he has made" (Psalm 145:8–9), and in whose house we can dwell forever (Psalm 23). "He" would be like the one described in virtually every sura (chapter) of the Qur'an as "the compassionate, the merciful." Such a God, who is like a father welcoming home a prodigal son, does not *exist*! But the *experience* of feeling welcome, safe, and at home in relationship with the universe is exquisitely real *and is the essential and existential truth of authentic spirituality*

My mother put it in needlework which now graces a wall in our home: Happiness Is Still Homemade. Christians emphasize belonging to a "church home." The apostle Paul based his egalitarian vision of a peaceful world on a dated image of home, family, and benevolent father. Traditional Confucianism similarly uses antiquated notions of family relationships (ancestors included) which can symbolize belonging to and feeling at home in the universe. Confucianism is so focused on the unity of everything under heaven here and now ("the celestial kingdom") that many Confucians insist that their worldview is not a religion but a way of viewing the universe and a way of life. Biographer Ray Monk says that the music loving twentieth century philosopher Wittgenstein regarded "the feeling of being 'absolutely safe' as paradigmatic of religious experience." Hymn writer Isaac Watts saw God as "a Shelter . . . and our Eternal Home." Another great spiritual visualizes a "sweet chariot, comin' for to carry me home." Will Thompson drives the home theme home with his sentimental hymn: "Softly and tenderly Jesus is calling, Come home, come home, Come home, come home, Ye who are weary, come home!" In all this imagery I see amazing consensus on what it means to sing a mystical song of life transcending death.

There are both personal (psychological) and social/political (socio-logical) aspects of authentic spirituality. The personal aspect in Buddhism is apt to be described in terms of serenity, whereas in biblically-based religion personal spirituality tends to be related more to images of feel-ing confident, safe, and at home in the universe. The social and political aspect of ethical/historical biblically-based spirituality is expressed in the non-supernatural language of "doing justice" or "the Reign of God," or being followers of "The Way" of peace and liberation through ecological awareness, justice, and compassion rather than through violent conquest or economic exploitation. Likewise, the central goal of authentic Islam is to create a compassionate community (*ummah*) focused on social and economic justice. Nature/culture spirituality (e.g. Buddhism, Taoism) is more likely to express its social, political, non-supernatural and ecological practicality in terms of facing reality—struggling with ethical challenges, programs, and policies in the context of "The Way" (Tao) life really is. St. Paul's expression "life in the Spirit" is apropos to any authentic spirituality in both personal and social/political dimensions.

On the subject of struggling with ethical challenges, I return once more to the issue of martyrdom and self-sacrifice in connection with the emphasis on compassion. We rightly admire non-violent resisters against evil (like Jesus) who often end up giving their lives for the sake of others. But we can't all rush to be martyrs in this way, partly because if everyone did so, evil would win. Furthermore, the "others" for whom we must show compassion or set aside our own self-interests are often those closest to us whose welfare is best served by our continuing presence. The kind of questions on my mind here are: Can we blame or condemn, for example, the collaborationist Jews of Jesus' day who cooperated with Roman au-thority, or devious gay people who are forced to dissemble in order not to lose their livelihood or even their very lives, or folks who lied to Nazis in order to protect Jews? In short, what about situations where there is a stark choice between "adapt or die"?

I have mentioned the capitalist economic system occasionally in these pages. Should we give this system total free reign, abolish it through revolution, or tweak it with regulations and reforms? Does its encourage-ment of competitive self-interest make it, as Winston Churchill memorably said, "the worst possible system—except for all the others"? My point here is simply that we must not underestimate the complexity of the ethical issues involved when we participate in the struggle to be compassionate partisans of justice, liberation, peace and love.

It was easier for early founders of religions to envision spreading their message to the whole world because they did not realize how large and diverse the world actually is. We can forgive them for the occasional arrogance in their missionary zeal. Nevertheless and beyond reproach, authentic spirituality is powerfully present in the New Testament vision of "God's reign" bringing an egalitarian world of peace, justice, love and compassion. Authentic spirituality is also present in the Qur'an's vision of a just community where mercy and compassion are the rule, and in the Hebrew Scriptures' vision of mercy, truth and egalitarian justice rolling down like waters! (While it may not yet be fully realized economically and politically, many of us already live in what a 2010 Time Magazine article matter-of-factly described as "an increasingly egalitarian culture.") The Buddhist and Taoist emphasis on facing Reality with compassion ex- presses a similar understanding that authentic spirituality must bear the practical fruits of justice, liberation, and peace.

It's probably safe to say that most people do not understand the sym- bolic nature of biblical and other theological language as I have described it here; many will continue to take God, heaven, angels, etc. more literally than I believe they should. The same might be said about most people per- haps not understanding or appreciating my "psych yourself out" version of scientifically compatible, evidence-based Buddhism. There likely will always be folks who do not appreciate the abstract and symbolic meaning of "unconditional grace" that I am so keen to promote, or the complex terminology that Buddhism uses—Reality (Suchness/Tathata), Seamless Whole (Shunyata), Insight (Satori), Awareness, Awakened Consciousness, Enlightenment, Nirvana, Contingency, Emptiness, Non-duality. Is there really anyone who can claim to fully and absolutely understand "the whole thing?" Yet anyone who trusts their "in the moment" experience does understand "Ultimate Reality" on some level—when they enjoy a sunset, family and friends, good meals, creative work and play, great music, a great book, traditions, a good laugh or cry, sexuality, and more.

I sometimes cuss my computer's seemingly erratic behavior, but I nevertheless very much appreciate it as one of the true miracles of post- modern science and technology. One of its beauties is how quickly it can tell me that "God" appears 701 times in this book. I don't think it matters whether or not spiritual nonbelievers use the word God. The important thing from my point of view is that the word be understood by those who do use it as *a symbolic, poetic, and artful "manner of speaking" about the Ultimate Mystery of Existence,* and as *a way of imagining a God's-eye view or an Ultimate Reference Point for understanding everything.* Neither the word "God" (described by Joseph Campbell as "Reality beyond all categories of thought") nor this Mystery are going to go away.

We would all do well to raise our consciousness about how we use religious language. We would also do well to heed Wilber's words from *Integral Spirituality* that one doesn't have to be an expert or read endless books in order to glimpse non-duality, the Radiant All, or the Seamless Whole—in order to say with conviction and awareness "I am the universe happening." I think it would be cool to say "You are the universe happening" to the undiscerning child as part of an infant baptism ritual, and then to let hope spring eternal that the child would come to appreciate what this expression means.

God-talk is often arrogant. But sometimes it only seems to be so because it has set for itself the task of trying to be the most comprehensive, mind-bending, language-stretching venture we can undertake. I always come back to Gordon Kaufman's wise observation that "God" is the symbol we use as "the ultimate point of reference for understanding everything—every value, every experience, every desire, every act of imagination." I also like to call theology "the attempt to talk about the un-talk-about-able." God-language is an attempt to encounter and engage the Ultimate Mystery of Life, so it is bound to be inadequate, mind-boggling, or paradoxical. Occasionally, Spong seems to slip back into theism by referring to God as "Who." But it is always clear that he understands the huge difference between personifying God as "a Being," and seeing divinity as being expressed most fully in the lives of loving human persons. A fully developed human consciousness of eternity and of love in all its dimensions opens us up to face the realities of life and death—eating, drinking and being merry, *both because tomorrow we die and because today we are alive!* Personified theism creates an all-too-limited God who caters to our wishful thinking. Fully developed human consciousness of "sacred eternity" understands spirituality (religion) as a consummate creative art form that celebrates human values, especially our myriad contingent relationships.

Ken Wilber frequently uses the same metaphors of transcendence and depth that John Shelby Spong finds so meaningful. These musings from Wilber's *Brief History of Everything* provide a fine example of a symbolic, poetic, artful, and meditative manner of speaking about transcendent spiritual consciousness and our relationship to Ultimate Mystery (pages 62–63):

> "The very Spirit in us is invited to become self-conscious, or even, as some would say, superconscious . . . Are the mystics and sages insane? Because they all tell the same story, don't they. The story of awakening one morning and discovering that you are one with the All, in a timeless and eternal and infinite fashion . . . I think the sages are the growing tip of the secret impulse of evolution. I think they are the leading edge of the self-transcending drive that always goes beyond what went before. I think they embody the very drive of the Kosmos toward greater depth and expanding consciousness. I think they are riding the edge of a light beam racing toward a rendezvous with God."

Spong puts it this way, " . . . we ought to look again at the mystics: they might turn out to be the means through which the essence of yesterday's religion can be transformed into tomorrow's spiritual understanding." Mathematician/philosopher Bertrand Russell wrote "what you call God is very much what I call infinity." A skeptic about religion, he has nevertheless been described as embracing "transcendent mysticism." This kind of mystical humanism is not about superstition, numerology, elixirs of immortality, or other esoterica. Einstein wrote: "The most beautiful and most profound religious emotion that we can experience is the sensation of the mystical, and this mysticality is the power of all true science." True science can always help to increase our awareness of being one with the All. Ethical-historical monotheism makes a distinction between God and the Cosmos in order to emphasize the Holiness and Mystery of the Divine. In this type of monotheism we are in a sense separate from the Divine and can only have a relationship with "God"—expressed in Martin Buber's famous "I and Thou." Elaine Pagels has suggested the phrase "I *am* Thou" to express the alternative understanding and awareness of being completely one with The All, the unity of the human and the divine (emphasized especially in Eastern Orthodox Christianity and in Buddhism)—the depth experience of enlightened, mystical, spiritual serenity.

In her discussion of the intensely visionary, emotional and psychological aspects of mystical experience, Karen Armstrong writes: "It is a mistake for the visionary to see these mental apparitions as objective or as anything more than *symbols of transcendence.*" (italics mine) Noting the etymological connection between the words myth, mystic, and mystery,

Armstrong stresses that mystical spirituality involves an imaginative encounter with the ineffable, "pushing language to its limits," bypassing the merely intellectual in order to experience transcendence. This is not a journey to a God "out there" but a psychological experience of the awe, wonder, and mystery of Reality. In her view, imaginative and mystical forms of worship, devotion, and meditation are needed to counterbalance the moral activism that can run amuck and wear us down.

Elaine Pagels explains that the quest for mystical experience accounts in part for the popularity of the bizarrely symbolic and artistic apocalyptic literature of "revelation." At its most intense level, the "vision quest" is understood as a deliberate encounter with madness, darkness, or overwhelming light. The person who risks such an experience and survives may then be seen as one who now has special spiritual qualifications. In some ways this book is asking the reader to risk taking this kind of new look at spirituality, belief, faith. I imagine that a lot of strong feelings have been dredged up. I hope there have been among them some helpful "aha!" moments.

My own understanding of religion—and of the Bible in particular—has changed dramatically over the years. By the time I graduated from a traditionalist Lutheran high school, I was close to being a Christian fundamentalist. But during my senior year I wrote a long paper on the issue of how the 66 "books" of the Bible were chosen, a topic which clearly indicated that I was disinclined to accept without question everything I was being taught. My view of Christianity started to change when I arrived at college, and even more so at seminary where I began to understand the historical-critical method of studying the Bible. One seminary professor, Roger Jordahl, taught us to describe this method as "radical literalism" because it indicated how one meaning of "literal" must include the process of scouring every nuance and clue, every letter and word in biblical literature, utilizing every other related literary source or technique of scientific analysis, in order to discover as much as we could about the creation of this literature which has come to be considered sacred. There would be questions about who really wrote, edited, chose and collected this material; about when and where this process took place and the motivations of those involved; about the copying and transmission of sacred texts; and about how conscious the writers and editors were of the degree to which their material was historical, theological, or mythological. This kind of revealing inquiry about the nature and background of the Bible and of other sacred literary art forms continues to result in the creation of books like this one.

While my outlook on religion has indeed changed, an important thing has not changed. In fact, I value it now more than ever—and it has been in the forefront of this entire book. Whoever chose the little saying that was placed next to my picture in our high school yearbook decided to make this observation about me: "Opportunity is rare; a wise man will never let it go by him." Part of the reason this line was quite appropriate is that I was a very studious guy. Perhaps the sudden death of my 39-year-old father when I was 12 years old also had something to do with it. My present perspective, however, is that I already understood then as I do even more now the importance of *carpe diem*, of seizing the day. *Carpe diem* (we studied Latin in high school!) is not about a desperate scramble to have it all, to experience every possible thrill, to pack every day with absolute maximum productivity—or to save the world.

Carpe diem is simply about life! To reduce the Jesus stories to the idea that his main purpose in life here on earth was to die, is an unfortunate form of literalism and non-metaphorical thinking. The Jesus stories are about living—living to promote justice, peace, life, love and compassion, all the while wishing and praying (as in Gethsemane) that it would not be so risky to do so! Mohandas Ghandi, Abraham Lincoln, Rosa Luxemburg, Leon Trotsky, Susan B. Anthony, Coretta Scott King, Martin Luther King Jr., Harvey Milk and so many others also lived to advance these values. The Jesus stories, the Buddha stories, the story of Mohammed's great concern about the growing gap between rich and poor in his own tribe, and the stories of many other folks such as these, are about seizing the day for the sake of life, love, peace and justice.

Seizing the day is also about realizing along with the author of Ecclesiastes that when all is said and done we don't have ultimate wisdom, we don't have all the answers. We only have Ultimate Mystery. We only have each other. We only have our contingent relationships in which we find meaning and ever-expanding consciousness. *Carpe diem* is about being able to arrive at the end of one's life rejoicing at having been alive, and without major regrets—without feeling that one's priorities have been misplaced, valuable opportunities missed by a mile, relationships squandered in the pursuit of mere things, and moments of spiritual awareness not savored. In other words, one should rest gracefully in the hope of having lived a life that is a reasonably good version of the universe happening.

Subject Index

Abelard, Peter, 100
absolutism, 48, 95, 113, 116–17
Abraham, 81, 89, 115
Adam and Eve, 155, 192–93
Addison, Joseph, 19
agnostic, ix, 28–30, 110, 112, 199,
  219, 223
Alain de Botton (Religion for Atheists),
  31, 112
Alexander, Eben, 208–09
Allah, 8, 26, 76, 113, 120, 160, 214
allegory, 8
Allen, Woody, 18, 51, 176, 190, 220
allusion, 15, 167
ambiguity/ambiguous, 29, 57, 113, 152,
  155, 166
angels, 6, 17, 19, 73, 76, 122, 154, 196,
  198, 200, 205, 210, 228
Anglican/Episcopal, xvii, 23, 24, 41,
  43, 182
anthropomorphic, 8, 52, 160
AntiChrist or Anti-Christ, 59, 99
anti-intellectualism (and scientific
  illiteracy), 116, 162, 212
apocalypse/apocalyptic, xviii, 73, 99,
  125, 135, 145–47, 149, 151, 231
Arendt, Hannah, 105
Armstrong, Karen, x, xiv, xv, 2–8, 10,
  26, 30, 43, 45, 55–57, 91, 104,
  141, 194, 230–31
artistic (freedom, license, metaphor,
  etc.), xii–xiv, 1–11, 14, 18, 23–
  24, 29–32, 39, 42, 45–57, 63–71,
  74–83, 87, 92, 95–96, 99, 104,
  107, 109, 117, 120, 122, 127,
  148, 151, 158–60, 167–68, 170,
  179, 181, 184–85, 187, 194, 202,
  204, 206–09. 214–15, 231

art and science, 6, 21, 33, 170
Asia, 3, 46, 55, 116, 125, 175, 182
Athanasius/Athanasian (Creed), 59, 90
astronomy, astronomer, 12–13, 42, 159,
  202
atheism/atheist, ix, x, xvii, 3, 11, 23–33,
  35, 37–45, 47, 49, 51, 53, 55,
  57, 59, 61, 63, 65, 67, 69, 112,
  160–61, 170, 179–80, 182, 191
Athitakis, Mark, 163
atonement (theories/interpretations
  of), 33, 52, 71–74, 77–84, 89,
  98, 100–02, 156, 202
attitude, xi, 14, 23, 28, 34, 40–41, 50,
  53, 58, 62, 68, 91, 94–96, 102,
  104, 112–114, 119–20, 128, 132,
  140, 149, 160, 173, 177, 180,
  187, 196, 198, 211, 223–24
Aulen, Gustav, 71, 77, 83, 89, 100–02
authoritarianism, 15, 26–28, 39, 64, 74,
  80–81, 84, 112, 114–15, 120,
  160, 190

Babylon, 46, 74–75, 84, 100
Bach, Johann Sebastian, xx, 7, 18, 158,
  217
Bartok, Bela, 49
Batchelor, Stephen, 38, 170, 191, 224
Bahai, 15
Baldwin, James, 214
Ball, Philip, 14
Barnes, Julian, 199
Barth, Karl, xiv, 61, 156
Bauer, Walter, 77, 92
Bawer, Bruce, 66
beatific vision, 134, 137

233